SHUSTERMAN'S PRAGMATISM

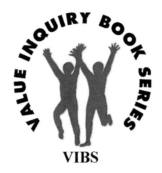

VIBS

Volume 244

Robert Ginsberg
Founding Editor

Leonidas Donskis
Executive Editor

Associate Editors

a volume in
Central European Value Studies
CEVS
Emil Višňovský, Editor

SHUSTERMAN'S PRAGMATISM
Between Literature and Somaesthetics

Edited by

Dorota Koczanowicz and Wojciech Małecki

Amsterdam - New York, NY 2012

Cover illustration: www.morgueFile.com

Cover design: Studio Pollmann

The paper on which this book is printed meets the requirements of "ISO 9706:1994, Information and documentation - Paper for documents - Requirements for permanence".

ISBN: 978-90-420-3486-0
E-Book ISBN: 978-94-012-0763-8
© Editions Rodopi B.V., Amsterdam - New York, NY 2012
Printed in the Netherlands

CONTENTS

Part Three:
SOMAESTHETICS

Introduction

Dorota Koczanowicz and Wojciech Małecki

While there have been numerous scholarly articles written on Richard Shus-terman, not to mention a few journal issues[1] and a monograph devoted to him,[2] the present volume constitutes the first collection of essays in English[3] to engage the work of this interesting philosopher—one of the most often translated pragmatists of the recent decades. Indeed, one task of this book is to shed light on why Shusterman is so widely read not only in different cultural contexts (the languages into which his books have been translated include Italian, French, German, Spanish, Portuguese, Polish, Hungarian, Russian, Slovakian, Chinese, Korean, Japanese, and others), but also within different disciplines, including literary, gender, education, and performance studies, philosophy, musicology, physiology and sports science, art, design, and archi-tecture theory, and human-computer interaction studies. Part of the answer is that, as in the case of any other important thinker, Shusterman is simply origi-nal: both in the sense of exploring various *terrae incognitae* (his 1991 essay "The Fine Art of Rap," for instance, was the first text on that subject by an aesthetician[4]), and of presenting an innovative approach to seemingly well-known subjects (his somatic interpretation of the problem of self-knowledge is a good case in point[5]). Yet one needs to mention here that his thought owes its wide appeal also to its remarkable flexibility, or rather to its refusal to grant to any "single ... school of thought" "a monopoly on philosophical insight,"[6] or to adopt the perspective of only one academic discipline. There is also the fact that Shusterman's work is unwilling to remain confined within the walls of academia as such. Shusterman's oeuvre, as he himself underscores in this vol-ume, situates itself *in between* many phenomena and fields, something which is partly reflected in the title of the present book.[7]

But before unfolding some of the more complex connotations of Shuster-man's in-betweenness, let us admit that the title *Between Literature and Som-aesthetics* may be understood as meaning basically a very simple thing. Namely, that the trajectory of Richard Shusterman's intellectual itinerary so far can be traced from his initial (almost exclusive) interest in the aesthetics of literature[8] to his recent focus on the topic of embodiment, which finds its expression in the new philosophical subdiscipline he coined over a dozen years ago and named "somaesthetics."[9] While this picture is generally accurate, it needs to be refined by saying that Shusterman has not abandoned literature *entirely* for the sake of the body, but has rather assigned to it a different role in his thought: it has been transformed from a topic of philosophical reflection to a medium through which he addresses not only the somatic, but also other matters, such as the nature of philosophy itself.[10] And by "medium" we mean here not only that Shusterman employs literary texts as illustrations of his views on embodiment and yokes the concept of literature to theorize the nature and tasks of philosophy, but also that he crosses the contested boundary between literary and philosophical discourse in his own writings—something which must be rather intriguing in light of the fact that when, in the beginning of his career, he actually focused on the subject of literature, his philosophical voice was rather dry, abstract, and as remote from literariness as possible. Briefly put, it was the tone of an analytic philosopher, which Shusterman was at that time.[11]

And here we can turn to another interstitial space in which Shusterman operates, that between different philosophical schools or traditions. For while it is true that—as he himself admits—at some point he converted from analytic to continental philosophy (particularly the thought of Theodor W. Adorno), only to eventually become a pragmatist,[12] some traces of his earlier philosophical commitments still permeate his thought, making it an interesting and unorthodox amalgam of these three theoretical orientations (even if the pragmatist ingredient dominates). Thus his repudiation of analytic philosophy's science-envy (an envy which often manifests itself in pathological formalization, specialization, and technicality for its own sake), has not prevented him from inheriting from that tradition the attention to the clarity of discourse, well-crafted structure of argument, and conceptual precision, which are surely commendable features even if they at times makes his "philosophical prose" sound a bit "stilted," as he himself has put it.[13] His experience with continental thought, in turn, seems to have instilled in him a conviction (for which the ground was prepared by his frustration with some problems of analytic aesthetics that he discusses in the opening essay), that there are things which simply evade conceptualization or atrophy and pour through our fingers when submitted to logical analysis; that sometimes it is to the literary that we must turn to philosophize; and that philosophizing, far from being a metadiscourse unfolded from a God's eye perspective is—at least to some extent—the philosopher's "unconscious memoir" (as Nietzsche put it)[14] and is also steeped in politics through and through.

Lastly, but most importantly—pragmatism. Given the character of Shusterman's thought, it would be tempting to say that what he has absorbed from the pragmatist tradition is its emphasis on practicality, its insistence that instead of dealing with "the problems of philosophers," philosophy—in Dewey's formulation—should focus on "the problems of men" and women.[15] Yet it is rather the case, as Shusterman's autobiographical texts indicate, that this insistence has always constituted one of his firmest convictions, and when he actually discovered pragmatism for himself he embraced it precisely because it was a form of theorizing that allowed him to embody this conviction better than any other philosophy he had known before.[16] Importantly, the melioristic imperative to employ philosophical reflection in order to improve the current realities (either through constructive or deconstructive strategies)[17] is not the only way in which pragmatism allowed Shusterman to embody philosophy.

Another, and no less important, way is related to pragmatism's corporeal naturalism, which, after Darwin, treats humans as thoroughly embodied creatures, where "thoroughly" signifies that this embodiment includes every aspect of human life, our minds and thoughts included.[18] This, however, does not mean that the point of Shusterman's somatic pragmatism is to reduce mental phenomena to the electrical activity of neurons, as instead of choosing one, materialistic, side of the mind-body discussion, he rather formulates—following Dewey—the strong ontological postulate of the existence of one body-mind.[19] He treats what is usually called "body" (and which he prefers to denominate "soma," in order to avoid the many unfortunate philosophical meanings that former word has accreted since Plato[20]) not as a physiological mechanism or mere prison of the soul,[21] but rather as a sentient, experiencing and experienced corporeal being.[22]

This theoretical move, that is, synthesizing body and mind, might well be considered a natural consequence of pragmatism's general holistic approach,[23] and such holism can be further seen in Shusterman's belief that not only there is no absolute ontological gap between each human being and her environment (we are constituted and constantly reshaped by it and vice versa) but there is also no such gap between what we customarily call the natural and the sociocultural environment, or nature and culture.[24] To demonstrate the advantages of such a position, let us contrast it with a presumption that is still well-entrenched in the West and claims that the body constitutes the natural, biological or animal pole of the human being, as opposed to the mental or cultural pole thereof. First of all, as Shusterman argues, this claim flies in the face of the undeniable fact that not only are our mental processes dependent on physiological ones (say, malnutrition impairs the movement of our limbs to an equal extent that it does so with the movement of our thoughts), but also that from the very first moment of their coming into being, our bodies are shaped by "culture," for instance, by the culturally determined nutritional habits of the mother, which in turn partly determine the physical features of the fetus.[25] With age that influence only deepens, also due to the operation of diverse corporeal norms that are imprinted in our bodies in the process of socialization (some of them being undeniably oppressive, like the norm "that 'proper' women speak softly, stay slim, eat dainty foods, sit with their legs close together, assume the passive role or lower position in (heterosexual) copulation"[26]), and which, as a result of recent technological advancements, have gained hitherto unimagined possibilities of dissemination and implementation. This only contributes to what Shusterman dubs the somatic turn of contemporary Western societies and whose paradoxical nature he describes as follows:

As telecommunications render bodily presence unnecessary, while new technologies of mediatic body construction and plastic cyborg-surgery challenge the very presence of a real body, our culture seems increasingly fixated on the soma, serving it with the adoring devotion once bestowed on other worshiped mysteries. In postmodern urban culture, gyms and fitness centers proliferate, largely replacing both church and museum as the preferred site of self-meliorative instruction, where one is obliged to visit in one's leisure as a duty to oneself, even if it involves inconvenience and discomfort. Ever more money, time, and pain is being invested in cosmetics, dieting, and plastic surgery. Despite mediatic dematerialization, bodies seem to matter more.[27]

Of course, it might be observed that Shusterman is hardly saying anything new here, as the aforementioned points have been recycled for decades in philosophy and in the humanities in general. Yet while Shusterman would be ready to accept that charge to some extent (admitting with William James that pragmatism is programmatically but a new name for some old types of thinking[28]), he would add that if those points themselves are not novel, then what he does with them surely is. To be more exact, as Shusterman complains, contemporary philosophy and the humanities have indeed been mainly concerned with endlessly *recycling* such points in the machinery of academic discourse—that is, refining, discussing, analyzing, and contextualizing them—but philosophy and the humanities have been, sadly, less interested in employing those points to change the current state of things. As a result, contemporary theory of the body, lacks "something that the individual can directly translate into a discipline of improved somatic practice," a deficiency only exacerbated by this theory's lack of any "structuring overview or architectonic" that could "integrate its very different, seemingly incommensurable discourses into a more productively systematic field."[29] Shusterman is trying to remedy both these lacks through aforementioned somaesthetics, that is, a field "devoted to the critical, ameliorative study of one's experience and use of one's body as a locus of sensory-aesthetic appreciation (aesthesis) and creative self-fashioning."[30]

So without discarding theoretical reflection on the somatic altogether (this reflection in fact constitutes one of its fundamental elements), somaesthetics pays much attention—within what Shusterman calls its "pragmatic" branch—to "proposing specific methods of somatic improvement and engaging in their comparative critique."[31] A good exemplification of "pragmatic somaesthetics" at work is Shusterman's 2008 book *Body Consciousness*, where, among other things, he attempts to propose some concrete solutions to the problems of women's emancipation and racism. As far as the first of these problems is concerned, Shusterman's main target is the contention, which he attributes to Simone de Beauvoir, yet sees also in contemporary feminist thinkers such as Iris Marion Young, that "…by improving their awareness of bodily experience, women would be reinforcing their passivity and withdrawal from the world into immanence as well as underlining the very dimension of their being (namely, bodily experience) that most expresses their oppression."[32] In contrast to that, Shusterman tries to demonstrate that bodily experience and various somatic techniques that rely on it, such as Alexander Technique or Feldenkrais Method, not only do not condemn women to deeper subjugation, but in fact can be employed as an instrument of emancipation; something which should become clear "once we recognize the body's irreplaceable instrumentality for all our action" and perception.[33]

This recognition lies also at the root of Shusterman's somaesthetic approach toward racism, whose etiology, as he argues, can often be attributed to the "unacknowledged visceral reactions" that are provoked by racial others. Naturally, in such cases "racial and ethnic enmity resists resolution through logical means of verbal persuasion" (as the problem here is not a set of beliefs on the racial or ethnic other, which can be refuted discursively, but rather a certain unarticulated revulsion that one may feel independently of one's beliefs) and "...as long as we do not consciously attend to these deep visceral feelings we can neither overcome them nor the enmity they generate and foster."

> Disciplines of somaesthetic awareness—continues Shusterman— involving a focused, systematic scanning of our bodily feelings, is first helpful in identifying these disturbing somatic sensations so that we can better control, neutralize, or overcome them. If we can do no more than merely "put up with" them, in Wittgenstein's words, we have at least the ability to identify and isolate them in our consciousness, which better enables us to take a critical distance from them and avert their infecting our political judgments.[34]

Leaving aside the question of the efficacy of this solution, let us point out that this and the previous citations illuminate another aspect of the in-betweenness, or hybridity, of Shusterman's thought, namely, its interdisciplinarity. After all, giving advice on mastering one's bodily feelings is impossible (at least insofar as we want our advice to be reliable) without the knowledge of their underlying neurophysiological mechanisms, a knowledge for which one needs to reach beyond philosophy—to neurology and psychology. Not to mention the fact that the somaesthetic analysis of corporeal norms, and *a fortiori* any suggestions for their improvement, necessitate consulting the resources provided by sociology, art history, cultural, gender, and even literary studies.[35] What is more, as we said above, somaesthetics transcends not only the borders of particular academic disciplines, but also the confines of what is conceived (at least today) as the domain of academia, and it does so through its "practical" branch, which, as Shusterman puts it,

> ...is not a matter of producing texts, not even texts that offer pragmatic methods of somatic care; it is instead about actually pursuing such care through intelligently disciplined practice aimed at somatic self-improvement (whether in representational, experiential, or performative modes). Concerned not with saying but with doing, this practical dimension is the most neglected by academic body philosophers, whose com-

mitment to the discursive logos typically ends in textualizing the body. For practical somaesthetics, the less said the better, if this means the more work actually done. But because, in philosophy, what goes without saying typically goes without doing, the concrete activity of somatic training must be named as the crucial practical dimension of somaesthetics, conceived as a comprehensive philosophical discipline concerned with self-knowledge and self-care.[36]

Of course, the injunction that academic philosophers actually engage in "disciplined practice aimed at somatic self-improvement" (which means, yes, that they should work their bodies as part of their philosophical activity), may raise eyebrows among its addressees, and some of them may even protest that it is a blasphemous betrayal of the ages long tradition of philosophy.[37] Yet as is usually the case with the most ardent, or at least most vocal, defenders of any tradition, in doing so these philosophers would demonstrate a blatant ignorance of the very tradition the purity of which they would be trying to protect from contamination. For, as Shusterman reminds us after Pierre Hadot, in ancient Greece "…the gymnasion, the place where physical exercises were practiced, was the same place where philosophy lessons were given,"[38] while "[r]ecognition of somatic training as an essential means toward philosophical enlightenment and virtue lies at the heart of" the thought of such founding fathers of Western philosophy as Diogenes the Cynic, Socrates, and even Plato himself.[39] And since we are on the subject of ancient philosophy it is worth mentioning that the idea of practical somaesthetics is partly a consequence of Shusterman's involvement in the general project (inspired by Hadot and Foucault, but also by Asian thinkers such as Confucius and Mencius, and today pursued by the likes of Martha Nussbaum and Stanley Cavell) of the rehabilitation and reanimation of the ideal of philosophy as a way of life.

With this remark we would like to finish our discussion of the main elements and themes of Shusterman's thought and if there is no need to explore them further here, it is because they, and some other elements that we have not mentioned, are given an in-depth treatment in the texts that follow, both in those written by Shusterman himself and by his commentators. And so Shusterman's approach to literature and to aesthetics in general (including the aesthetics of self-creation), is discussed in the papers by Kacper Bartczak, Anna Budziak, Dorota Koczanowicz, and Wojciech Małecki, which form the first section of the volume (entitled "Literary Theory and Philosophy of Art"). These papers touch, too, on his ethics of self-fashioning and conception of philosophy as an art of living, as do the essays by Jerold J. Abrams and Sami Pihlström. Pihlström's and Abrams' papers, in turn, belong to the second section ("Epistemology, Metaphysics, Ethics, and Politics"), which includes also Don Morse's text, which interrogates Shusterman's holism, and Adam Chmielewski's piece, which analyzes and puts in the context of urgent political matters Shusterman's plea for a fallibilistic approach in religion.[40]

The theme of the third section is "Somaesthetics" and it contains papers by Monika Bokiniec, Robert Dobrowolski, Martin Jay, and Krzysztof Skowroński, though it must be noted that various aspects of somaesthetic reflection are also tackled in the aforementioned essays by Abrams and Budziak. As is clear from this description, and as Richard Shusterman emphasizes in his reply to them, some papers could well belong to a different section than that in which we eventually placed them. But this overlapping is understandable given the interrelatedness of various elements of Shusterman's thought and its "hybridity," and we hope the reader will find our grouping of essays helpful.

One final thing that probably should to be explained in this place is the prevalence of Polish names in the list of contributors, and what lies behind it is the fact that the volume originates in a conference on Shusterman's philosophy which was organized by the editors of the present volume in 2008 in Poland, where—it must be noted—for more that fifteen years Shusterman has had a considerable, and positive reception. To be more substantive, thus far three of his books (*Pragmatist Aesthetics*, *Practicing Philosophy*, and *Body Consciousness*) have been translated into Polish and have been widely read by academics and students. His numerous essays have also been published in translation in various Polish journals (some of them were collected in a special anthology published in 2007[41]). It is also worth mentioning that he is frequently invited to Poland to give talks and seminars, and that his work has been discussed in prominent periodicals there. Given these circumstances, it came as no big surprise that our efforts to organize the aforementioned event, and subsequently to prepare and publish this volume, met with an overwhelmingly positive reaction from various Polish institutions and colleagues, and therefore we would like to conclude with expressing our gratitude to them.

But most of all, we would like to thank the main protagonist of the volume, Richard Shusterman, for participating in the conference and for writing both a special essay for this volume and an in-depth yet comprehensive response to the papers contained herein. We thank him for his unceasing encouragement of our work on his thought and on pragmatism in general. Thanks go also to all the participants in the conference and to those authors who (like Jerold J. Abrams, Martin Jay, Don Morse, and Sami Pihlström) did not attend the event yet agreed to contribute to the volume.[42] Both the conference and the volume would not have come into being without financial support provided by the Institute of Polish Philology, University of Wrocław, and University of Lower Silesia, for which would like to thank them from this place. Thanks are extended, too, to David Schauffler, who proofread the manuscript. Finally, we are grateful to Emil Višňovský, the editor of the series in which this book appears, for his supporting the project from the very beginning, and to Krystyna Wilkoszewska and Leszek Koczanowicz for their advice and help with this and other projects.

This book was supported by a grant from the Faculty of Philology, University of Wrocław.

NOTES

1. See, for instance, the essays contained in *Action, Criticism, and Theory for Music Education*, 1 (2010). Cf. the special symposia on Shusterman's work published in *The Journal of Speculative Philosophy*, 16:1 (2002), pp. iv–38, and in *The Journal of Aesthetic Education*, 36:4 (2002), pp. 84–115.
2. Wojciech Małecki, *Embodying Pragmatism: Richard Shusterman's Philosophy and Literary Theory* (Frankfurt am Main-New York: Peter Lang, 2010).
3. Note that there has already been a French collection on Shusterman's work: *Penser en Corps: Soma-esthétique, art et philosophie*, ed. Barbara Formis (Paris: L'Harmattan, 2009).
4. See Richard Shusterman, "The Fine Art of Rap," *New Literary History*, 22 (1991), pp. 613–632.
5. See Richard Shusterman, "Self-Knowledge and Its Discontents," *Philosophy of Education Archive* (2007), pp. 25–37, http://ojs.ed.uiuc.edu/index.php/pes/article/view/1432/179 (accessed October 10, 2009).
6. See p. 11 of this volume.
7. One notes that the concept of in-betweenness has been used in the contemporary humanities rather carelessly, by which we mean that it seems that nowadays everything can be assigned an interstitial status, and in fact is assigned that status so often that the very notion of in-betweenness has begun to lose meaning. Yet as far as Shusterman is concerned, it is indeed very hard to resist classifying him as simultaneously occupying diverse liminal spaces.
8. See, for instance, Richard Shusterman, "The Anomalous Nature of Literature," *British Journal of Aesthetics*, 18:4 (1978), pp. 317–329; "Aesthetic Blindness to Textual Visuality," *Journal of Aesthetics and Art Criticism*, 41:1 (1982), pp. 87–96; and *The Object of Literary Criticism* (Amsterdam: Rodopi, 1984).
9. See, for instance, Richard Shusterman, *Body Consciousness: A Philosophy of Mindfulness and Somaesthetics* (Cambridge: Cambridge University Press, 2008). Even though somaesthetics is still a relatively new element in the academic landscape it has already become the subject of many articles and chapters in books. See, for instance, Gustavo Guerra, "Practicing Pragmatism"; Kathleen Marie Higgins, "Living and Feeling at Home: Shusterman's Performing Live"; Casey Haskins, "Enlivened Bodies, Authenticity and Romanticism"; and Martin Jay, "Somaesthetics and Democracy: Dewey and Contemporary Body Art"—all four articles published in *Journal of Aesthetic Education*, 36:4 (2002), pp. 55–69, 84–102; Jerold J. Abrams, "Pragmatism, Artificial Intelligence, and Posthuman Bioethics: Shusterman, Rorty, Foucault," *Human Studies*, 27 (2004), pp. 241–258; Peter J. Arnold, "Somaesthetics, Education, and the Art of Dance," *Journal of Aesthetic Education*, 39:1 (2005), pp. 48–64; Eric C. Mullis, "Performative Somaesthetics: Principles and Scope," *Journal of Aesthetic Education*, 40:4 (2006), pp. 114–7; Simo Säätelä, "Between Intellectualism and 'Somaesthetics,'" *Filozofski Vestnik*, 20:2 (1999), pp. 151–162; Ken Tupper, "Entheogens & Education: Exploring the Potential of Psychoactives as Educational Tools," *Journal of Drug Education and Awareness*, 1:2 (2003), pp. 145–161; Bryan S. Turner, "Somaesthetics and the Critique of Cartesian Dualism," *Body & Society*, 14:3 (2008), pp. 129–133; Deanne Bogdan, "Musical Spirituality: Reflections on Identity and the Ethics of Embodied Aesthetic Experience in/and the Academy,"

Journal of Aesthetic Education, 37:2 (2003), pp. 80–98. Cf. also articles and chapters in languages other than English, for instance, David Zerbib, "Richard Shusterman: les effets secondaires d'une philosophie douce," *Le Monde des Livres* (20 Nov 2007), p. 12; Monika Bakke, "Wszystkie przyjemności: duże i małe" [All Pleasures Great and Small], *Czas Kultury*, 1 (2003), pp. 27–34; Dorota Koczanowicz, "Sztuka i życie: Teoria estetyczna Richarda Shustermana" [Art and Life: Richard Shusterman's Aesthetic Theory], in *Doświadczenie sztuki, sztuka życia: Wymiary estetyki pragmatycznej* [The Experience of Art and the Art of Living: Dimensions of Pragmatist Aesthetics] (Wrocław: Wydawnictwo Naukowe Dolnośląskiej Szkoły Wyższej, 2009), pp. 159–66. For Shusterman's own reflections on the reception of somaesthetics, see, for example, Richard Shusterman, "Somaesthetics and the Revival of Aesthetics," *Filozofski Vestnik*, 28:2 (2007), pp. 135–149.

10. See Shusterman's own remarks on that topic in "Od literatury do somatoestetyki" [From Literature to Somaesthetics: An Interview with Richard Shusterman, conducted by Wojciech Małecki], *Teksty Drugie*, 6 (2009), pp. 198–200.

11. Note that Shusterman was, for instance, the editor of the important volume *Analytic Aesthetics* (Oxford: Blackwell, 1989).

12. See, for example, Richard Shusterman, *Pragmatist Aesthetics: Living Beauty, Rethinking Art*, (New York: Rowman and Littlefield, 2000, 2nd ed.), p. xvii–xviii.

13. Richard Shusterman, "Human Nature at the Schlachtensee," in *Aesthetics in the Human Environment*, ed. Pauline von Bonsdorff and Arto Haapala (Lahti: International Institute of Applied Aesthetics, 1999), p. 46.

14. Friedrich Nietzsche, *Beyond Good and Evil: Prelude to a Philosophy of the Future*, trans. Walter Kaufmann (New York: Vintage, 1966), p. 13

15. John Dewey, "The Need for a Recovery of Philosophy," in *The Middle Works of John Dewey*, vol. 10, ed. Jo Ann Boydston (Carbondale: Southern Illinois University Press, 1985), p. 46.

16. See, for example, Shusterman, *Pragmatist Aesthetics*, p. xvii–xviii; cf. Richard Shusterman, "Życie, sztuka i filozofia" [Life, Art, and Philosophy: An interview conducted by Adam Chmielewski], in *O sztuce i życiu: Od poetyki hip-hopu do filozofii somatycznej* [On Art and Life: From Hip-Hop Poetics to Somatic Philosophy], trans. and ed. Wojciech Małecki (Wrocław: Atla 2, 2007), p. 19.

17. See, for example, Richard Shusterman, "Popular Art and Education," *Studies in Philosophy and Education*, 13 (1995), p. 207; cf. *Pragmatist Aesthetics*, pp. 20, 45.

18. See, for example, Richard Shusterman, "What Pragmatism Means to Me: Ten Principles," *Revue française d'études américaines*, 124 (2010), pp. 61–62.

19. See Shusterman, *Pragmatist Aesthetics*, p. 280 and *Practicing Philosophy: Pragmatism and the Philosophical Life* (New York and London: Routledge, 1997), p. 233n12. Cf. John Dewey, *Logic: The Theory of Inquiry*, in *The Later Works 1925–1953*, vol. 12, ed. Jo Ann Boydston (Carbondale: Southern Illinois University Press, 1986), p. 32; Thomas M. Alexander, "Dewey, Dualism, and Naturalism," in *A Companion to Pragmatism*, ed. John R. Shook and Joseph Margolis (Malden: Blackwell, 2006), pp. 184–192; and Robert B. Brandom, "When Philosophy Paints Its Blue on Gray: Irony and the Pragmatist Enlightenment," *boundary 2*, 29:2 (2002), p. 5.

20. Cf. Richard Shusterman, *Performing Live: Aesthetic Alternatives for the Ends of Art* (Ithaca: Cornell University Press, 2000), p. 250n1.

21. See *ibid.*, p. 146.

22. Cf. William James, "The Experience of Activity," in *Essays in Radical Empirism* (Cambridge: Harvard University Press, 1976), p. 86; and Shusterman, *Body Consciousness*, p. 135.
23. See Shusterman, "What Pragmatism Means to Me," p. 64.
24. Cf. Shusterman, *Pragmatist Aesthetics*, p. 7; and "Convention: Variations on the Nature/Culture Theme," in *Surface and Depth: Dialectics of Criticism and Culture* (Ithaca: Cornell University Press, 2002), pp. 108–122.
25. Not to mention the fact that they determine also the child's own gustative habits. See Richard Shusterman, "Somaesthetics and Burke's Sublime," *British Journal of Aesthetics*, 45:4 (2005), pp. 338–339.
26. Richard Shusterman "Somaesthetics: A Disciplinary Proposal," *Journal of Aesthetics and Art Criticism*, 57:3 (1999), pp. 303–304.
27. Shusterman, *Performing Live*, p. 137.
28. See Shusterman, *Pragmatist Aesthetics*, p. 263. Cf. William James, "Pragmatism: A New Name for Some Old Ways of Thinking," in *Pragmatism and Other Writings*, ed. Giles Gunn (New York: Penguin Books, 2000), pp. 1–132.
29. Shusterman, *Performing Live*, p. 141.
30. *Ibid.*, p. 138.
31. Shusterman, *Body Consciousness*, p. 24.
32. *Ibid.*, p. 97.
33. *Ibid.*, p. 99. Cf. Shusterman, "Pragmatism and East-Asian Thought," *Metaphilosophy*, 35 (2004), p. 26; Shusterman, *Practicing Philosophy*, p. 41, and Richard Shusterman, "Thinking Through the Body, Educating for the Humanities: A Plea for Somaesthetics," *Journal of Aesthetic Education*, 40:1 (2006), p. 2.
34. Shusterman, *Body Conciousness*, p. 130. Cf. David A. Granger, "Somaesthetics and Racism: Toward an Embodied Pedagogy of Difference," *The Journal of Aesthetic Education*, 44:3 (2010), pp. 69–81.
35. See Shusterman, *Body Consciousness*, p. 23. Cf. Shusterman, *Pragmatist Aesthetics*, p. 272.
36. Shusterman, *Body Consciousness*, p. 29.
37. See, for instance, Shusterman, *Pragmatist Aesthetics*, p. 279. Cf. Richard Shusterman, "Somaesthetics and Education: Exploring the Terrain," in *Knowing Bodies, Moving Minds: Towards Embodied Teaching and Learning*, ed. Liora Bresler (Dordrecht: Kluwer Academic Publishers, 2004), p. 59.
38. Pierre Hadot, *Philosophy as a Way of Life: Spiritual Exercises from Socrates to Foucault*, ed. Arnold Davidson (Oxford: Blackwell, 1995), p. 102. Cited in Shusterman, *Body Consciousness*, p. 16.
39. Shusterman, *Body Consciousness*, p. 17.
40. See Richard Shusterman, "Fallibilism and Faith," *Common Knowledge*, 13:2–3 (2007), pp. 379–384.
41. See Shusterman, *O sztuce i życiu*.
42. In particular, we would like to thank Martin Jay and the University of Illinois Press for giving us permission to include in this volume his essay "Somaesthetics and Democracy: Dewey and Contemporary Body Art," which originally appeared in *The Journal of Aesthetic Education*, 36:4 (2002), pp. 55–69. Copyright 2002 by the Board of Trustees of the University of Illinois.

A PRAGMATIST PATH
THROUGH THE PLAY OF LIMITS:
FROM LITERATURE TO SOMAESTHETICS

Richard Shusterman

I

This volume of collected essays discussing my work in pragmatist philosophy provides me with a valuable occasion for reviewing my philosophical trajectory and its impact on others rather than simply following my well-entrenched habit of looking ahead to new topics and projects that attract my philosophical libido. When the editors asked me not only to respond to the papers but also to contribute an opening essay for the volume, I decided that this essay could usefully trace how I came to pragmatist philosophy and how I was led from my initial focus on literary theory to a much broader philosophical project that eventually generated the interdisciplinary field of somaesthetics. Since this volume takes my pragmatism as its starting point and focus, and since a recent monograph on my aesthetics also explicitly confines itself to my pragmatist writings,[1] I think it would be useful here to explain why I came to embrace pragmatist philosophy (in mid-career), and more particularly how both pragmatism and somaesthetics emerged from my earlier work in analytic philosophy.

Intellectual curiosity and the belief that no single method or school of thought has a monopoly on philosophical insight have led me to work with many different philosophical traditions. Though my movements between analytic philosophy, continental theory, pragmatism, and East-Asian thought might give the impression of chaotic aimless wandering, there is, I believe, considerable coherence of fundamental orientation in my different transitions. For instance, certain themes—such as anti-essentialist pluralism, the primacy of practice for guiding our theoretical efforts and for judging their fruits, and an empirical spirit in theorizing that looks at language and action in their actual (socially embedded and historically changing) contexts rather than in some pure ethereal world of abstraction—have directed my thought from my earliest writings in analytic philosophy of literature to my most recent explorations in somaesthetics.[2] Moreover, in surveying my publication history, I discern a fairly consistent direction in the evolution of my thought.

In this paper I would like to briefly outline one aspect of that evolution by reviewing the main path of my research in the field of aesthetics in terms of an underlying theme that I was initially unaware of but that I increasingly recognize as a central (albeit often implicit) factor or engine that guided my developing research trajectory. That trajectory begins firmly within the realm of literary theory—my very first publication being "The Anomalous Nature of Literature" and my first book *The Object of Literary Criticism*—but it has by now taken me into the broad, interdisciplinary field of somaesthetics. And when I review my trajectory of thirty-two years in aesthetics, I realize that it has been largely driven by an underlying theme that permeates my discussions of the very diverse topics I have treated: a continuing struggle with the various limits that define the aesthetic field, and often also with the limits defining academic philosophy in general.

When I was still a student at Oxford specializing in analytic aesthetics, my first three publications were papers protesting the limits of prevailing monistic doctrines in the philosophy of literature: theories claiming that poetry (and by extension literature in general) is essentially an oral-based performative art without real visual import, and theories arguing that beneath the varying interpretations and evaluations of works of art there was nonetheless only one basic logic of interpretation and one basic logic of evaluation (though philosophers differed as to what that basic logic was and whether it was the same for both interpretation and evaluation). When I proposed contrastingly pluralistic accounts of interpretive and evaluative logic, while suggesting that literature could be appreciated in terms of sight as well as sound, I was not consciously aiming at transgressing the prevailing limits. I was more interested in being right than in being different or original, and I saw myself as working fully within the limits of analytic aesthetics.[3]

My initial decision to concentrate on the field of literature was motivated by the analytic critique of essentialism—too much bad aesthetic theory had resulted from taking what was obviously true in one art and then generalizing it for all arts. This key tenet of Wittgensteinian and Austinian analytic philosophy of art, which I first learned in Jerusalem, was reinforced in my doctoral studies at Oxford. But despite my focus on literature I came to see that to understand it properly (indeed to understand its special features or singularity), I had to relate it to the other arts and thus go beyond the limits of working merely in *literary* theory. So while *The Object of Literary Criticism* (based on my Oxford dissertation) formulated its analysis of work-identity and ontological status and the logics of interpretation and evaluation in terms of literary works, I also indicated how some dimensions of this analysis could be applied to other arts.

In my second book, *T. S. Eliot and the Philosophy of Criticism* (1988), I also sought to focus on issues in philosophy of literature by selecting a paradigmatic literary figure as the prism for my inquiries into such issues as objectivity, subjectivity, pleasure, history, and tradition in critical judgment and reasoning, while deepening my study of interpretation. But once again I found that my investigation inevitably took me beyond the limits of literature, because Eliot himself came increasingly to realize that literature and its criticism were significantly shaped by sociohistorical factors and broader cultural ideologies. My philosophical analyses thus followed his lead by going into more than literary matters, such as the analysis of tradition and the interpretation of culture and its historical changes.

By examining Eliot's turn from his early objectivism to a more historicist, hermeneutic stance, I was moreover impelled to read more deeply into hermeneutic theory and other schools of continental philosophy that emphasized the sociohistorical shaping of art and criticism. Thus, though the book's declared philosophical approach remained analytic philosophy, its topics led me to explore other philosophical perspectives. If its first chapter "Eliot and Analytic Philosophy" explored how that philosophy's new ideas and ideals shaped Eliot's early objectivist literary and critical doctrines, the book's final chapter "Pragmatism and Practical Wisdom" highlighted the pragmatic dimension of Eliot's critical theory while relating it both to classical and contemporary versions of pragmatist philosophy. This made me increasingly appreciative of the rich variety, powers, and resources of philosophical pragmatism.

When, in the late 1980's, I thus expanded my horizons to embrace pragmatism more explicitly, I became conscious of pushing at the limits of analytic aesthetics, though I considered my work to be largely continuous with the basic topics and modes of reasoning of analytic philosophy, much in the way that Nelson Goodman, Richard Rorty, Hilary Putnam, and Joseph Margolis were combining pragmatist insights with analytic styles of argument.[4] And in using some continental philosophy for inspirational insight (from Nietzsche and Adorno to Foucault and Bourdieu), I could assure myself that the most respected analytic philosopher of art, Arthur Danto, had constructed much of his art theory on Hegelian ideas.

Of course, when my book *Pragmatist Aesthetics* (1992) devoted its largest chapter to the analysis and advocacy of hip hop, I could no longer pretend to myself that I was essentially working within the traditional limits of analytic or even pragmatist aesthetics. Colleagues who used to be very friendly began to identify me as a sensationalist transgressor of hallowed boundaries of academic philosophy, reminding me through painful words or even more painfully silent shunning that I had passed beyond limits that defined acceptable work in analytic aesthetics.[5] Though my new work continued to command a distanced respect (and was even appreciatively used by most analytic colleagues to save them the time of reading pragmatist and continental authors for themselves), I could no longer fully be trusted. My subsequent turn to somaesthetics, crowned by my professional training as a somatic educator in the Feldenkrais Method, confirmed my image as what the Germans call a *Grenzgänger*, a border-crosser, a transgressor of boundaries.[6] The French, for their part, have also characterized me as a "nomad philosopher" and *passeur culturel* (a term hard to translate into English because "cultural smuggler" sounds too criminal and narrow while "cultural mediator" too bureaucratic and bland). Whatever its translation, the term was used to suggest that my philosophical explorations crossed well-defined boundaries and sought to import new ideas and topics from across the standard disciplinary borders that divide philosophical schools (or even broader philosophical traditions) from each other and from other domains of thought and life. Like it or not (and initially I greatly disliked it), my image had evolved from a mainstream, Oxford-trained analytic aesthetician into a limit-defying provocateur, who had to be kept at some distance from the inner circles of power within the mainstream aesthetics establishment however much it still accorded my work a respectful hearing.

Pierre Bourdieu once suggested to me, in conversation, a sociological explanation of my philosophical trajectory: my bi-national, transcultural background tends to make boundary crossing (and pluralistic vision) a necessity of life, and this would promote a habitus of cultural pluralism and transgressing limits that would likely be mirrored in philosophical work. Though I had seemed to achieve insider status in Anglo-American analytic aesthetics (as editor of an important Blackwell collection on that topic and as a tenured professor in Temple University's philosophy department that was famous for analytic aesthetics), this insider persona could not really fit with my entrenched habitus as a displaced intellectual, a wandering Jew who had left America for Israel at age sixteen, and who then experienced outsider status there and again at Oxford before returning, in my mid-thirties, as an academic stranger to the United States, though frequently departing again for long periods of research and teaching in France, Germany, and Japan. Perhaps Bourdieu's explanation was right. But rather than going further into this line of social self-analysis (which I elsewhere explore in an overtly autobiographical essay[7]), I wish to suggest in this essay a much broader hypothesis: that the play of limit transgression is a central feature of the field of aesthetics in the West, a key aspect of its history and structure. If I am right, my trajectory reflects not simply the personal hang-ups of an unsettled mind but also a deep current in the history of aesthetics.

II

Modern Western aesthetics defined itself from the beginning as transgressing boundaries and exceeding limits. Baumgarten introduced aesthetics precisely to extend philosophy beyond the limits of conceptual knowledge and into the sphere of sensory perceptions and what he calls "the lower cognitive faculties." As he insists in paragraph 3 of *Aesthetica*'s "Prolegomena," one of aesthetics' goals is "improving knowledge also beyond the borders of the distinctly knowable" ("*Die Verbesserung der Erkenntnis auch über die Grenzen des deutlich Erkennbaren hinaus vorantreibt*"). There is a basic logic at play here: to justify a new philosophical discipline or science like aesthetics, Baumgarten must argue that the new field is needed to go beyond the limits of the studies we already have, that it occupies a place beyond the boundaries defined by other fields. Hence Baumgarten likewise defends the need for aesthetics by saying it goes beyond the limits of *Rhetorik* and *Poetik* by comprehending a larger field ("*Sie umfasst ein weiteres Gebiet*") by including also objects of other arts. Nor can aesthetics be simply equated with criticism or with art, Baumgarten argues, because criticism in general includes critique of logic while aesthetics is said to deal specifically with matters of sensibility, and because aesthetics is claimed to be a science (*Wissenschaft*) rather than just an art.[8]

Beyond Baumgarten, the modern field of aesthetics can be seen as an attempt to go beyond the limits of older philosophies of beauty, sublimity, and taste to engage a much wider domain of qualities and judgments relating to our pleasurable and meaningful experience of art and nature. We can likewise see the essential move of Hegelian aesthetics (and other aesthetic idealisms) as moving beyond the limits of sensuous and nonconceptual experience and instead toward the idea of art as purveying the very highest spiritual truths, albeit in a somewhat sensuous form. Moreover, we can certainly see modernity's progressive revolutions of artistic forms and styles in the same Hegelian spirit of dynamic movement that progresses by meeting and overcoming determinations of boundaries.[9]

We may have forgotten the limit-defying trend in aesthetics because the dominant Anglo-American aesthetic school of the last half century, analytic aesthetics, has been keen to insist on defining limits and on policing them. Initially, it had the best of reasons to stress the need for more recognition of limits and distinctions in order to remedy the limit-defying confusions of the dominant aesthetic idealism of the early twentieth century, perhaps most powerfully exemplified in Benedetto Croce. As I have elsewhere argued, analytic aesthetics emerged from dissatisfaction with the wooly vagueness of idealist, Hegelian-inspired aesthetic theories such as Croce's that affirm a more unbounded aesthetics whose project is limit defiance.[10]

Croce's project was shaped by a struggle to defend the transcendent power of aesthetic insight from the limitations of encroaching positivisms with respect to art's meaning. If one positivism confined artistic creation and evaluation to the strict rules of genre criticism, another reduced art to historical and sociological causal explanations, such as Hippolyte Taine's famous formula that art could be defined and explained simply in terms of "race, milieu, and moment."[11] For Croce, who defines the aesthetic in terms of a basic formative power of intuition that pervades all meaningful perception, aesthetics cannot be confined to a narrow domain of poetics and fine arts nor to questions of natural beauty. The aesthetic instead is a fundamental principle of intuitive perception that pervades the experienced world as a whole. All the world, Croce argues, is essentially a matter of aesthetics, since "all this world is intuition," "it is nothing but intuition or aesthetic fact."[12]

Identifying intuition with expression and language, and insisting that the nature of intuitions and language is "perpetual creation" and change, Croce argues that any attempt to limit aesthetic intuition to fixed boundaries, categories, or meanings is as useless and perverse as "to seek the immobility of motion." Traditional limits of aesthetic genres and rhetorical categories are thus completely swept away: "Expression is an indivisible whole," Croce claims, hence "a philosophical classification of expressions is impossible," for there are no essential distinguishing principles or fixed "formal differences" to justify such categorial limits, only differences of degree and context and changing convention. The same goes for the alleged limits between artist, critic, and audience; and even art and non-art. "The limits of the expressions and intuitions that are called art, as opposed to those that are vulgarly called non-art, are empirical and impossible to define. If an epigram be art, why not a single word?" Challenging not only the limits but even the standard distinctions between disciplines, Croce declares that "philosophy of language and philosophy of art are the same thing." By asserting that traditional aesthetic distinctions cannot rely on fixed essential principles since aesthetic perception is always a matter of the changing play of language and experience, yet failing to equally insist that pragmatic distinctions can nonetheless be usefully made, Croce's theory falls into a much wider essentialism, a monism of the world as intuition-expression or language. (Deconstruction, I have argued, in pursuing a very similar argument against the foundations and fixity of genre and disciplinary distinctions, also tends to fall into the trap of linguistic essentialism where all the world is nothing but text.[13])

Analytic aesthetics emerged as a power in the mid-twentieth century by attacking the influential Crocean view for the dreary, vague, and apparently useless monotony of its distinction-demolishing essentialism. By that time, art no longer needed to be defended against positivist, reductionist explanatory models, whether of traditional rhetoric or of sociological determinism. This was because more autonomously aesthetic varieties of art criticism and literary criticism had by then been firmly established, for example that advocated by the New Criticism. Croce's early analytic critics did not generally maintain that the genre distinctions Croce dismissed could be justified by appeal to real metaphysical essences or to tradition. On the contrary, they themselves offered critical revisions of traditional essentialisms about art and its genres. But they did maintain that that in order to talk illuminatingly about art, one must draw some distinctions and respect some limits of signification in one's theoretical terms; and that to define these boundaries more clearly and maintain them more consistently could promote better ways of talking about art.

Monroe Beardsley, for example, in distinguishing the perceptual object from its physical base and authorial intention, explicitly argued that since there is no essence of the aesthetic object to be discovered, we have "to propose a way of making the distinction" which itself can only be justified pragmatically. "One can only point to the conveniences of adopting it, the inconveniences of rejecting it, ... [and] its own inconveniences."[14] Similarly, John Passmore, in complaining of "the dreariness of aesthetics" prescribed the remedy of "a ruthlessness in making distinctions," in drawing limits that may "seem arbitrary" but can be justified pragmatically by the fact that certain distinctions or limits can structure the aesthetic field in a way that "gives rise to interesting generalizations."[15] He even suggested that "the dullness of aesthetics arises from the attempt to construct a subject where there isn't one," "that there is no aesthetics and yet there are principles of literary criticism, musical criticism, etc.," and that general aesthetics should be abandoned "for an intensive special study of the separate arts," whose specific differences should be respected.

But most analysts in aesthetics still pursued projects of finding general limits to distinguish aesthetics from other fields. J. O. Urmson, my supervisor at Oxford, for example, argued that "[w]e should expect to find a criterion which allows us to distinguish the aesthetic, the moral, the economic, the intellectual, and other evaluations by a single *fundamentum divisionis*," and that "to call an appreciation aesthetic has as part of its point the effect of ruling out the moral as irrelevant."[16] Stuart Hampshire devoted an entire article "Ethics and Appreciation" to arguing likewise that ethical and aesthetic judgments were entirely different in logical form, and that aesthetics should confine itself to the limits of its own subjective and particularist logic.[17]

III

The history of analytic philosophy's attempts to draw firm and convincing distinctions can instructively illustrate how aesthetics tends to resist clear and strict limits. Analysts such as Beardsley and Urmson tried to distinguish the aesthetic from the non-aesthetic in terms of the former's being narrowly concerned with the perceptual appearance or surface "look of things."[18] Yet this appearance-based limit was shown to break down once we realize that what we know about an artwork's material properties and purpose will in fact affect, and should affect, how that work appears to us, thus reversing the primacy of appearance over non-perceptual knowledge in aesthetic appreciation.

Other analysts, such as Frank Sibley, tried to draw a sharp aesthetic/non-aesthetic limit in terms of the alleged logically anomalous and independent status of aesthetic terms, the claim being that such terms were neither rule-governed nor conditioned by and inferable from any set of non-aesthetic features of the artwork but instead rely on aesthetic taste alone for their application.[19] Yet closer analysis showed that this alleged independence from non-aesthetic properties could not be maintained, since aesthetic properties must be at least causally and ontologically dependent on the work's other properties, and since it was also clear that the prominent presence of some non-aesthetic properties (such as great size, mass, weight, bulky shape) could entail that certain aesthetic properties (such as delicate fragility) would not be appropriate for describing the work.[20] Moreover, predicates such as unity and balance seem to straddle the alleged distinction because they can be conceived in both aesthetic and non-aesthetic (computational) terms.

Similarly, the attempt to limit aesthetics to a realm devoid of all ethical considerations met the insurmountable difficulty that ethical content often so deeply pervaded the artwork's meaning that the work could not be properly understood without attending to its ethical dimensions. Attempts to distinguish a special aesthetic attitude or a special aesthetic experience that is limited to artworks and natural beauty (and arises always and only in their presence) have likewise proven very problematic—indeed so problematic that analysts have persistently questioned whether the notions of aesthetic attitude and aesthetic experience are at all useful for defining the field.

Increasingly aware of the problem of determining the limits of the aesthetic, analytic philosophers have devoted increasingly greater attention to defining instead the limits of art. Two different limit-defining projects can be noted here: first, drawing the boundaries of the realm of art as a whole in contrast to the rest of life and what Danto calls "mere real things"; and, secondly, defining the specific borders of individual artworks, that is, the borders that mark off a true instance of the given work (say a genuine text or performance of *Hamlet*, or an authentic copy of an etching) from objects that are inauthentic presentations, copies, or forgeries of the artworks they claim to be. Both these projects aim at perfectly covering the extension of the concepts they define (whether art as a whole or a particular artwork) by providing a verbal formula that would fit all and only the right objects for the concept in question: namely, with respect to the general concept of art, those objects that are accepted as works of art; or, with respect to a particular artwork, those objects or events that are accepted as authentic instances of the particular work in question (in painting most often this is a single instance).

Any proposed definition of this sort can be challenged by bringing counterexamples that its verbal formula would either wrongly cover or fail to cover and so would either wrongly include or exclude from art's domain or from the particular artwork's authentic instances. The proposed definition is thus shown to be either too wide or too narrow; its motivating ideal is perfect coverage, and I have therefore called this definitional style "the wrapper model of theory." For like the better food wraps, such theories of art transparently present, contain, and conserve their object—our conventional view of art. They aim to preserve rather than transform art's practice and experience. Like the condom, another form of elastic transparent wrapper (which the French aptly designate "*preservatif*"), such definitions aim to preserve the conventional limits of art (and thus art itself) from contamination by art's exciting yet impure enveloping environment while at the same time preserving that environment from art's potential to create new life by its penetration beyond the limits that seek to compartmentalize it within the established artworld and within the established criteria of legitimately authentic performances or instances of a particular artwork.

Let us first consider the issue of defining the limits of the particular artwork's identity. This was of crucial importance to analytic aesthetics as part of its preoccupation with art's objects that in turn arose from academic criticism's preoccupation with objective critical truth, which seemed to demand a clearly defined object to serve as the standard of truth. Thus Beardsley claimed, "The first thing to make criticism possible is an object ... with its own properties against which interpretations can be checked," and artworks therefore must be such "self-sufficient entities" whose properties and meaning are independent of their contexts of genesis and reception.[21] The object of art becomes a fetishized "icon" whose limits of identity and authenticity must be strictly defined and protected from fakes and corruptions.[22] But we see in Nelson Goodman's influential theory of work-identity how the need for precisely defining the work's identity leads to the paradoxical result of defining it independently of its aesthetically important properties, since such properties are too vague and variable for providing clear definitions. For Goodman, the identity of a musical work must be defined only by the notes of the score, because only the notes are clearly definable and defining. This means that he admits that the most miserable performance without actual mistakes counts as a fully authentic instance of the musical artwork "while the most brilliant performance with one wrong note does not."[23] But what is the real point of defining an artwork to preserve it, if the aesthetically important properties of that work are not meant to be preserved? Is it not more fruitful to concentrate on preserving or enriching the aesthetic values of aesthetic experience, even if this involves admitting some wrong notes or letters or reproductions? Such analytic perversities helped push me toward pragmatism, as did the analytic attempts to define art in general.

The most influential of these attempts to define art have likewise tried to do so without appealing to the notion of the aesthetic (whose limits and essence the analysts had earlier failed to effectively define). Instead these theories define art in terms of something beyond aesthetic perception but alleged as necessary for shaping such perception in appreciating art—namely, the artworld, a notion that Arthur Danto introduced to analytic aesthetics through his beloved example of Warhol's *Brillo Boxes*, and that George Dickie then interpreted in terms of the institutional theory of art. That institutional theory, which defines an artwork as simply any "...artifact upon which some person or persons acting on behalf of a certain social institution (the artworld) has conferred the status of candidate for appreciation,"[24] is purely procedural and formal. It leaves all substantive decisions and principles to the artworld. By stressing this social context through which art is generated and provided with properties not directly exhibited to the senses (properties that distinguish between Warhol's *Brillo Boxes* and their visually identical counterparts), the institutional theory can explain how art can have a definitional essence without its objects sharing a core of exhibited aesthetic properties. The theory's success in covering all and only authorized artworks is matched by its explanatory poverty. It provides no explanation of the reasons or constraints for proposing artworld membership, no explanation of the artworld's history and structure or of the artworld's relationship to the wider socio-cultural and polit-ico-economic world in which the artworld is embedded and by which the artworld is significantly shaped.

Danto rejects the institutional theory of art as lacking explanatory value because of its historical emptiness. Ignoring Wölfflin's insight that not every-thing is possible at every time, the institutional theory fails to consider the historical conditions that structure the artworld and that therefore shape and limit its participants' actions in creating and interpreting art. It cannot explain why Warhol's work would not have been accepted had Warhol produced it in fin-de-siècle Paris or *quattrocento* Florence but could be art in Manhattan in the 1960s. The explanation, Danto argues, depends on the history of art and art theory, because objects are artworks only if they can be interpreted as such by the artworld. Thus, the *Brillo Boxes* as a work of art required an interpreta-tion to that effect, both creatively by Warhol and responsively by his audi-ence; and the artworld "required a certain historical development" to make that interpretation possible.[25] And since the artworld is but an abstraction from the artistic, critical, historiographical and theoretical practices that constitute art's history, art is essentially a complex historical practice that must be de-fined and understood historically.

So far so good; but Danto also insists on viewing the structure and histo-ry of the artworld simply in terms of "its own internal development," in essen-tial isolation from history's wider social and cultural contexts, economic fac-tors, and political struggles. This compartmentalization from the rest of life is part and parcel of Danto's insistence that the distinction between art and reali-ty is absolute. But, as Danto surely knows, relations between the wider life-world are significantly formative of directions in the artworld. Why was it Warhol's *Brillo Boxes* rather than Duchamp's much earlier *objets trouvés* (or readymades) that so strongly captured Danto's and the wider public's interest and thus more decisively transformed our notion of contemporary art? Is not the wider social and cultural revolution of the 1960s part of the explanation, along with the ever-increasing power of consumerist culture and of popular media culture to which Warhol himself was so attached? How can we explain the emergence of graffiti art and the work of Keith Haring and Jean-Michel Basquiat without looking to social and cultural movements such as hip-hop that were initially beyond the established limits of the artworld?

By faithfully representing our established concept of art and insisting on its objects' radical distinction from "mere real things," Danto's theory best realizes the dual goals of wrapper definitions: accurate reflection and com-partmental differentiation that set art apart from the rest of life.[26] My dissatis-faction with the value of these goals helped push me toward the path of prag-matism. If all substantive decisions as to what counts as art are left to the internal decisions of the artworld as recorded by art history, then what useful purpose does simply reflecting those decisions in a philosophical formula serve, apart from appeasing the old philosophical urge for theory as mirroring reflection of the real?

Accurate reflection seems an eminently valuable philosophical ideal when reality is conceived in terms of fixed, necessary essences lying beyond ordinary empirical understanding. This is because an adequate representation of such reality would always remain valid and effective as a criterion for assessing ordinary understanding and practice. But if art's realities are the empirical and changing contingencies of art's historical career, then the reflective model seems pointless. For here, theory's representation neither penetrates beyond changing phenomena nor can sustain their changes. Instead, it must run a hopeless race of perpetual narrative revision, holding the mirror of reflective theory up to art's changing nature by representing its history.

Danto tries to avoid this worry by insisting that art, despite its changing history, has a defining and unchanging "transhistorical essence" that "is always the same." His claim is that there is "a fixed and universal artistic identity" or "unchangeable" essence of art, even an "extrahistorical concept of art," but that this essence merely "discloses itself through history."[27] Likewise, though this defining essence determines the limits of art (by marking art off from what is not art), it does not in any way limit how art can appear, since aesthetic properties are excluded from this essence. So in that sense, for Danto, anything could be a work of art though many things are not works of art.

The problem with this essentialist strategy is that the definition it provides is not at all helpful in telling us how to recognize a work of art, which is one of the reasons why essential definitions were sought. Nor does Danto's notion of essence provide effective criteria for evaluating art or making stylistic suggestions for creating art, which are the other important practical motives for seeking an essential definition of art. Both good and bad artworks, Danto realizes, must have the very same essence, since both are works of art by virtue of that essence, and that essence is not at all a matter of aesthetic or artistic quality.[28] Danto's essentialist strategy moreover fails to define art's essence in a sufficiently specific way. His two criteria for the essence of an artwork (which he admits are too "meager" to "be the entire story") are to "have a content or meaning" and "to embody its meaning."[29] Yet iconic signs and all sorts of cultural objects also satisfy these criteria, and so do most intentional actions. A real-life kiss has meaning and embodies it. But that does not make it a work of art; though, of course, one could stage a kiss as an artwork or represent one as Klimt and Rodin did so sensually.

Art's mutable history, however, need not be merely represented in theory (essentialist or otherwise); pragmatism urges that this history can also be made through theoretical interventions. So pragmatism also rethinks the roles and limits of aesthetic theory and philosophy. No longer content with simply analyzing realities and concepts, pragmatism seeks to improve them and thereby promote better experience. Such theoretical activism does not entail abandoning philosophy altogether by forsaking its traditional project and self-image as the wholly disinterested pursuit of truth. For philosophy's most powerful achievements were not always, if ever, really governed by this goal. Certainly Plato's aesthetic theory cannot be seen as disinterestedly representing the nature of art. It was clearly a politically motivated response to the pressing problem of whose intellectual leadership (art's ancient wisdom or philosophy's new rationality) should guide Athenian society at a time of troubled change, political dissension, and military defeat. The influential political theories of Thomas Hobbes and John Locke were also responses to political crisis and were shaped by political motives. Moreover, the very ideal of pure, neutral reflection typically disguises an impure bias. Fixation on the facts often reflects the interest of a conservatism that is happy to reinforce the status quo by representing it in definition, or is simply too timid to take part in the messy struggle over the shaping of culture. The fetishism of disinterested knowledge obscures the truth that philosophy's ultimate aim is to benefit human life rather than serving pure truth for truth's sake. If art and aesthetic experience are crucial forms of human flourishing, then philosophy betrays its role if it merely looks on with neutrality without joining the struggle to extend their breadth and power.

IV

For such reasons I turned from analytic philosophy to pragmatism, while also enlisting insights from hermeneutics, critical theory, and poststructuralism that challenge in different ways some of the problematic assumptions and limits of analytic aesthetics: its fetishized concern with precisely defining art's objects that are presumed to have a fixed identity, unity, and ontology; its exaggerated sense of art's demarcation from the rest of life and autonomy from wider social and political forces that in fact penetrate even into very forms of artistic expression; and its essentially descriptivist conceptual approach that typically eschews revisionary projects and socio-political engagement so as to represent and reinforce the established cultural status quo.[30]

If analytic theory is essentially demarcational—seeking to define by delimiting the concepts, it analyzes in terms of wrapper definitions of extension, then the pragmatism I practice tries to be more transformational in style. Though beginning with a recognition of the established meanings and limits of the concepts it treats, the pragmatist examines whether a concept's range can be usefully extended (or narrowed) in places where its borders seem vague and flexible enough to allow such extension (or restriction) without destroying the concept's principal meaning and value but rather making it more meaningful and useful in improving our aesthetic understanding and experience. Recognizing that Dewey's definition of art as experience was hopelessly inadequate as an extensional or wrapper theory, I argued (in *Pragmatist Aesthetics*) that it was nonetheless useful as a transformational theory, because its emphasizing aesthetic experience could not only help break the hold of object fetishism in contemporary art, aesthetics, and culture but could also be used to help acquire artistic legitimacy for popular arts (such as rap music) that provided powerful aesthetic experience but were not yet granted genuine aesthetic or artistic status.

My own subsequent proposal to define art as dramatization was likewise not at all aimed at perfect wrapper coverage of the extension of art but instead to highlight two crucial aspects of art—intensity of presence and formal framing—that have generated conflicting theories that divide contemporary aesthetics.[31] The concept of dramatization connotes both intensity of meaningful appearance, action, or experience (which generates theories that define art in terms of immediate, captivating presence or experience). But it also connotes the formal framing of an action, appearance, or experience through a historically established conventional framework that differentiates what is framed from the ordinary flow of life. This second feature lies at the core of contemporary theories that define art in terms of its historically constructed social differentiation from other realms, theories such as Pierre Bourdieu's, Danto's, and Dickie's. In proposing the idea of art as dramatization my aims were also transformational in that the definition will take us beyond the conventional limits of established art by applying also to forms of ritual and athletics that display significant artistry and aesthetic experience but do not fall under the concept of art. It can also apply, as I have recently argued,[32] to practices of love-making, the so-called erotic arts, whose status as art and potential to provide intense and artistically dramatized aesthetic experience has been neglected in the West. Its exploration forms part of my current research program in somaesthetics.

V

Somaesthetics, of course, is a natural extension of my work in pragmatist aesthetics. Bringing aesthetics closer to the realm of life and practice, I realized, entails bringing the body more centrally into aesthetic focus, since all life and practice—all perception, cognition, and action—is crucially performed through the body. Somaesthetics was thus conceived to complement the basic project of pragmatist aesthetics by elaborating the ways that a disciplined, ramified, and interdisciplinary attention to bodily experience, methods, discourses, and performances could enrich our aesthetic experience and practice, not only in the fine arts but in the diverse arts of living. It originated as an attempt to go beyond the limits not only of Baumgarten's neglect of somatic cultivation in his original project of aesthetic cultivation, but also beyond the rejection of body and desire that is so prominent in the Western tradition of philosophical aesthetics from Shaftesbury and Kant through Schopenhauer and into the present, despite the fact that body and desire are so prominent in Western art and literature, even in its religious forms.

But the roots of my somaesthetic project extend beyond my interest in revitalizing aesthetics. The project was inspired equally by the ancient idea of philosophy as a way of life and my efforts to apply the pragmatist tradition to revive this idea in order to overcome the limits of philosophy's institutionalized confinement as a purely academic practice of teaching, reading, and writing texts. Thus, it is in my book *Practicing Philosophy: Pragmatism and the Philosophical Life* (1997) that I first discussed the idea of somaesthetics in an explicit way by using this term.[33] For me, the notion of philosophy as an art of living (rather than an "art of dying" as Plato's *Phaedo* described it) entails that embodiment should be a meaningful aspect of philosophical practice since it is an essential aspect of life. Philosophers in the ancient world were assessed not simply by the words they wrote or spoke but by the virtue of their actions and the quality of their comportment. Confucius thus could suggest to his disciples that he simply give up lecturing and teach (as nature does) by exemplary wordless behavior; and Mencius indeed praised this style of teaching: "His every limb bears wordless testimony."[34] Somaesthetics thus offered a way of reminding contemporary readers that philosophy could and should be practiced with one's body and not be limited only to the life of the mind. In showing how philosophical practice engages with political issues of democracy, justice, freedom, and liberal society, *Practicing Philosophy* also highlighted the body as our primordial mode of experience and instrument of action. Though *Practicing Philosophy* contains my most focused discussion of political theory, I had already broached political questions of democracy, justice, and freedom in my work in aesthetics. For most readers, this has been most evident in my advocacy of hip hop and other forms of popular art, but I had already learned from Eliot the lesson that aesthetic issues always go beyond the limits of art and are shaped by social and political factors: "'Pure' artistic appreciation is ... only an ideal, when not merely a figment."[35]

Somaesthetics involves an attempt to go beyond the conventional limits of philosophical aesthetics as mere theory by insisting on a practical dimension of actually cultivating somatic disciplines. Though Baumgarten originally conceived aesthetics as a discipline that one studied also through practical aesthetic exercises, he rejected somatic exercises from the field because he associated the body with mere flesh devoid of capacity for perception (*aesthesis*). My concept of soma as a living, purposive, sentient, perceptive body or bodily subjectivity provides an altogether different direction. We can, as I have tried to demonstrate, improve our perceptive faculties through better use of the soma. Because the most convincing demonstrations of this truth are not in verbal arguments but in lived perceptual experience, there is great importance to the actual experience of somaesthetic exercises that heighten perception. I have therefore felt obliged not only to lecture on somaesthetics but also to give practical workshops that convey and underline its practical dimension.[36] These workshops exhaust a great amount of time and energy that I would otherwise be happy to devote to reading and writing, but they are necessary for insuring that somaesthetics goes beyond the limits of a mere theoretical discursive pursuit; and indeed they have proven extremely rewarding in offering a different way of transmitting my philosophical ideas.

Finally, somaesthetics, even in its more theoretical pursuits, goes beyond the typical disciplinary limits of philosophy. Though I initially conceived it as entirely nested within philosophy, most likely as a subdiscipline of aesthetics, I soon realized that it would be more fruitfully pursued as an interdisciplinary field. It should enlist a variety of disciplines (such as history, sociology, cosmetics, anatomy, meditative and martial arts, physiology, nutrition, kinesiology, psychology, and neuroscience) that enrich our understanding of how we experience and use the body in appreciative perception, aesthetic performance, and creative self-fashioning and that can provide or test methods for improving such experience and use. Anatomy and kinesiology, for example, can help explain how greater flexibility in the spine and ribcage can increase one's range of vision by enabling greater rotation of the head, while, on the other hand, more intelligent use of the eyes can conversely (through their occipital muscles) improve the head's rotation and eventually the spine's.

Some critics express the worry that this breaking out of philosophy's disciplinary limits risks making somaesthetics an incoherent and unstructured field with no center relating to aesthetics. In particular, the interest in natural science is feared as an invasive impertinence to aesthetic theory. But I believe that aesthetic research should be properly informed by the best relevant scientific knowledge; and the sciences that explain somatic functioning are surely relevant to the question of enhancing somatic experience, use, and beauty. Renaissance art and art theory provide a good precedent for the use of science, since they clearly owe much of their success to the study of anatomy, mathematics, and the optics of perspective. The central, structuring focus of somaesthetics is the body's use in appreciative perception (*aesthesis*) and aesthetic self-fashioning, and there are certainly many matters that fall outside its limits. Issues in formal logic and income tax hardly seem to pertain to the field, but there is little point to outlaw their possible relevance a priori from the outset. If some aspect of knowledge can be convincingly shown to relate importantly and productively to somaesthetics' central concerns, then somaesthetics can reinterpret or extend its borders at that precise place to take it in, recognizing that limits (just like concepts) can still function when they are flexible and vague. Somaesthetics, moreover, contains some structuring distinctions that provide some organizing borders within the field. The different branches of analytic somaesthetics (essentially descriptive theory), pragmatic somaesthetics (comparative evaluation of methodologies of practice), and practical somaesthetics (actual performance of somatic disciplines) have already been elaborated too often to warrant repetition here.

Instead I wish to close by briefly considering another kind of limit with which somaesthetics is concerned and which has been especially emphasized by some important contemporary French philosophers, such as Georges Bataille and Michel Foucault. It is not so much a conceptual limit or disciplinary boundary but an experiential one, which they sometimes call "limit-experience" (*expérience-limite*) and which they describe as an experience of violent intensity, typically involving some violent form of somatic transgression that is also typically a transgression of moral as well as somatic norms.[37] The value of these limit-experiences lies not simply in their experiential intensity that seems related to the intense sublimities of aesthetic experience, but especially in their power to transform us by showing us the limits of our conventional experience and subjectivity and by introducing us to something fascinatingly powerful beyond those limits, an "*au delà*" of what we are and know. Is somaesthetics committed to such limit-experiences? And what would such commitment imply about its general viability and value—in pragmatic, ethical, social, and health-related terms?

Certainly, somaesthetics is committed to studying the use of such forms of limit-experiences, but that does not imply a commitment to advocating them as the best way to enlarge our somaesthetic capacities and to achieve wider transformational improvements of our selves and self-knowledge. In fact, there is growing evidence from recent studies in psychology and neurophysiology that indicate the dangers of such sensory violence for our powers and pleasures of perception. These studies reinforce perspectives of the old Weber-Fechner law of psychophysics which explains how increased intensity of stimulus reduces the power to perceive and appreciate smaller sensory differences—thus tending to generate a spiral effect where ever stronger stimulation is demanded to meet the rising sensory thresholds, habits, and needs. Somaesthetics can therefore involve also a critique of the limits (cognitive, aesthetic, as well as practical, moral, and social) of these violent limit-experiences, while also exploring other limit-experiences that deploy more gentle, subtle means to probe a wide range of somaesthetic limits (limits of sensory attention, somatic flexibility, habitual breathing rhythms, and muscular tensions) that can equally achieve powerful experiences of transformative exultation that expand the self.

Moreover, somaesthetics should not limit itself to the realm of ecstatic limit-experiences. There is a range of different somaesthetic limits that we fail to appreciate in everyday life, and a better experiential knowledge of them could significantly improve the ways we live. Lacking the sensitivity to sense these limits—such as the border between satiating our hunger and being full, between engaging perceptual interest and over-stimulation, between proper tonus for postural poise and excessive muscular contraction—has led all too much of our population to problems of obesity, insomnia, and chronic back pain. We often do not perceive these borders because our somaesthetic awareness has not been sufficiently sharpened and sensitized to grasp them. The problems arising from failure to recognize such limits might be called the somaesthetic pathologies of everyday life; and it is the topic of another paper.[38]

NOTES

1. Wojciech Małecki, *Embodying Pragmatism: Richard Shusterman's Aesthetics and Literary Theory* (Frankfurt am Main-New York: Peter Lang, 2010).
2. When I was asked in 2009 to write a preface for the French translation of my first book, *The Object of Literary Criticism* (Amsterdam: Rodopi, 1984), written before I had any interest in pragmatism, I was surprised on rereading the book in French translation how certain pragmatist themes were already powerfully present in my work (probably through the influence of Wittgenstein and Austin). For more details on the continuity of this work with my later work in pragmatism, see "Préface à l'édition française," in Richard Shusterman, *L'objet de la critique littéraire* (Paris: Questions Théoriques, 2009), pp. 7–12.
3. See Richard Shusterman, "The Anomalous Nature of Literature," *British Journal of Aesthetics,* 18 (1978), pp. 317–329; "The Logic of Interpretation," *Philosophical Quarterly,* 28 (1978), pp. 310–324; "The Logic of Evaluation," *Philosophical Quarterly,* 30 (1980), pp. 327–341.
4. In my "Introduction" to *Analytic Aesthetics* (Oxford: Blackwell, 1989), I explore how some pragmatist perspectives can be seen as convergent with and even formative of some important approaches in analytic aesthetics.
5. See Richard Shusterman, *Pragmatist Aesthetics: Living Beauty, Rethinking Art* (Oxford: Blackwell, 1992).
6. I briefly mentioned the idea of somaesthetics (or more precisely *Somästhetik*) in my book *Vor der Interpretation* (Wien: Passagen Verlag, 1996), but the first time I really discussed it was in *Practicing Philosophy* (London: Routledge, 1997). I first outlined the structure of somaesthetics, in Richard Shusterman, "Somaesthetics: A Disciplinary Proposal," *Journal of Aesthetics and Art Criticism,* 57 (1999), pp. 299–313, revised and reprinted in the second edition of *Pragmatist Aesthetics* (New York: Rowman & Littlefield, 2000), two further chapters in *Performing Live* (Ithaca: Cornell University Press, 2000), and in too many subsequent papers to list here. My fullest treatment of somaesthetics (a field that goes far beyond the traditional questions of art and aesthetics) is in *Body Consciousness: A Philosophy of Mindfulness and Somaesthetics* (Cambridge: Cambridge University Press, 2008). For a detailed bibliography on somaesthetics including articles and books by other authors, see http://www.fau.edu/humanitieschair/Somaesthetics_Bibliography.php and http://wise.fau.edu/humanitieschair/Somaesthetics_Bibliography_Others.php.
7. Richard Shusterman, "Regarding Oneself and Seeing Double: Fragments of Autobiography," in *The Philosophical I: Personal Reflections on Life in Philosophy,* ed. George Yancey (New York: Rowman and Littlefield, 2002), pp. 1–21.
8. My citations from Baumgarten are from the bilingual (Latin-German) abridged edition of this work, Alexander Baumgarten, *Theoretische Ästhetik: Die grundlengenden Abschnitte aus der "Aesthetica"* (1750/58), trans. Hans. R. Schweizer (Hamburg: Felix Meiner, 1988), pp. 3, 5.
9. I raised these same points in "Somaesthetics at the Limits," *Nordic Journal of Aesthetics,* 35 (2008), pp. 7–23, and redeploy its arguments here.
10. See Richard Shusterman, "Analytic Aesthetics, Literary Theory, and Deconstruction," *The Monist,* 69 (1986), pp. 22–38. For an account of Croce's relationship

to pragmatist philosophy, see my "Croce on Interpretation: Deconstruction and Pragmatism," *New Literary History*, 20 (1988), pp. 199–216.

11. See Hippolyte Taine, *History of English Literature*, trans. Henri van Laun (New York, 1886), 18, as qtd. in William K. Wimsatt and Cleanth Brooks, *Literary Criticism: A Short History* (Chicago: University of Chicago Press, 1954), p. 532.

12. See Benedetto Croce, *Aesthetic as Science of Expression and General Linguistic*, trans. Douglas Ainslie (London: Macmillan and Co., 1922), pp. 22–23, 26, 30, 110–113, 146, 197–198, 234, 247.

13. See Richard Shusterman, "Analytic Aesthetics, Literary Theory, and Deconstruction," and also Richard Shusterman, "Deconstruction and Analysis: Confrontation and Convergence," *British Journal of Aesthetics*, 26 (1986), pp. 311–327.

14. See Monroe C. Beardsley, *Aesthetics: Problems in the Philosophy of Criticism* (New York: Harcourt, Brace, 1958), pp. 52–53.

15. See John Passmore, "The Dreariness of Aesthetics," in *Aesthetics and Language*, ed. William R. Elton (Oxford: Blackwell, 1954), pp. 45–50, 55.

16. See J. O. Urmson, "What Makes a Situation Aesthetic?" in *Aesthetics: Contemporary Studies in Aesthetics*, ed. Francis J. Coleman (New York: McGraw-Hill, 1968), pp. 360, 368.

17. See Stuart Hampshire, "Logic and Appreciation," in *Aesthetics and Language*, p. 169.

18. See Monroe C. Beardsley, *Aesthetics*, pp. 29–52; J. O. Urmson, "What Makes a Situation Aesthetic?" *Proceedings of the Aristotelian Society*, supp. 131 (1957), pp. 72–92.

19. See Frank Sibley, "Aesthetic Concepts," *Philosophical Review*, 68 (1959), pp. 421–450.

20. For these and other criticisms of Sibley's theory, see Ted Cohen, "Aesthetic/Nonaesthetic and the Concept of Taste: A Critique of Sibley's Position," *Theoria*, 39 (1979), pp. 113–152; Peter Kivy, *Speaking of Art* (The Hague: Martinus Nijhoff, 1973); Gary Stahl, "Sibley's Aesthetic Concepts: An Ontological Mistake," *Journal of Aesthetics and Art Criticism*, 29 (1971), pp. 385–389.

21. See Monroe C. Beardsley, *The Possibility of Criticism* (Detroit: Wayne State University Press, 1970), p. 16.

22. See Monroe C. Beardsley, *The Verbal Icon: Studies in the Meaning of Poetry* (University of Kentucky Press, 1967).

23. See Nelson Goodman, *Languages of Art* (Oxford: Oxford University Press, 1969), pp. 120, 186, 209–210.

24. See George Dickie, *Aesthetics* (Indianapolis: Bobbs-Merrill, 1971), p. 101; and *Art and the Aesthetic: An Institutional Analysis* (Ithaca: Cornell University Press, 1974). I provide a more detailed critique of his theory in *Pragmatist Aesthetics*, pp. 38–40.

25. Arthur C. Danto, *The Transfiguration of the Commonplace* (Cambridge: Harvard University Press, 1981), p. 208.

26. *Ibid.*, ch. 1.

27. Arthur Danto, *After the End of Art* (Princeton: Princeton University Press, 1997), pp. 28, 187, 193.

28. *Ibid.*, p. 197; and Arthur Danto, *The Madonna of the Future* (New York: Farrar, Straus, and Giroux, 2000), p. 427.

29. Danto, *The Madonna of the Future*, p. xix.

30. For more on these themes, see Shusterman, *Pragmatist Aesthetics*.

31. See Richard Shusterman, *Surface and Depth* (Ithaca: Cornell University Press, 2002), ch.13.

32. See Richard Shusterman, "Asian Ars Erotica and the Question of Sexual Aesthetics," *Journal of Aesthetics and Art Criticism*, 65:1 (Winter 2007), pp. 55–68.

33. Richard Shusterman, *Practicing Philosophy: Pragmatism and the Philosophical Life* (New York: Routledge, 1997), pp. 128–29, 176–77.

34. For more on these points, see my "Pragmatist Aesthetics and East-Asian Thought," in Richard Shusterman, *The Range of Pragmatism and the Limits of Philosophy* (Oxford: Blackwell, 2004), pp. 13–42.

35. T. S. Eliot, *The Use of Poetry and the Use of Criticism* (London: Faber, 1964), p. 109. For more on this topic and more generally on Eliot's philosophy of criticism, see Richard Shusterman, *T. S. Eliot and the Philosophy of Criticism* (London and New York: Duckworth and Columbia University Press, 1988).

36. For some clips of one such workshop, see http://projetasc.free.fr/index.php/2009/11/10/conscience-du-corps/.

37. See Michel Foucault, "How an 'Experience-Book' is Born," in *Remarks on Marx: Conversations with Duccio Trombadori*, trans. R. James Goldstein and James Cascaito (New York: Semiotext(e), 1991) and Georges Bataille, *Inner Experience* (Albany: SUNY Press, 1988).

38. See Richard Shusterman, "Muscle Memory and the Somaesthetic Pathologies of Everyday Life," *Human Movement*, 12:1 (2011), pp. 5–16.

Part One

LITERARY THEORY
AND PHILOSOPHY OF ART

One

THE IDEA OF EMOTION IN T. S. ELIOT AND IN RICHARD SHUSTERMAN

Anna Budziak

> Only emotion endures.
> Ezra Pound[1]

The present study is located at the frontiers of philosophy, psychology and literature. Its inspiration comes from philosophy, but one of its foci is a literary doctrine: by focusing on the concept of emotion, it explores the affinities between Richard Shusterman's somaesthetics and T. S. Eliot's theory of poetry. In his much-celebrated essay "Tradition and the Individual Talent," T. S. Eliot addressed the problem of verbally expressing feeling and emotion, but those two categories seem to overlap. However, even if Eliot slightly confused the qualities of feeling and emotion in "Tradition," his preference was definitely for feeling. The questions of how his preference developed and how his theory of emotion matured beyond the conclusions of "Tradition" can be explored more deeply if approached from the perspective provided by Richard Shusterman's pragmatist somaesthetics.

Shusterman's philosophy—like Eliot's literary doctrine—is about living and experiencing not only about writing or about the recently aggrandized *écriture*. Certainly, the close connectedness of literature, philosophy and living has been asserted by thinkers such as Hans-Georg Gadamer, Martha Nussbaum, and Alexander Nehamas. However, the link between somaesthetics and Eliot's poetic theory is especially intimate. It is firm not only because Shusterman wrote on Eliot,[2] but also because both Eliot's literary theory and Shusterman's philosophy are embedded in American pragmatism which, as this essay seeks to show, influenced their ideas of affectivity. Eliot's literary sensibility is rooted in that strain of pragmatism which is represented by John Dewey, Herbert Mead and William James, and which, as Shusterman has it, "insists on the essential, ineliminable embodiment of our experiences" and on their "organic, physiological roots."[3] It is anchored in this version of pragmatism, which stresses the biological foundation of human experience and the physiological element of affectivity. However, James's naturalistic approach to emotion was a feature distinctive only of Eliot's early poetry—respecting the later period of Eliot's creativity, James's biological pragmatism seems insufficient for a poet who starts exploring questions concerning the ethical and cognitive aspects of emotion. With time, the problem of emotion in Eliot changes from the issue of how to adequately express emotion in poetry to the problem of how to understand and to master it in the existential sense. When speaking of emotion in his later essays, Eliot turns more and more decidedly towards his older masters: to Aristotle, whom he recommends as "a moral pilot of Europe,"[4] and to Aquinas, with whom he was initially acquainted through the work of Jacques Maritain. In 1926 Eliot described Saint Thomas as the unparalleled "intellectual monument" within the Catholic Church[5] and perceived him as restoring "the principles of order and lucidity,"[6] or providing the foundations for harmony and clarity.

1. Within American Pragmatism

A. The Postmodernist Horizon and Richard Shusterman's Somaesthetics

As conceptualized in somaesthetics, emotion has at least four important aspects: judgmental, transformative, aesthetic, and somatic. The judgmental aspect has often been de-emphasized in the Platonic strain of philosophy: since emotion arises in the sphere of *alogon* and seems to be the opposite of the lucid *logos* of discursive thought, it has been contemptuously consigned to oblivion. However, somaesthetics rehabilitates the concept of intelligence as defined in terms broader than "thematized thinking and discursive reasoning"[7] by positing that intelligence involves understanding, which is not necessarily dependent on interpretation. Such understanding, like emotion (and not in contrast to it), can be rational without being verbalized. Its rationality is also recognized in contemporary psychology as evidenced in the work of Patricia Greenspan and Robert C. Solomon, and in literary theory and criticism as represented by Martha C. Nussbaum, Greenspan, and Solomon, who see emotion as evaluative and judgmental. In her *Love's Knowledge: Essays on Philosophy and Literature*, Nussbaum speaks of the "cognitive role of emotion" and the "epistemological value of feeling."[8] She explains Plato's reasons for chasing poets from the Republic as related to such an outlook on life as poetry offers by giving prominence to chance events and feelings; and she champions Aristotle's claim that emotions are necessary in practical wisdom. Nussbaum decidedly rejects the views of Plato and the Stoics that emotional judgments are by nature false.[9] Greenspan further questions the stoical tradition which relegates emotion and feeling to the realm of the irrational. She supports this view by observing that the lack of emotional empathy in psychopaths not only endangers their would-be victims but also threatens those psychopaths' own prospects. She also reminds us that the emotional development of children forms the basis for their intellectual progress.[10] Solomon, on the other hand, states that emotions not only resemble judgments but also are judgments. He notes that the similarity between feelings and judgments is clear, for example, in the case of those kinesthetic judgments that prevent us from falling when we are walking and skating on ice. These instantaneous decisions are made all the time in a non-reflective, nondeliberative and inarticulate way.[11] On those occasions, we judge as we feel. Accordingly, in Shusterman's somaesthetics the idea of emotion as judgmental is connected with the concept of the non-discursive immediacy of the lived experience. As Shusterman puts it in his *Practicing Philosophy*, "[p]roprioceptive discriminations beneath the level of thematized consciousness structure our perceptual field, just as unformulated feelings ([Deweyan] 'expansions, elations, and dejections') influence our behavior and orient our thinking."[12] Such non-discursive immediacy of thought, it should be noted, is captured in Eliot's famous metaphor of a rose, when Eliot says that thought should be as immediate as a feeling or a bodily sensation, or as "the odour of a rose."[13]

Feelings—all these "expansions, elations, and dejections"—are recognized in Shusterman's philosophy as forming a part of aesthetic experience, as shaping our perceptions and affecting our cognitive processes, as well as "orienting [our] thinking" or molding our selves. In "The End of the Aesthetic Experience," Shusterman presents the weaknesses of the analytical and phenomenological definitions that render the aesthetic experience in terms of a demarcational concept separating what is aesthetic from what is not. In their place, he recommends that we should restore the idea of the aesthetic experience as evaluative and affective, and he endorses this view by invoking those theoreticians for whom the aesthetic experience was an event arousing emotions—specifically, an event stirring joy. In particular, Shusterman refers to Dewey's claim that the experience of art is affective, to Monroe Beardsley's observation that it "is intrinsically enjoyable," and to T. S. Eliot's maxim that appreciation of the poem amounts to "enjoy[ing] it for the right reason."[14]

Enhancing our judgments and our sense of beauty, emotion also has the power to transform our selves. This transformative aspect of emotion is highlighted by Shusterman's references to mystical states. Shusterman reminds us that mystical states induce "self-surrender in the quest for self-transformation"[15]: with overwhelming emotion—as in the experience of deep religious ecstasy or of intense appreciation of art—the old self is swept away and replaced with the new Self. Indeed, in mystical states, the sense of the "phenomenal ego" is replaced with the experience of "the true Self": such a Self is called *Atman* in Hinduism, and it is described as "the *spark*, the *center*, the *apex of the soul*"[16] in Christian mysticism. However, this awesome and overpowering emotion, as stressed by Shusterman, is not elation sought for its own sake; rather, it appears along with, and as a result of, one's striving for excellence. Naturally, such endeavors will effect self-transformation not only in the religious but also in the agnostic sphere. As with religious ecstasy, so with the work of a genius, an industrious and earnest search for perfection can result in finding "another, higher self," which is a reward coming not as the goal but as a by-product of such striving. These humble endeavors prepare one for "self-abandonment," for the moment of "letting go,"[17] for self-dispossession or, as expressed by ancient Greek philosophy (whose word Shusterman uses, echoing Ralph Waldo Emerson), for the self's possession by a *daimon*.[18]

Thus, the category of emotion as it appears in Shusterman's philosophy comprises judgmental, aesthetic, and transformative aspects. In particular, emotion's aesthetic and judgmental value is combined with its transformative power. Emotion constitutes part of our impression of beauty and it enhances our judgment but it can also radically alter our familiar sense of the self. These three qualities, in turn, are closely related to the physical, or somatic, status of emotion. As conceptualized in Shusterman's philosophy, emotion—being significant in the choices we make and conducive to self-transformation as well as enhancing aesthetic experience—has a markedly bodily character. The bodily aspect of emotion, as illustrated by Shusterman, is clear in the religious experience of Saint Teresa. Her religious elation not only involves the mind but also affects the body. In Shusterman's words,

> ...the overwhelming spirituality of religious experience is often expressed and heightened by a deeply somatic deliciousness that St. Teresa describes as 'penetrating to the marrow of the bones,' enthralling and transfiguring us. The terms 'rapture' and 'ecstasy' convey this idea of being seized and transported outside ourselves by pleasure so intense that it sometimes seems almost painful to endure.[19]

The mystical states constitute the condition where the body and the mind co-exist in a special harmony and in which knowing and feeling are one. The coordinated faculties of knowing and feeling, which are characteristic of the mystical states, take us back to the judgmental and cognitive aspects of emotion. Indeed, in his anthology of mysticism F. Crossfield Happold points out that mystical states possess, among many other features, a *noetic* quality, which means that "they are also the states of knowledge."[20] However, these experiences are ineffable; they are unaccountable for within the bounds of discursive logos. Interestingly, speaking of this ineffability, Happold deploys phrases which are strikingly reminiscent of Eliot's wording in "The Metaphysical Poets," where Eliot describes the poet's mind as "constantly amalgamating disparate experience": as comprising the experiences of "fall[ing] in love" and of "read[ing] Spinoza" and the sensations produced by "the noise of the typewriter or the smell of cooking."[21] Happold, in turn, speaks of the impossibility of adequately accounting for an analogously wide range of experiences: the "...toothache, the smell of a rose, ... sensation of being in love, ... [or] the pleasure which comes to one when listening to a great symphony."[22] The mystic apprehends the world as the Eliotean poet does: in a momentary suspension of the discursive, at the point where a sensation meets a thought.

Admittedly, the problem characteristic for philosophy—of how to understand, evaluate and shape emotion—is ontological and ethical. But philosophy also signals emotion's ineffability which comes with emotion's physical rather than purely mental status. Trite as this observation may appear, intense emotion requires silencing the discursive. The incapacity of the discursive *logos* for accommodating emotion is also noted in somaesthetics. Indeed, Shusterman refutes the hegemony of the verbal, or of interpretation, and restores the sub-sentential to a place of prominence in the process of understanding. Emotion, then, can be expressed by all those non-verbal signs which in his "Postmodernism and the Aesthetic Turn" are described as "tingles, spasms, gestures, urges, and all intuitive understandings beneath the level of the sentence."[23] But how to account for emotion when all that one has at one's disposal are sentences? How to express emotion within language, but beyond its discursive *logos*? This is the task for poetry as seen by T. S. Eliot: emotion can be explained by a philosopher, but it must be expressed by a poet. To express emotion within a sentence but beyond the linguistic *logos* means liberating language from the rule of the one-to-one equivalence and from the principle of verbal non-contradiction. This kind of freedom is offered by the language of poetry, it is given through the rhetoric of symbolism, paradox, or oxymoron—by the pointedly foolish speech. The problem of ineffability which Shusterman signaled in his postmodernist philosophy, Eliot had attempted to solve in his high-modernist literary theories. Eventually, the issue of expressing emotion in poetry finds its specifically Eliotean resolution in the doctrine of the objective correlative. In order to express emotion in poetry, Eliot provides his reader with an image of emotion's physical equivalent: a physical feeling or sensation, or a situation which evokes them.

B. The Impact of James's Pragmatism

Eliot's insistence on the bodily aspect of emotion brings this essay home—to William James's biological, naturalistic pragmatism. A shift to James's psychology of emotion has its justification also in the fact that during his time at Harvard (1906-10, 1911-14) Eliot actually remained within the sphere of James's influence. Admittedly, Eliot wrote his doctoral dissertation on Francis H. Bradley's idealism and under the guidance of another idealist, Josiah Royce, whose lectures also impacted on Eliot's idea of literary tradition (a notion rooted in German idealism and, as Trevor Pateman observes, influenced by the American idealism of Royce[24]). However, the intellectual climate in the Harvard of Eliot's day was far from homogenous: Bertrand Russell visited America and disseminated his logical atomism through lectures in "symbolic logic," which were attended by the 26-year-old Eliot[25]; George Santayana presided over the circle of Harvard aesthetes, and William James was working on his philosophy combining physiology and psychology. Thus, the ambience was by no means uniformly idealist. In his student days in America, Eliot was influenced by Russell's analytical spirit, confronted with Santayana's "feline aestheticism,"[26] and exposed to James's pragmatism.

James's version of pragmatism, highlighting the biological foundation of the self, differed from Royce's "absolute pragmatism," which insisted on the objective reality of ideas. As described by John Herman Randall, Royce's "absolute pragmatism" is a philosophy in which reality becomes "a universe of ideas or signs which occur in a process of being interpreted by an infinite community of mind."[27] There arises an interesting parallel between the modernist and postmodernist pragmatist disagreements. The insistence on interpretation—the chief characteristic of Royce's philosophy—is also a feature of Rorty's pragmatism, in which reality and the experiencing self are subject to endless re-interpreting. Thus, Royce's idealism, or "absolute pragmatism," anticipates Rorty's version of pragmatism, whereas the tradition of the naturalistic pragmatism of James is developed in the somaesthetics of Shusterman. James and Royce, debating and arguing over each other's views, nevertheless maintained an unfailing and lifelong friendship. Their differences notwithstanding James's empiricism and naturalism commanded respect from Royce. Eventually, the ripples of the philosophers' friendship reached the shores of literature. James's views, filtered into the literary work of Eliot, then Royce's doctoral student, and became reflected in the poet's view of emotion.

To William James, emotion is not a mental condition but a physical state; it is involuntary, pre-conscious and corporeal. James reverses the order which his predecessors had introduced when speaking of emotion and of its bodily demonstration, or feeling. He claims that emotion does not precede the bodily manifestation; rather, emotion is the result, or more specifically, an equivalent—or "correlative"—of the bodily reaction. James states, that "...we feel sorry because we cry, angry because we strike, afraid because we tremble, and not that we cry, strike, or tremble, because we are sorry, angry, or fearful, as the case may be."[28] In his essay "What is an Emotion", published in 1884, James plainly asserts that emotion is limited to physical sensation—"feeling ... *IS* the emotion,"[29] or emotion is feeling—and describes feelings (equated with emotions) exclusively in the language of physiology, for instance, as the changes in the functioning of the smaller blood vessels and arteries. Admittedly, James's extreme view may pose some practical difficulties, since, even at present, it might be impossible to find a specific behavioral pattern or a physiological reaction exactly matching the feeling of nostalgia or melancholy. A short quotation should give a flavor of James's radical way of thinking about affectivity:

> Hardly a sensation comes to us without sending waves of alternate constriction and dilatation down the arteries of our arms. The blood-vessels of the abdomen act reciprocally with those of the more outward parts. The bladder and bowels, the glands of the mouth, throat, and skin, and the liver, are known to be affected gravely in certain severe emotions, and are unquestionably affected transiently when the emotions are of a lighter sort.[30]

Emotion is "no mind-stuff." On the contrary, a reduction of the emotional to the mental would erase affectivity, as in James's hypothesis when he imagines that "...if [he] were to become corporeally anaesthetic, [he] should be excluded from the life of the affections, harsh and tender alike, and drag out an existence of merely cognitive or intellectual form."[31] Such an "I" (or "he" as envisaged in James's text) would lead the life of the coldly aestheticist Eliotean figures from "The Love Song of J. Alfred Prufrock": the life of a "patient etherised upon a table"[32] and of Prufrock himself, lost in his futile cogitations.

Eliot's "The Love Song of J. Alfred Prufrock" was written in the years 1910-11. It was completed in Paris but begun when Eliot was a student at Harvard, and it precedes by six years "Tradition and the Individual Talent," the essay which reflects the early stages of Eliot's grappling with the problem of emotion in the sphere of literary theory. In "Tradition and the Individual Talent"—which Eliot described as "juvenile,"[33] despite his being 32 at the time he wrote it—Eliot's view of feelings and emotions is rather uncertain. On the one hand, Eliot treats the categories of "feelings" and "emotions" as if they referred to the same affective quality. On the other hand, however, he juxtaposes these terms. On the occasions when they are seen as contrasted, Eliot favors feelings; in his words, "great poetry may be made without the direct use of any emotion whatever: composed out of feelings solely."[34] Some indications of this preference can be found in Eliot's Harvard days. Indeed, at the time Eliot was writing his doctoral thesis, he intimated that he understood feelings in the Jamesian way by posing a challenging question which attracted the attention of his interpreters. He asked: "Why should anger be any less objective than pain sensation?"[35]

The ambiguity complicating Eliot's "Tradition"—the ambivalence yielded by mixed references to "emotions" and "feelings"—is eventually resolved in an essay published in 1926, "The Metaphysical Poets," in which feelings are clearly identified with bodily sensations. In "The Metaphysical Poets," Eliot solves the problem which he perceives as the stylistic impasse threatening English poetry, stranded, between the diction of Milton and Dryden—both of them stilting emotion—and the tradition of the Romantics who poured out individual passions in poetry. Eliot answers the Romantics' appeal to "look into our hearts and write" with his poetic—and characteristically Jamesian—advice to "look into the cerebral cortex, the nervous system, and the digestive tracts."[36] The Eliotean "heart" is no longer a metaphor for vague emotionalism—it is made of organic tissue and beats in the biological body. Biology is respected in Eliot's critical work. In his essay "The Perfect Critic," the nineteenth-century essayist and literary critic Charles Augustine Sainte-Beuve and the symbolist, Rémy de Gourmont, are placed on the humanities pedestal next to Aristotle.[37] Notably, what brings Sainte-Beuve, de Gourmont, and Aristotle together is the fact that they all received an education and did research in matters of physiology.

Fundamentally, then, in his early theory of poetic expression, Eliot understands feelings as physical sensations. The word "emotion," in contrast, is used by him to designate sentimentalist, rather than late Romantic, limp and tepid, reflexivity. Eliot sums up his view of emotion as both bodily and *noetic* by criticizing the lack of these features in emotions as expressed by English poetry. Specifically, in an essay published in *The Little Review* in 1918, "In Memory [of Henry James]," Eliot comments on what he thought deplorably sentimental in English poetry by stating: "In England ideas run wild and pasture on the emotions; instead of thinking with our feelings (a very different thing) we corrupt our feelings with ideas; we produce ... the emotional idea evading sensation and thought."[38]

2. Under the Aristotelian and Thomist Impact

A. From the Aesthetic to the Ethical

Within the span of some ten years, from 1919 to 1929, Eliot's view of emotion underwent significant changes. Over this decade, Eliot's interests gradually shifted from the issue of expressing emotion to the problem of understanding emotion and of conceiving emotion not only as felt in one's body but also about the other. In his preoccupation with the question of emotion, Eliot moved from the purely aesthetic to an ethical stance, though he never forgot emotion's physical nature and its *noetic* aspect. In "Tradition and the Individual Talent" Eliot is preoccupied with a question of aesthetics, namely how to express emotion, and not so much with the ontological problem of what an emotion is. He does not consider emotion as directed towards the other, nor as inscribed into a system of passions, affects, virtues or vices. In "Tradition" Eliot emphasizes the "artistic emotion" and the drama's "structural emotion" rather than the individual poet's feeling: "It is not in his personal emotion, the emotions provoked by the particular events in his life, that the poet is in any way remarkable or interesting. His particular emotions may be simple, or crude, or flat."[39] The poet's business is to escape from such "personal" emotion through the process of creation, to replace emotion with a poetic form.

The formalistic aspect of Eliot's preoccupation with emotion is stressed by Lee Oser, who contends that in *The Sacred Wood* Eliot's major concern is how to translate the felt emotion into an "artistic emotion" and that, consequently, this collection of essays becomes Eliot's contribution to the "debate in modern philosophy about the relation between aesthetics and morality." Eliot's stance, as observed by Oser, is similar to the position of Bernard Bosanquet, a theoretician to whom *catharsis* would be reduced to an exclusively aesthetic feeling, "an art emotion." Indeed, Oser claims that Eliot's intellectual cast is markedly different from the attitudes represented by the philosophers who—as James and Dewey do—regard emotion primarily as a bodily feeling to be lived through rather than to be merely analyzed. In Oser's

view, Eliot's analytical slant—his "obsession with the *le mot juste*," an attitude redolent of "linguistic idealism"—makes his theory of emotion also veer
away from Aristotelianism, where emotions were presented as binding people
and making them desire things, not only as significant because of their artistic
relevance. Unlike in Eliot's literary theory, within the realm of "Aristotelian
anthropology *all* feeling is not in perception; feeling, by virtue of its interpersonal character, by its very depth precedes the self." So Oser concludes that
Eliot's endeavor to join "a tradition linking Aristotle, Aquinas and Dante" was
thus an "impossible task."[40]

However, in those literary essays which Eliot wrote after "Tradition and the
Individual Talent," his purely formalistic stance dissipates. His frigidly aestheticist
and analytical, almost *flâneurian*, attitude to emotion eventually changes. It should
be noted that "Tradition," despite its prevailingly formalistic bias, includes the
germs of Eliot's later, more comprehensive view of emotion and is justifiably
regarded as Aristotelian. If in 1917, the year of writing "Tradition," Eliot was in
equal measure Aristotelian and Jamesian through his emphasizing the physical
aspect of affectivity, then in his later essays, he was predominantly an Aristotelian
through his understanding of emotion as socially binding.

Oser is correct that in 1917 Eliot's interest in the question of feeling and
emotion was purely aesthetic in the sense of being analytical; yet with time,
Eliot's interest in emotion acquired a dimension which was prominently ethical. Admittedly, in his early caustically ironic verses, as well as in his "juvenile" "Tradition," Eliot seems bent on taking an aestheticist flight from emotion. But at the time of writing "The Metaphysical Poets," "Shakespeare and
the Stoicism of Seneca" (1927), and especially "Dante" (1929), he no longer
nonchalantly dons the cloak of neo-classicist literary taste—he speaks as a
straightforward moralist.[41] He does not recommend an escape from emotion,
but rather the mastery and understanding of the self's affective side. Such
understanding can be acquired when personal affections and passions are
viewed within a larger perspective: not as the unrelated thrills, "ecstasies" and
"shocks" that appear in Eliot's early poetry but as a part of an intellectual and
emotional spectrum covering the "depth" of passion, as in Dante, and span-
ning its "width,"[42] as in Shakespeare. Poetry, then, shall reintegrate the emotional, the intellectual and the everyday sensuous. Eliot stresses the importance of this synthesis in his "Shakespeare and the Stoicism of Seneca" by
recommending a "transmutation" or "metamorphosis" of the personal emotion
"every poet starts from" into the communicable, shared form of a poem. Appropriately, then, while discussing Eliot's theory of impersonality, Hugh Kenner notes that poetry allows poets to share their vulnerability in a way which
renders them invulnerable, or to use his exact words, "the ritual of art allows a
man to express an emotion without exposing his wounds."[43] In his essay on
Shakespeare and Seneca, Eliot speaks not only of the exactitude of expression—or of finding an objective correlative for emotion—but also of the clarity of feelings. He distinguishes between "precise emotion" and hazy emotion-

alism and claims that "[t]o express precise emotion requires as great intellectual power as to express precise thought."[44] With this statement, Eliot puts the emotional on a par with the intellectual.

Yet, though the mature Eliot values Shakespeare's diversity, Shakespearean comprehensiveness is less appealing to him than Dantean system and order. The issue of emotional order, invoked in his literary criticism, recurs in Eliot's later poetry. For example, in "East Coker," in a passage of poetic confession, Eliot cautions against poetry's "deteriorating / In the general mess of imprecision of feeling, / Undisciplined squads of emotion"[45]. It is not "feeling" and "emotion" as such that are to be avoided, but only vagueness and lack of discipline that may occur in the affective sphere—the "mess" of excitations or a flicker of compensatory sensationalism so characteristic of Prufrock's consciousness and of Gerontion's histrionic posing.

In contrast to the aestheticist sensibility depicted in "Prufrock," the vision underlying Dante's *Divine Comedy* accommodates emotion within an ethically ordered universe. Eliot comprehensively presents his views on Dante in two essays: "Dante" (1929) and "What Dante Means to Me," originally a lecture given at the Italian Institute in London in 1950, and published in *To Criticize the Critic*, in 1965. For Eliot, *The Divine Comedy* "...is a complete scale of the depths and heights of human emotion. ... Every degree of the feeling of humanity, from lowest to highest, has, moreover, an intimate relation to the next above and below, and all fit together according to the logic of sensibility."[46] Hence, the Dantesque suffering—which either leads to, or completes, emotion—is functional: it is inscribed into the pattern of redemption from the passions that has been relentlessly pursued. Such suffering, which naturally involves feeling and emotion, is as purging as it is transformative. Meaningful (or redemptive) suffering would be hard to find in Eliot's early poetry, that is, in the verses he wrote before 1927. In his early, avowedly classicist stage (which, paradoxically, was also the period of modernist avant-garde experimentation), Eliot would not use references to Dante in order to introduce a meaningful moral hierarchy, but only to create a bathetic effect, in order to provide a degrading comparison to the poem's *persona* or to the described events. His early protagonists occupy a limbo-like space which, in David Wallace's metaphor, is described as neither Hell, nor Purgatory, but "the vestibule of Hell."[47] They suffer from nervousness, uncertainties, apprehensions and self-doubt, experiencing emotions which, in the post-1927 Eliotean terminology, would be denominated as "vague."

B. The Thomist Order

Increasingly, Eliot would value emotion's interpersonal and binding powers, as they are emphasized in Aristotle, and recognize emotion's cognitive and transformative aspects, as they are highlighted by the medieval thinker and saint for whom Aristotle was "*the* philosopher," by Saint Thomas Aquinas.

Admittedly, Eliot warns against simplistically translating the emotional appeal of poetry into an intellectual system of philosophy—against translating Dante into Aquinas,[48] or, in other words, against viewing *The Divine Comedy* as a poeticized *Summa Theologica*. But Eliot certainly acknowledges the emotion-structuring impact of philosophy.

In accordance with the Aristotelian tradition and in contrast to the stoical school which recommended liberation from passions, or *passiones*, Saint Thomas regards emotions and feelings (*sensualitas*) as good, although, as it is put by Stefan Świeżawski, a Polish interpreter and commentator of Saint Thomas, "they should be kept on a tight rein, brought under control and used properly."[49] The Thomist universe of emotions is strictly hierarchized.[50] Thus, as Świeżawski explains, the Thomist *ratio universalis* guides *ratio particularis* (or, the individual intellect), which, in turn, governs *vis cogitativa* (or, the power of judgment) presiding over *sensualistas*. *Sensualitas*, as such, is an amoral sphere, and emotions are shared with the animal world.[51]

Significantly, Aquinas speaks of emotions not only as linking us to the animal world, not only as fitting in with the sensuous, but also as belonging to the intellectual sphere. Emotions comprise both sensation and thought. More specifically, Saint Thomas distinguishes between *passio*, or the sensuous feeling, and *affectus*, or the same feeling of love, anger or pleasure, however regarded as freed from the domain of sensuality.[52] In other words, *affectus* is *passio* so transformed that it loses its sensuous object and its bodily characteristics: it desires or detests things universal. For instance, as Aquinas explains in his *Treatise on the Human Nature*, the sensual versions of anger (*ira*) and lust (concupiscence) have their intellective equivalents:

> ...there is some concupiscence that cannot pertain to sensory appetite, but only to intellective appetite, the will. There is, for example, the concupiscence for wisdom, concerning which Wisdom 6.21 says, *the concupiscence for wisdom leads to the eternal kingdom.* There is also a kind of anger (*ira*) that cannot pertain to sensory appetite, but only to intellective—when, for example we are angry about vice. ... Therefore the irascible and the concupiscible ought to be distinguished in the intellective appetite, as in the sensory.[53]

Likewise, delight (or *delectatio*) not only has its sensuous manifestation but also can occur within the sphere of intellect.[54] To support his view of the affective side of intellect, Aquinas refers to Aristotle, though cautiously guarding his references to *De Anima* with the assertion that "it is not necessary to put any faith in the words of that book."[55] So he invokes Aristotle's idea of the predominantly intellectual soul as a substance, which comprises also "the non-rational part," thus including the emotions of "concupiscence and anger."[56]

The Thomist universe of emotions is orderly, but organically connected rather than mechanistically segmented. Besides, due to its hierarchical nature, it allows for the expansion of the reign of reason over man's impulsive nature. Indeed, to explain the position of passions, Aquinas invokes the metaphor of a "political" rule of will and reason over *sensualitas* from Aristotle's *Politics*[57]: the Thomist anger and desire, though they belong to the sensuous sphere, are ultimately subjugated to reason and will, the faculties which rule them in a political and regal way, *"politico et regali"*, meaning that their imperatives, even if they do not have to be obeyed, shall be at least respected.

C. The Aristotelian Bonding

The orderly quality of Thomist emotions had great appeal to Eliot when he was struggling for paradigms with which to render emotion as not only impersonal but also communicable in poetry. Eliot admired the universe of Saint Thomas in Dante. However, underlying Acquinas, Dante's universe has older foundations in the Aristotelian way of thinking, which philosophy Eliot recommends as providing guidelines for modern sensibility.[58] Emotion in Aristotle is interpersonal, *noetic* and ethical. While in the *Poetics*, Aristotle notes the cognitive aspect of emotions; in *The Nichomachean Ethics*, he explains how emotions connect people. Outlining his theory of tragedy in *Poetics*, Aristotle presents emotion as inalienable from the scenes of "recognition." It accompanies *anagnorisis*, which Aristotle defines as "change from ignorance to knowledge, disclosing either a close relationship or enmity."[59] Clearly, the emphasis of this definition falls upon the cognitive element ("change from ignorance to knowledge"), but its latter part refers to the affective nature of human bonding ("close relationship or enmity") involving consanguinity, friendship or hostility. Thus, human drama in Greek tragedy not only is played out on the border between innocence and experience but also develops as a continuous dialectic of the cognitive and the affective, or of the known and the felt.

In *The Nichomachean Ethics*, in the section "Friendship is a Necessity," Aristotle speaks of affection as arising among friends, comrades, and parents and their children. It is a binding force. Whether affection is directed towards people or, as often happens, misdirected exclusively towards oneself or inanimate objects, it varies in its intensity and is liable to change, as friendship can change into tyranny if one of the equals become subordinated,[60] or as pleasurable sensation changes into overindulgence if pursued beyond measure or exclusively for this sensation's sake. The accidental, or contingent, character of pleasure in Aristotle and in Eliot is noted by Shusterman, who underlines Eliot's view, which echoes Aristotle's, that pleasure "completes the activity" rather than is pursued for its own sake.[61] Diverted from the other and directed to the self, or dissociated from activity, emotion becomes perverted. Such a course of emotional perversion is depicted in Eliot's early personae—in his dandyesque Prufrock, hysterical Gerontion, and the emotionally callous young man from the "The Portrait of a Lady"—whose potential for affection is detached from the care for the other and turned into mere affectation. Their capacity for feeling, or, as Eliot understood it in his earlier writings, their ability to experience sensation, degenerates into craving for sensationalism, a quality which Aristotle (both in his ethics and in his aesthetics) considers to be needless.[62]

Shusterman emphasizes yet another Aristotelian facet in Eliot's attitude to the problem of emotion: emotion can be "educated and refined." Elaborating on Eliot's pragmatist inclinations, Shusterman indicates Eliot's adherence to the Aristotelian idea of *phronesis*, or of practical wisdom, and refers to Eliot's conviction that "the betterment of social life. ... requires 'a moral conversion' involving 'the discipline and training of emotions.'" He observes that Eliot's stress on the importance of practice, of "discipline and training,"[63] parallels Aristotle's concern "with feeling the right feelings" and his recommendation that "emotions can be educated and refined by habituation and discipline,"[64] and also that it corresponds with Aristotle's emphasis on the proper cultivation of feeling.

Aristotelian and Thomist influences in Eliot are entwined. Both tendencies, however, bear the impact of Jamesian thought. In Eliot's writings, the philosophies of those classics were planted on the fertile soil of James's mixture of philosophy, psychology and physiology. James's naturalistic pragmatism aided Eliot in solving the problem of how to express emotion in poetry, whereas the works of Aquinas and Aristotle helped him to understand emotion in order to evaluate and to cultivate it. In other words, while James's theory of emotions was invaluable in solving the problem of Eliot's aesthetics, Aristotle and Aquinas, in his later years, provided Eliot with the conceptual foundations for his ethics. James's theory, drastically reducing emotion to autonomic and motor functions, could not answer questions concerning causation and value: What is the role of will and reason in emotional response? What arouses emotions? What is their proper object, or do they have any object at all? Are they morally justifiable? Are they destructive or motivating? How do they differ from moods, or do they? In the light of James's theory, these questions would be meaningless. But they acquire importance in the context of Aristotle's philosophy and Aquinas's thought, both of which describe emotion as aiding the cognitive processes, binding, and gradable (as in the *Poetics* and *The Nichomachean Ethics*), or subject to evaluation, discipline and training (as in Aristotle's *Nicomachean Ethics* and in Aquinas's *The Treatise on Human Nature*). Incorporating Aristotle and Aquinas in his poetic theory and practice, Eliot nevertheless retained the lesson of James's philosophy and never rejected the importance of the bodily aspect of emotion.

The above features are also reflected in the idea of emotion which appears in Shusterman's somaesthetics: in emotion's judgmental, aesthetic, and transformative qualities and in its biological nature. At the root of this analogy in viewing emotions—a confluence which develops between Eliot's poetic theory and Shusterman's somaesthetics—lie respect for biological naturalism and an optimistic conviction that emotions can be ameliorative and ameliorat-

ed, and that discipline and training can lead to an increased richness and refinement of feeling. Eliot's and Shusterman's ideas on emotion, as noted
above, are also related through their philosophical antecedents. Behind Shusterman's approach to emotion, and buttressing Eliot's theory of feeling, stands
Aristotelianism. Moreover, Eliot's creativity, apart from its philosophical
Aristotelian lineaments, shows the sensibility-structuring impact of Saint
Thomas, the philosopher whose principles of *consonantia, integritas*, and
claritas Shusterman invokes in his outline of the criteria of beauty.[65] Finally,
with regard to their concepts of affectivity, Shusterman's somaesthetics and
Eliot's poetic theory have a shared point of intellectual origin in James's pragmatism, in his recognition of the corporeality of selfhood and, consequently, in
his foregrounding of that component of emotion which is physiological.

NOTES

1. Ezra Pound, "A Retrospect" in *Modern Poetics: Essays on Poetry by Yeats, Pound,
   Frost, Eliot, Williams, Hopkins, Ransom, Moore, Stevens, Cummings, Crane,
   Auden, Thomas, Jones, Lowell*, ed. James Scully (New York: McGraw-Hill,
   1995), p. 42.
2. See, for example, Richard Shusterman, *T. S. Eliot and the Philosophy of Criticism*
   (New York: Columbia University Press, 1988); Richard Shusterman, *Surface
   and Depth: Dialectics of Criticism and Culture* (Ithaca: Cornell University Press,
   2002), pp. 139–158; Richard Shusterman, "A Tension in Eliot's Poetics," *British
   Journal of Aesthetics*, 20 (1980), pp. 248–253; Richard Shusterman, "Eliot's
   Pragmatist Philosophy of Practical Wisdom," *The Review of English Studies*, ns
   40 (1989), pp. 72–92; Richard Shusterman, "Wilde and Eliot," *T. S. Eliot Annu-
   al*, 1 (1990), pp. 117–144.
3. Richard Shusterman, "Interpretation, Mind and Embodiment," *Psychological Inquiry*, 5 (1994), p. 258.
4. T. S. Eliot, *Selected Essays* (London: Faber and Faber, 1976), p. 60. On the exploration of Eliot's Aristotelism, see, for instance, Anna Budziak, "Between Metaphysics and Physics: Aristotelian and Postmodernist Perspectives in T. S. Eliot's
   Theory of Poetic Expression, the Mind and the Soul," *Anglica Wratislaviensia*,
   45:1 (2008), p. 9.
5. Eliot, *Selected Essays*, p. 342.
6. Peter Ackroyd, *T. S. Eliot* (London: Hamish Hamilton, 1984), p. 155.
7. Richard Shusterman, "Intellectualism and the Field of Aesthetics: The Return of the
   Repressed?" *Revue Internationale de Philosophie*, 220 (2002), p. 328.
8. Martha C. Nussbaum, *Love's Knowledge: Essays on Philosophy and Literature*
   (Oxford: Oxford University Press, 1992), pp. 7, 175.
9. *Ibid.*, pp. 10–23, 40–43.
10. Patricia Greenspan, "Emotions, Rationality, and Mind/Body," in *Philosophy and
    the Emotions. Royal Institute of Philosophy Supplement 52*, ed. Anthony Hat-
    zimoysis (Cambridge: Cambridge University Press, 2003), p. 115.

11. Robert C. Solomon, "Emotions, Thoughts and Feelings: What is 'Cognitive Theory' of the Emotions and Does it Neglect Affectivity?" in *Philosophy and the Emotions*, p. 10.
12. Richard Shusterman, *Practicing Philosophy: Pragmatism and the Philosophical Life* (New York: Routledge, 1997), p.166.
13. Eliot, *Selected Essays*, p. 287.
14. Richard Shusterman, "The End of Aesthetic Experience," *Journal of Aesthetics and Art Criticism*, 55 (1997), pp. 34, 37.
15. Richard Shusterman, "Somaesthetics and Care of the Self: The Case of Foucault," *Monist*, 83:4 (2000), p. 545.
16. F. Crossfield Happold, *Mysticism: A Study and an Anthology* (Harmondsworth: Penguin, 1970), pp. 48–49.
17. Richard Shusterman, "Genius and the Paradox of Self-Styling," in *Performing Live: Aesthetic Alternatives for the Ends of Art* (Ithaca and London: Cornell University Press, 2000), pp. 214, 216.
18. *Ibid.*, p. 204.
19. Shusterman "The Case of Foucault," pp. 544–545.
20. Happold, *Mysticism*, p. 45.
21. Eliot, *Selected Essays*, p. 287.
22. Happold, *Mysticism*, p. 45.
23. Richard Shusterman, "Postmodernism and the Aesthetic Turn," *Poetics Today*, 10:3 (1989), p. 617. For Shusterman's rehabilitation of the non-discursive, see his "Interpretation, Mind and Embodiment"; see also his "Beneath Interpretation," in *The Interpretive Turn: Philosophy, Science, Culture*, eds. David R. Hiley, James F. Bohman, and Richard Shusterman (Ithaca: Cornell University Press, 1991), pp. 102–128. For Shusterman's rehabilitation of Dewey's idea of non-discursive experience, see Shusterman, *Practicing Philosophy*, p. 158. For Shusterman's critique of textualism, see Shusterman, *Practicing Philosophy*, p. 174.
24. Trevor Pateman, "Tradition and Creativity: T. S. Eliot 'Tradition and the Individual Talent,'" in *Key Concepts: A Guide to Aesthetics, Criticism and the Arts in Education* (London: Falmer Press, 1991), pp. 2–3. http://www.selectedworks.co.uk/tradition.html, accessed 4 June 2008.
25. See, for instance, Ackroyd, *T. S. Eliot*, p. 50.
26. Jonathan Freedman, *Professions of Taste: Henry James, British Aestheticism and Commodity Culture* (Stanford: Stanford University Press, 1990), p. 122. See also Ackroyd, *T.S. Eliot*, p. 35.
27. John H. Randall, Jr., "Josiah Royce and American Idealism," *The Journal of Philosophy*, 63:3 (1966). p. 63. http://www.jstor.org/stable/20238249, accessed June 2008.
28. William James, "What is an Emotion?" *The Mind*, 9 (1884), pp. 188–205. *Classics in the History of Psychology* online, ed. Christopher D. Green, p. 190. http://psychclassics.yorku.ca/James/emotion.htm, accessed 2 June 2008.
29. *Ibid.*, pp. 189–190.
30. *Ibid.*, pp. 191–192.
31. *Ibid.*, pp. 193–194.
32. T. S. Eliot, "The Love Song of J. Alfred Prufrock," in *The Complete Poems & Plays of T. S. Eliot* (London: Faber & Faber, 1969), p. 13, line 3.
33. Brian Lee, *Theory and Personality: The Significance of T. S. Eliot's Criticism* (London: The Athlone Press, 1979), pp. 92–93.
34. Eliot, *Selected Essays*, p.18.

35. Mowbray Allan, *T. S. Eliot's Impersonal Theory of Poetry* (Cranbury, NJ: Associated University Presses, 1974), p. 78.
36. Eliot, *Selected Essays*, p. 290.
37. See T. S. Eliot, *The Sacred Wood: Essays on Poetry and Criticism* (London: Methuen; New York: Barnes and Noble, 1964), pp. 13–14.
38. Allan, *T. S. Eliot's Impersonal Theory of Poetry*, p. 76.
39. Eliot, *Selected Essays*, pp. 19–21.
40. Lee Oser, "T. S. Eliot and the Case of the Vanishing Ethics," *Literary Imagination*, 4:2 (2002), pp. 222–224.
41. On Eliot as a moralist and as the proponent of a particular, prejudiced and intransigent social and political ethos, see, for instance, Rossell H. Robbins, *The T. S. Eliot Myth* (New York: Henry Shuman, 1951); Rajendra Verma, *Royalist in Politics: T. S. Eliot and Political Philosophy* (London: Asia Publishing House, 1968); Roger Kojecky, *T. S. Eliot's Social Criticism* (London: Oxford University Press, 1972); William M. Chace, *The Political Identities of Ezra Pound and T. S. Eliot* (Stanford: Stanford University Press, 1973); Michael North, *The Political Aesthetics of Yeats, Eliot and Pound* (Cambridge: Cambridge University Press, 1991). On Eliot's insistence that criticism has ideological and moral aspects, see Shusterman, *T. S. Eliot and the Philosophy of Criticism*, pp.145–147. On the Aristotelian tradition of ethics in Eliot, see Shusterman, *T. S. Eliot and the Philosophy of Criticism*, pp. 195–205. On Eliot's attitude to the moral tradition represented by Walter Pater and Matthew Arnold, see Anna Budziak, "Pater and Eliot: The Case of Aestheticizing Ethics," in *PASE Studies in Literature and Culture* (Łódź: Wydawnictwo Uniwersytetu Łódzkiego, 2008), pp. 79–85.
42. Eliot, *Selected Essays*, p. 265.
43. Hugh Kenner, *The Invisible Poet: T. S. Eliot* (London: Methuen, 1966), p. 27.
44. Eliot, *Selected Essays*, p. 135.
45. T. S. Eliot, "East Coker," sec. 5, in *The Complete Poems & Plays of T. S. Eliot* (London: Faber & Faber, 1969), p. 182.
46. Eliot, *Selected Essays*, pp. 268–269.
47. Peter Lowe, "Dantean Suffering in the Work of Percy Shelley and T. S. Eliot: From Torment to Purgation," *English Studies*, 4 (2004), p. 330.
48. Eliot, *Selected Essays*, p. 136.
49. Tomasz z Akwinu [Thomas Aquinas], *Traktat o człowieku: Summa teologii 1, 75–89, [The Treatise on Human Nature: Summa Theologiae 1, 75–89]* trans., intro., and commentary Stefan Świeżawski (Kęty: Wydawnictwo Antyk, 2000), p. 364.
50. See, for instance, Thomas Aquinas, *The Treatise on Human Nature: Summa Theologiae 1, 75–89*, trans., intro., and commentary Robert Pasnau (Indianapolis & Cambridge: Hackett Publishing, 2002), Question 81, Article 3.17–50, pp. 113–114.
51. Tomasz z Akwinu, *Traktat*, pp. 364, 367 .
52. *Ibid.*, p. 385.
53. Thomas Aquinas, *The Treatise*, Question 82, Article 5.1.5–13, p. 124.
54. Tomasz z Akwinu, *Traktat*, p. 385.
55. Thomas Aquinas, *The Treatise*, Question 82, Article 5. 71–72, p. 125
56. *Ibid.*, Question 85, Article 5.3, p. 124.
57. *Ibid.*, Question 81, Article 3.55–64, p. 114.
58. See, for instance, Eliot, *Selected Essays*, p. 60.
59. Aristotle, *Poetics*, trans. and intro. Malcolm Heath (London: Penguin Books, 1996), sec. 52a, p.18.

60. Aristotle, *The Nicomachean Ethics*, original trans. James A. K. Thomson, further rev. Hugh Tredennick and Jonathan Barns (London: Penguin Books, 2004), pp. 200–201, 220–223.
61. Shusterman, *T. S. Eliot and the Philosophy of Criticism*, p. 135.
62. For Aristotle on "defective plots," see *Poetics* 17; 51b–52a.
63. Shusterman, "Eliot's Pragmatist Philosophy," p. 80.
64. *Ibid.*, p. 79.
65. See Shusterman, *Practicing Philosophy*, p. 38.

Two

NEO-PRAGMATIST MODELS OF SELF-DEVELOPMENT AND THE POETIC SUBJECTIVITY IN JOHN ASHBERY'S POETRY

Kacper Bartczak

John Ashbery has puzzled critics for decades now. His poetic is a highly original amalgam of quite various and remote traditions. Difficult to classify, his poems represent an avant-garde aesthetics which, however, maintains complex communication with more traditional styles. Among the most elusive issues informing the difficulty of Ashbery's writing is the role and position of the poetic subject. Taking his cue from major American traditions, and enriching them with a great variety of foreign influences, merging mainstream assumptions with some of the most eccentric poetic ideas, Ashbery has offered a significant modification of the role and shape of poetic subjectivity. In this essay I am interested in showing how Ashbery's multi-vocal, elusive stylistics could be approached and discussed from the point of view of neo-pragmatist aesthetics. I am particularly interested in the writings of Richard Rorty and Richard Shusterman. In my view, they represent a healthy alternative to some more text-oriented readings, primarily deconstruction.

The evolution of Ashbery's poetic voice contains an internal discussion over the notion of poetic subjectivity, as the poet was searching for his own stance amidst his rich artistic and literary fascinations. As it has developed, Ashbery's stance is a brilliant oscillation between a provisional voice that seems to emerge from his opaque meditations, and the almost complete obliteration or disappearance of this voice. To elucidate the rhythm and significance of this oscillation, I will first present a discussion of the most interesting models of subjectivity offered by neo-pragmatist thought. Having sketched these philosophical and aesthetic perspectives, I will then return to Ashbery's poetry.

1. Richard Rorty's Models of Self-Development: the Ironist

Rorty's revival of pragmatism creates possibilities for two models of subjectivity and self-creation: the model, or life, of the liberal ironist, and the model of the strong poet. These models are Rorty's compilation of motifs appropriated from his own pragmatist theories of language and the self, from his interpretations of the lives of Nietzsche, Heidegger, Derrida, and novelists, notably

Proust, Nabokov, and James. They are interesting inasmuch as they afford a platform for retaining modes of subjectivity in today's theoretical discussions, thus bringing back the idea of individual responses to a thoroughly rhetorical, discourse-ridden culture. The hope these models present is that the subject may continue as an authentic being even after the realization that it is a constructed, rhetorical figure, a creation of historical contingencies or of prevailing discourses of the culture.

The liberal ironist has freed herself from the old dream of making up a final system of describing the universe in terms which will not be redescribed. Becoming free of that dream automatically means to be freed of the idea of the essential self—an analogue of the essence of the Universe or Nature. This newly-got liberty corrects the foundational project of western culture—the project of getting to know oneself. The ironist knows and accepts a situation in which each acquired state of mind is a transition in the development of one's individual, entirely linguistic understanding of oneself and one's relation to the world. Rorty calls such understanding self-description. While a metaphysician might still yearn for a self-description that would cease to be a description and become a final truth, the ironist is free of such illusions and knows—actually expects—these descriptions to be changeable. The ironist treats her self as a text, a rhetorical set, in which there is no single element that is not liable to further revision. The ironist has nothing—or rather *is* nothing—but these rhetorical descriptive sets. That is why they are defended with conviction, when needed, as the only available platforms for action. This is where Rorty begins to talk about the western intellectual as a member of the "literary culture": an ironist who is well-enough educated and has enough time and intellectual curiosity to expose herself to other self-descriptions, the images that people in different cultures hold of themselves.

As a result, the ironist project of self-creation consists in setting up conditions for the re-description of her current self-image by putting it in the context of other such constructs and, possibly, absorbing, borrowing, or incorporating their elements into her own self-descriptive network, playing off the old against the new, the local and familiar against the remote and alien. This process of redescription by recontextualization is best achieved through literature—Rorty stresses the role of the novel here, and his understanding of the genre is similar to that offered by Milan Kundera—rather than by philosophy. Since self-descriptions are thoroughly rhetorical creations, they may best be understood through works of imagination which themselves are based on rhetoric—not on the logos of argumentation. It is the novel that tells us why people are willing to assume ways of life and forms of self-understanding that would look aberrant or weird from exclusively rational perspectives. So the ironist or the intellectual seeks close encounters with other texts of self-understanding in the hope that her own text will become larger. This is why Rorty's model is a self-creative model—it carries on the traditional philosophical task of suggesting modes of good life, methods of bettering one's self.

The self-enlargement through self-redescription is a means toward greater autonomy, or a kind of transport, a redemption, which earlier intellectuals of the West sought either in the Platonic realm of ideal forms, or in God, or in Reason. Thus: "Literature offers redemption through making the acquaintance of as great a variety of human beings as possible,"[1] and the authors of the novel "do a lot for the plausibility of Bloom's suggestion that the spiritual education for the young might better be entrusted to imaginative literature than to religious tradition or the study of moral philosophy."[2]

It is important to note that while earlier cultural formations sought "re-demptive truths," Rorty would like to abandon this concept and instead stick only to "redemption." The "literary culture" gives up the hope for "redemptive truth"—a non-mutable final description of reality. However, it does encourage its members to seek something that is still "redemptive." "Redemption" is a word Rorty uses for a state of development in which a life-long reading practice, fueled with sheer fascination, ultimately brings autonomy from clichéd thinking.

2. Rorty's Strong Poet

Rorty's next model of self-creation is that of a strong mind who succeeds in redescribing not only himself but also, if not mainly, others, or more precisely the criteria and world-descriptions created by others. The purpose of this strongly willed person is to create his own criteria by which his own life will be judged. The primary purpose of the strong creator is to achieve autonomy from the gaze of others, to cull a space of self-reliance in which one reigns as the supreme spirit. The strong creator may then alternatively try to impose that autonomous space—with its laws—on the public sphere (Nietzsche is the primary example), or he may be free of that wish and contented with the achievement of a strong privacy (Proust). In both cases, however, the trick consists in devising a context in which to view the creations of others—the lives of others, their systems of thought, their characters—from a completely new perspective, one that will change previous creations by bringing forth those features and properties that could not be brought forth previously.

Needless to say, Rorty's model of the strong creator is a version of Harold Bloom's strong poet—a successful, if greedy, voracious, even aggressive —inheritor of the work of the predecessor, or of the whole preceding tradition. At least in his *Contingency, Irony, and Solidarity,* Rorty is happy to accept the major tenets of Bloom's theory, apparently undisturbed by the fact that Bloom's aims may be quite remote from the projects and self-creative scenarios entertained by Rorty himself. There are parts in Bloom's narrative that should be unpalatable to Rorty the pragmatist, the most obvious being the project of the realized solipsist, the phantasmagoric realist, who is an intensely antisocial creature. Rorty is of course aware of the problem and in his book he plays down Bloom's sublimities by the use of Wittgenstein's insistence that something like an entirely private language is impossible.

All this amounts to saying that Rorty's models of self-creation as presented in *Contingency, Irony, and Solidarity* do remain in an uneasy tension;
while on the one hand Rorty champions Bloom's strong poet, identifying him
with the Nietzschean hero who subjugates all the past accidents of his life-
story until he can say of the past: "thus I willed it," on the other hand Rorty
has to keep this beast at bay and remind the reader that no such projects are
final or complete. Rorty envisions a difficult balance between the strongly
willed self-creation and the pathos of the fact that no such projects are granted
completion, and that all of them, however strong, depend on the background
of the social. Thus Rorty hopes for a new kind of human being who will live
the contradiction of striving for full independence with the knowledge that no
such thing exists. He writes:

> …if we avoid Nietzsche's inverted Platonism—his suggestion that a life of
> self-creation can be as complete and as autonomous as Plato thought a life
> of contemplation might be—then we shall be content to think of human life
> as the always incomplete, yet sometimes heroic, reweaving of such a web.[3]

3. Rorty and Nehamas

Rorty's master of private narrative is very similar to the vision of the artist of
one's life offered by Alexander Nehamas, for whom the existence of the
strong creator—Nietzsche, Montaigne, Foucault—is actually a life-long composition of one's self on the basis of, or rather in a rebound movement from, a
text, or texts, of previous authors. Nehamas's strong heroes write their own
texts which grapple with the texts of mysterious predecessors (for instance,
Socrates) whose text or life is indeterminate but also radiates possibilities rich
enough to compel an endless interpretive process in which fascination may
mix with other strong feelings, even hatred. In the process, the re-interpreters
write their own selves and the textual self becomes an analogue, a more important and more real version of the real-life self. In fact there is no longer any
difference, as in these projects the rhetorical composition of a textual self is
the major content of one's life; writing is living and we are talking about the
art of living. Nehamas writes: "…one acquires or creates a self, one becomes
an individual, by integrating those materials with others acquired and constructed in the way."[4] The work of the predecessor is an accident on one's
way, but it becomes a strong accident in the sense that it compels one's attention and catalyzes the composition of one's own self. Neither the work nor the
life of the predecessor posits self-explicit meanings; these are scattered, and
the work of the interpreter is a painstaking life-long gathering or recomposing
of the alleged sense of the precursor. In so doing, however, interpreters gather
and compose their own selves.

Rorty agrees with that and works with the idea, borrowed both from Nehamas and Bloom, that it is through writing, through the work on one's texts, through the interpretive struggle with the works of the predecessors, that the self of the strong creator emerges. Rorty notes of Nietzsche, for example: "In the actual world Nietzsche was a twitchy, irresolute, nomadic nerd who never got a life outside literature,"[5] and he quotes Nehamas's discussion of Nietzsche and Proust in which Nehamas insists that the creation of the self is akin to the process of discovery of one's necessities, or the creation of one's necessities, since the line between the discovery and the making becomes blurred at this point. Rorty comments on this process: "He [Proust] had written a book and thus created a self which [others] could not have predicted or even envisaged."[6] For Rorty, as for Bloom, it is through such self-reliant, poetic strategies that Emersonian individuals progress in any field, be it poetry, philosophy, or science.

4. Shusterman's Critique

It is this potentially unhappy marriage of the liberal ironist, a social being and a creature always thirsty for conversation with others, and, on the other hand, the master of one's past, the often unsociable, anxiety-ridden virtuoso of private compositions, that is picked up and developed into a full-fledged criticism of Rorty by Richard Shusterman. Shusterman subjects both of Rorty's models to close scrutiny and finds contradictions and flaws. His initial complaint turns our attention to the discrepancy between Rorty's models. On the one hand, Rorty, consistent with his radical antifoundationalism, proposes a view of the human self as a centerless, contingent network of inscriptions, which has neither stable core nor essence. It is this self that the ironist recognizes and accepts, and on which she works to keep it going, which in the Rortean vision means to keep it evolving and expanding. On the other hand, though, Rorty promotes the vision of the strong poet, and Shusterman makes a viable critical point, noting that the model of the strong creator entails maximum concentration, focus, and often self-limitation. After all, the strong poet's vehicle for self-creation is the intensified agonistic conversation with the predecessor, in which intensity is achieved through focus, self-limitation, and obsessive attention to selected aspects of the predecessor's text. This means a check to the process of constant search for novelty, permanent self-exposure to novel works of art, new gurus, so far unexplored cultural propositions, etc. Shusterman observes:

> The aims of self-creation and of enrichment through endlessly curious self-redescriptions are not at all identical.... Boundless seeking for change can threaten the concentration necessary for creating oneself in a

strong and satisfying way. The curious ironist and the self-creating strong poet can represent, in fact, two quite different forms of aesthetic life.[7]

Shusterman's most serious criticism concerns Rorty's insistence on the radical inessentiality of the human self as well as on the pursuit of novelty. For the self to be able to enlarge itself, claims Shusterman, there must be a more palpable selfhood to enlarge, something more than a centerless web of cultural transcripts. Shusterman refers to Rorty's attempt to rewrite the Freudian model of a selfhood divided into blocked-off spheres—of id, ego, and superego—into a space of enhanced internal communication between alternative selfhoods, or concurrent self-narratives which reside within one person and which Rorty calls quasi-persons. Freud, reinterpreted by Rorty, equips us with tools to

> ...give up the urge to purification, [the urge] to achieve a stripped down version of the self ... it gave us a vocabulary that lets us describe all the various parts of the soul, conscious and unconscious alike, in homogenous terms: as equally plausible candidates for the 'true self.'[8]

On this model the aim of moral life is to maintain a lively, evolving discussion and cross-reference between the various coexisting self-narratives. Hopeful as this version of selfhood sounds, Shusterman notes its weakness, which lurks in the incessant disorder:

> If we abandon the aim of a unified, coherent self-narrative, for Rorty's chorus of inconsistent 'quasi-selves' constituted by alternative, constantly changing, often incommensurable narratives and vocabularies with no complex narrative able to make them all hang together, then the project of self enrichment becomes mythical and incoherent.[9]

For Shusterman it is misleading and unfair to suggest that only the kind of hectic or intellectually promiscuous life, full of changes of contexts, environments, and conversation partners, is worth living. He reminds us of other models that seek aesthetic contentment through greater focus or stability: "One could well choose the life of an earth-rooted, family bound farmer over a jet hopping, spouse swapping academic simply in terms of its aesthetic joys of order, coherence and harmony, which stem from a centrally structured and limited project of development."[10]

5. Apology for Rorty

The question is whether Rorty's self-creation projects might be defended against this critique. After *Contingency, Irony, and Solidarity* Rorty kept returning to the idea of reading imaginative literature—particularly the modernist novel—as a condition not only for self-creation but also for leading a good, authentic moral life. Two later essays can be of interest to us at this point: "Philosophy as a Transitional Genre," a chapter in his *Philosophy as Cultural Politics,* and a piece entitled "Redemption from Egotism: James and Proust as Spiritual Exercises." In these two texts, Rorty brings the two earlier models of a good life—that of the intellectually promiscuous ironist and that of the strong, self-composing mind—more closely together. His hope, in short, is that there is in fact no contradiction between the two. To put it briefly, the model found in these texts is that of a mind who comprises two movements which, although they seem contradictory and mutually exclusive, are in fact shown to be complementary. One movement is toward a greater variety of sources, descriptions, perspectives and vocabularies. These sources, already present in the description of the ironist in earlier work, are now shifted a little, as Rorty stresses the need for acquainting oneself with as many various types of human behavior, offered primarily by the novel (thought of as the chorus of a multitude of characters) as possible. This prowling search is what substitutes for the historical "redemptive truth" of earlier civilizations. If in earlier cultural formations—such as Socratic and Platonic philosophy, Christianity, or the Enlightenment—redemption was sought through contact with variously posited sources of power, cognitive or not but always non-human, or super-human, such as Logos, God, or Reason, in Rorty's "literary culture" the focus is on entering imaginative interactions with specific instances of human idiosyncrasy, a specificity that is never to be touched by the sort of too general principles offered by religion or philosophy, a specificity which is found only in literature. The exposure now is to a variety of human types as produced for us by the prophetic skill of a James or a Proust. Now, in contrast to the model proposed in *Contingency, Irony, and Solidarity,* it is not merely a collection of random aesthetic and cultural experiences that the philosopher advocates; rather, it is a complex discussion with a motley crew of literary characters who are a useful imitation of the varieties of life. But the main point is that collecting multiple perspectives, or participating in such multiple conversations, does not obliterate or dissolve the pursuant self. To the contrary, the gathered materials are used in the second, complementary movement, which we may call re-composition, or refitting, of the apparently loose strands into a new pattern, a very coherent one. Here the model is again Alexander Nehamas, with his interpretation of the lives of Montaigne, Nietzsche, and others, but also Nabokov in such texts as the essay, "The Art of Literature and Commonsense".

Nabokov's disclosure is a passionate defense of literary creation whose sole task and responsibility, against the "literature of ideas" and against the limited-mindedness of tedious commonsense, is the beautiful, continuous composition of trifles, details of existence, into splendid constellations of achieved harmony. For Nabokov, this is imagination's victory over chaos, time, and mundaneness; it is the ultimate "enlargement of the spirit." The creative mind is revealed in its splendor and glory through juxtaposition with the deranged one: "The madman is reluctant to look at himself in the mirror, because the face he sees is not his own: his personality is beheaded; that of the artist is increased."[11] Such increase of the self is effected through those moments of creation in which random daily observations and debris of living coalesce into

> ...a radiant second [in which] the motion of impressions and images is so swift that you cannot check the exact laws which attend their recognition, formation, and fusion and how exactly are all those parts correlated [sic]; it is like a jigsaw puzzle that instantly comes together in your brain with the brain itself unable to observe how and why the pieces fit, and you experience a shuddering sensation of wild magic, of some inner resurrection, as if a dead man were revived.[12]

Granted that this passage is highly charged with romantic elation, for Nabokov this state of transport to a region of bliss produces not only the shudder of awe, but also moral elevation. The writer stresses a number of times how such creative states make the world a better place. Among other reasons, they do so because from the perspective of the achieved pleasure, coherence, and harmony, evil and knavery look foolish, inconsistent, unattractive, ridiculous, stupid, and simply less real.

Rorty was fascinated by Nabokov's approach to the novel. For the philosopher, this project means the end to the dichotomy between strong self-creation and sensitivity to the suffering of others. On the new model, the more multiple the sources and descriptions, the larger the complexity of the network of human relations engaged (as in James and Proust), the greater is the possibility for compassion toward potentially remote kinds of forms of life. Although it would be hopeless idealism to suppose that reading imaginative novels will eliminate evil, Rorty is positive that education through the novel could help decrease the degree of callousness in a given community: "[a] poor lame boy trying to get his spastic brother out of the range of stones hurled by schoolchildren will remain a familiar sight in all countries, but a slightly less frequent one in countries where people read novels."[13] The greater the number of life-like characters we have been engaged with through immersion in novels of human variety—for example James and Proust—the greater our skills, intuitions, and expertise in dealing with others. In "Redemption from Egotism" Rorty insists that the purpose of reading novels is not hard-core knowledge of human essence, something Rorty calls "the knowledge that," but rather a skill or instinct, a grace in finding oneself among others, of being amidst the vast network of human interactions that is called culture or simply experience. The purpose of reading novels is something Rorty has called "an increased flexibility and sympathy in the making of moral decisions." Novels give us the intuitive skill of being with others, skills that will never be closed in any set of rules. But eventually such being is not different from strong self-creation. Dealing with others, with multiple others, is a tool subordinate in the adjacent, or parallel, project—that of self-composition. Rorty writes in "Redemption from Egotism":

> For the intellectual who finds James and Proust exalting, it is the hope that she will be able … to see her life in this world as a work of art— that she will be able one day to look back and bring everything together into some sort of a pattern…. Novel reading [unlike devotional reading which stresses self-cleansing], aims at encompassing multitudes rather than eliminating superfluities.[14]

This model of self-creation is far removed form Harold Bloom's achieved solipsism of the supreme strong poet. What Rorty seems to retain from Bloom is the idea of achieved autonomy and authenticity of the spirit, freed from clichéd motley of platitudes any culture is so good at equipping its young ones with. Rorty agrees with Bloom that it is only through the sustained exercise of reading literature that one achieves such a state of autonomy. But as for Bloom's related idea of the strong poet's achieved solipsism, Rorty is quite far from it. His "intellectual" enjoys a self-created autonomy of consciousness, a quite coherent and rather ordered entity, one that never forsook the idea of exposure to multiple sources. By this token, Rorty's later modified approach may be a response to a criticism like that of Shusterman's. It may also represent a balance between the claims of the strong creative subject and the need for external conversation that, as I am going to suggest next, is more suitable for discussions of complex poets like Ashbery.

6. Bloom on Ashbery's "Self-Portrait in a Convex Mirror"

Any discussion of the versions of the poetic self demonstrated or used in Ashbery's poetry should deal with Harold Bloom's original theory of poetry. Bloom, one of the most prolific literary critics in the US, has been a steady champion of John Ashbery's poetry. Applying to Ashbery's poems his highly complex theory known as "the anxiety of influence"—a strong critical tool combining motifs derived from Freud, Gnostic writings, Emerson, and Nietzsche—Bloom has pointed to Ashbery as a contemporary paradigm of the canonical writer, one who continues the tradition. In this case it is the canonical American tradition deriving from Emerson, Whitman, Dickinson, Stevens, and Crane. The form of continuity, according to Bloom's theory, is the strong agonistic misprision, or willed misinterpretation of the work of the predecessors. Bloom's model is a story of shaping and achieving poetic uniqueness; however, as such it is also a model of self-creation, as the creation of any self, textual or existential, is the same kind of process. For Bloom, it is the story of a complex process in which the beginner poet, found out by the viral presence of the dead predecessor, enters a duel in which what is at stake is nothing less than the emergence of the new poetic self.

On the way to poetic autonomy, the new poet reaches a stage in which the new vision succeeds in digesting and integrating the vision of the predecessor. In this way a new aesthetic value is created, and the adept enters the stage of achieved independence. It is a strong re-conceiving of the received text, a novel creation, something that Bloom, drawing heavily on Emerson's later musings on the nature of self-reliance, calls achieved solipsism. Bloom's process of poetic self-conception involves a rhythm of contraction and expansion, the most dramatic of which perhaps are the stages, or revisionary ratios, of *kenosis* and *askesis*. Especially in the latter, the ephebe attempts a self-mutilating sublimation of his earlier richer instincts, a contraction, a self-cleansing, in order to expel the traces of the predecessor, and limit his or her self to what is genuinely the original self. This stage is also called the stage of achieved solitude, or the stage of perfect solipsism, and in *The Anxiety of Influence* Bloom insists that it is constitutive of the American poetic canon, where the goal of the process is a "self-sustaining solitude," a much sharper version of solipsism than in the British Romantic poets.[15] The aesthetic representation of the achieved solipsism (or phantasmagoric-realism) is the perfectly enclosed roundness of the vision, which is a world-creating act, wonderfully washed of doubt. In it, "what the strong poet, like the solipsist, *means* is right, for this egocentricity is itself a major training in imagination."[16] In *Figures of Capable Imagination*, we find a further elaboration of this stage: "What the all-but-perfect solipsist means cannot be right, not until he becomes perfect in his solipsism and so stands forth as a phantasmagoric realist."[17] Elsewhere, commenting on a late essay by Emerson, Bloom argues: "...for Emerson, every trope burns away context, and when enough context has been dissolved, a new pragmatic center appears. An isolating substitution brings about a re-centering ... ultimately his vision of self-reliance is one that cheerfully concedes the final reliance of the self upon the self, its condition of perfect sphericity."[18]

Now, there is perhaps no better place in which the formula of achieved solipsism can be tested than John Ashbery's poem "Self-Portrait in a Convex Mirror." The poem is a meditation on a mannerist 1524 self-portrait by Francesco Mazzola, known as Parmigianino. The self-portrait is a rendering of the artist's reflection in a convex mirror. The image is thus distorted in such a way that the whole painting is an allegory of the process of achieving the perfect-sphericity of the achieved solipsism that Bloom sees as a crucial stage in poetic self-development. The painter's world is changed into a perfect sphere, the center of which is occupied by the poet's head; his gaze, at himself, signifying the reigning self of the accomplished solipsist. All else, just as in the Bloom excerpt quoted above, is a "burned out context," becoming a margin of the painter's vision, details or accidents of time and place, simply fitted into a homogenizing, time-suspending creative gesture. In his poem, Ashbery uses information provided by Vasari to present the painter at work, apparently undisturbed by a war threatening his life, foreign troops besieging Rome. These circumstances are lost on the artist, who is engrossed in his solipsistic, self-capturing project. The presence of the city, with its historical contingencies, signified metonymically by the window included in the painting, is mere backdrop: the window, its frames curved by the spherical optics of the painting, is bent appropriately to take its due place in the circle of objects commanded by the central consciousness, the Emersonian god of consciousness, or the "central man" of Wallace Stevens' poems.

And yet, surprisingly, when Bloom analyses the poem in the essay "The Breaking of Form," he almost entirely skips the oddity of Parmigianino's formal arrangement, concentrating instead on tracing the regular sequence of rhetorical tropes appearing in the six parts of the poem exactly as prescribed by Bloom's six revisionary ratios that the poetic self purportedly undergoes on the way to self-divination.[19] Meanwhile, many passages in the poem are engaged directly with the spherical oddity of the painting, amounting eventually to a discussion with the project of achieved solipsism. Not for Bloom, however. For him, whenever Ashbery tries to evade or displace Parmigianino's time-annulling aesthetic construction, such movements are the necessary swerves from the Emersonian tradition, or instances of acute self-limitation and sublimation. Bloom does not entertain the possibility that some passages of the poem may be an affirmation of contingency, an absorption of multiplicity and plurality, a de-centering of the self. In other words, the self-limiting movements may well be Parmigianino's, not Ashbery's; the poet having a genuine, free argument with the painter, uninhibited by the severe excisions of the "anxiety of influence."

It is true that the debate between the two modes of being—intense self-focus and immersion in the multiplicity of perspectives which the notion of the "city" symbolizes in the poem—is never resolved, and Ashbery keeps spawning ambiguities that make it ultimately impossible to separate one from the other. But whatever it does, the poem shows that the Bloomian strong-poet model, or the mind-frame of the re-centered subjectivity that for Bloom is the goal of the self-creative process, may be a much more porous or flexible entity than Bloom himself suggests. Ashbery's complex meditation on art, his self, the self of the painter, and the memory of his friend Frank O'Hara (whose name is a ghostly backing of "Francesco"), may be pointing out that artistic concentration and self-absorption is mysteriously related to the opening of the self onto the accidentality of temporal and special shifts, including the accidental intrusions of others. To put it differently, Ashbery's poem, much as it seems a perfect illustration of Bloom's agonistic theory of poetic self-reliance, contains a different model—that of Rorty's ironist self which lives only on external conversation. At one point Ashbery proposes the following formula for the being of the self: Our landscape

> Is alive with filiations, shuttlings;
> Business is carried on by look, gesture,

...
The backing of the looking glass of the
Unidentified but precisely sketched studio ...[20]

Bloom's theory alone has problems accounting for such fragments and thus for the complexity of the poet's monologue. As a result, some of Bloom's comments seem forced, preferring the strict pattern of the revisionary ratios to the more volatile freedoms of the poem. It is Rorty's pragmatist reminder of the social indebtedness of any self-creative project that might be a useful context in reading such complex postmodern poets as Ashbery.

7. Shusterman's Neo-Pragmatism, the Paradoxes of Self-Creation, and Poetry

The differences between Bloom's and Rorty's models of subjectivity point to an important problem inherent in Romanticism in general, and particularly acute in its American version: the ongoing tension between the claims of the strong self-reliant individual and the necessities of the community. Rorty's texts seem to provide a solution to the tension, attempting to create a balance, however fragile, between the two drives: the individual and the communal. And yet, even with his correction of the Bloomian sublimities of strong individual development, there is a deliberatness, a purposiveness suffusing Rorty's vision of the self-shaping processes, which may sometimes rely too strongly on the subject's unified and clear sense of its own position, goals, and course of action. Rorty's hero does not seem to allow space for the indeterminate and the elusive; here, the course of action is laid out as if by an academic professor, consciously planning her career, knowing beforehand, well in advance of the journey, what kind of enrichments will enlarge her self.

The problem with such a stance is that poetry reminds us of how unexpected and volatile the course of growth of the self may be. In Rorty's model, the unexpected is relegated to the sphere of the contingent: that with which the self will not be able to cope, that which is beyond the reach of the subject who is trying to see its route of progress by detailing its future, while being prepared for the sheer fact of human limitations. Poetry, meanwhile, seems to offer a different approach to the facticity of human limitations. Often, the development of the poetic subject consists in opening the self to the unexpected, preparing a more fertile ground on which to absorb and transform the indeterminacies of existence than is allowed in Rorty's models, even after they are corrected by a better balance between the care for the self and the care for others.

It is beyond the reach of any single essay to fully characterize this capacity of poetry to enter into more active exchanges between the determinate and the indeterminate in the development of the subject. Here, I would like to point to a useful way of tackling the problem, offering an alternative both to Rorty's uses of literature for the combined causes of the individual and the liberal community and to deconstruction—a critical formation given entirely to the study of the indeterminacy inherent in the decision-making and self-development processes. For this alternative I turn again to the neo-pragmatism of Richard Shusterman.

Shusterman's focus has been the reintegration of the cognitive, the mental and the bodily in a fashion that is a continuation of Dewey's conception of the self's dependence on its manifold interactions with its environment. Shusterman's continuous elucidation of the many ways in which the care of the bodily sphere becomes a form of care for the self, and, in spite of some criticisms, also care for the environment and the community, deserves a separate study. Here I will signal those Shustermanian motifs which are my present focus: his useful gloss on the specificities of the development of the self and its potential for poetics.

Inherited from Emersonian philosophy by both Rorty and Shusterman is the idea of the basic identity of such terms as self-reliance, poetic originality, and the uniqueness and separateness of genius. Viewed through neo-pragmatist lenses, these terms describe a nexus of attitudes which use the indeterminacies of human existence not as a limitation on the active shaping of subjectivity—as is the case in deconstruction—but in fact as the enabling condition of this process. By turning to Emerson and Wittgenstein, Shusterman reminds us of the complex interrelation, occurring in the midst of this nexus, between the known and the unknown, the calculable and the elusive, the controllable and the unruly. Put in Shusterman's terms, this interrelation is a useful tension extending to and from the sphere of the body-mind organism and its physical surroundings, both spheres being treated as a larger whole. For Shusterman the talent of the genius is its uncanny way of opening toward the forces which emerge in our interactions with the environment. On most occasions, we may remain unaware and unresponsive to them. The skill of the genius is to become conscious and responsive to these forces in such a way that they may enter and enlarge subjectivity by putting it in a completely new, so far unforeseen, position toward the environment.

Tracing the problematic of Emersonian and Nietzschean "becoming-who-one-is," Shusterman notes the many paradoxes that bring together the seemingly contradictory values of ordinariness and uniqueness, the given and the new, the discovery of the self's limits and the transcending of those limits. Most importantly, Shusterman retrieves the attention paid by the thinkers of self-creation—Emerson, Nietzsche, Wittgenstein—to the necessity of entering a curious rhythm in the process, an oscillation between the conscious effort at self-stylization and the gesture of self-abandon, forgetfulness, even obliteration of the known self. The instruction found in these writers often evokes self-cancellation; they speak of "squandering oneself," "living dangerously," "losing oneself occasionally." Following them, Shusterman corrects the conscious project of self-care, by insisting that we should want "to be surprised out of our propriety." He speaks of the integration of the "spontaneous nature and intentional striving into a higher harmony of action," following Emerson's idea that we should "place ourselves in such attitudes as to bring bigger forces about to do the work for us."[21]

If self-reliance is an ability to act—and this is the core aspect of the term in the Emersonian understanding—then the action in question is a result of the self's ability to obtain access to energies that are not entirely its own, or are its own in the sense of a potential. Emerson's and Nietzsche's insistence on the ability to surprise oneself and to bring oneself to such a threshold at which the bigger forces begin to work through the self, is the residue of the spiritual in the neo-pragmatist discourse of self-creation. In a fashion that seems to me much more useful than the discourses of deconstruction, this position offers a redefinition of subjectivity, making this sphere more flexible and more apt to deal with the demands of the modern world than the legend of the disappearance of agency.

Shusterman's Emersonian view on matters of self-creation could be paraphrased as an aesthetic of a self in search of such interactions with its surroundings that will enrich the self in ways that cannot be calculated beforehand. This is the self ever in pursuit not just of novelty, but of a kind of energy in which being and interaction with the world is a matter of aesthetics, without ceasing to be a matter of pragmatics and ethics. It is with this neo-pragmatist conception that I am now going to close my discussion by proposing an approach to the elusive and interpretation-resistant later poetry of John Ashbery.

8. Reading Late Ashbery

Ashbery's later poems are dreamscapes leading readers into regions of associations, images and linguistic formulations which sound safe and familiar, in order to gradually start disfiguring these familiarities. In contrast to Ashbery's earlier poetry, this process is refined, happening ever more imperceptibly, with the line between the real and the fantastic ever more elusive. These poems do not demonstrate any particular affinity with the idea of self-development, let alone that of self-creation. Not only uninterested in any sort of recognizable self, they may in fact speak against the idea of the self. In the beautiful and poignant late lyric "Life Is a Dream," a voice representative of this phase of the poet's oeuvre says: "A talent for self-realization will get you only as far as the vacant lot."[22]

And yet one should see such denials as complex strategies revoking the idea of the self, now returned to on a different level. I propose to treat Ashbery's later poems as attempts to create stances and positions of the self in which, as in Shusterman's analysis of the paradoxes of self-creation, the self consents to obliteration and abandonment of its safer contours, for the sake of differently prefigured, even if not entirely unknown, future integrity. This is consistent with Ashbery's aesthetic belief that the poet has to avoid self-repetition, self-cliché, and constantly strive to seek new constellations, new positioning of the material. This strategy coincides with the idea of seeking the being of the poetic voice through persistent scattering. However aesthetically refined, outlandish, bizarre, or scattered they may be, the materials included in Ashbery's poems do return to vaguely personal motifs. There is a sense in the main pieces of the later Ashbery that the poet continues a concealed, indirect, but also deliberate and intense discussion of, or rather with, himself, with his own story as a man and poet. As a poet who has stressed on numerous occasions that he has no sense of his self, he is also a poet who, increasingly in the later poetry, engages with the topics of self-understanding, self-inspection, even autobiography. But in Ashbery this impulse, so natural to the lyric, so typical of aging poets, never obliterates the aesthetic of indeterminacy. To the contrary, it makes use of it.

Ashbery's assembling operations evoke the theme of the return of the personal, or the play with the personal, play with an idea of a subject, perhaps a biographical identity. Autobiographical self-reference appears as a version of the literary effort, its counterpart, its shadow, or resonance, as if the poet were visiting his real life from time to time or taking a perspective on it from the windows of his poetic chambers. Those visits are not in the confessional mode. Yet, without reaching for the gestures of confessional poetry, Ashbery continues to engage the idea of his real-life self as a fruitful vehicle for the poem.

The following possibility becomes available: the constellations of the materials of the poem are the constellations of the self. Ashbery's assemblages begin to work as digressions, footnotes, or veils behind which there shimmers the idea of somebody's real life. The so-called real life becomes enmeshed in aesthetic compositions; the two spheres integrate and begin to reverberate in one another. Here is an example of this rich play with the personal that is representative for the quasi-biographical strategy in Ashbery's later poetry. Possibly referring to Harold Bloom's theory of the development of poetic originality, the poem is entitled "The Problem of Anxiety":

Fifty years have passed
since I started living in those dark towns
I was telling you about.
Well, not much has changed. I still can't figure out
how to get from the post office to the swings in the park.
Apple trees blossom in the cold, not from conviction,
and my hair is the color of dandelion fluff.

Suppose this poem were about you—would you
put in the things I've carefully left out:
descriptions of pain, and sex, and how shiftily
people behave toward each other? Naw, that's
all in some book it seems. For you
I've saved the descriptions of chicken sandwiches,
and the glass eye that stares at me in amazement
from the bronze mantel, and will never be appeased.[23]

Here's a mixture of lucidity and mystery typical of Ashbery. The first stanza seems to present reports from the life of the speaker. The reports are mostly dry and ordinary, although they are enriched by a darker, more mysterious note. The addressee of this seemingly mundane postcard communication is reminded of some "dark towns" inhabited by the speaker. There is a possibility here that the mundane report contains allusions to the life of poetry writing. The "dark towns" may be a poetic trope for the loci of poetic imagination, possibly echoing Eliot's London, but the reader need not make much use of the allusion at this point. What matters is the atmosphere of the bizarre that subtly enters the flat statements. Their dryness and down-to-earth quality become opaque, ripe with mystery. Could they reverberate with meanings beyond the fictive?

The time span mentioned in the first line seems to correspond with the span of Ashbery's poetry writing career. Moreover, the image of the blossoming apple trees may remind us of Ashbery's childhood at his grandparents' apple orchard farm in Sodus, New York. The assumption that Ashbery is playing with his biography, however vague, is reinforced in the first line of the second stanza, which does propose a suggestion that the bland, cliché-ridden surface of the previous lines may in fact be an attempt, however failed or ironic, at tackling the personal theme. By saying "suppose this poem were about you," the poet is in fact asking, "what if the deadpan story of the previous stanza was really about me?" This would of course mean that he is trying to talk about himself, but finds it difficult or impossible. Indeed, the tone shifts a little, and the poem mentions exclusions, the necessity of selection, of screening, leaving things out. The more substantial, emotionally authentic story of the real self—"descriptions of pain, and sex, and how shiftily/people behave toward each other"—is considered briefly, as an alternative to the preceding platitudes, only to be rejected. Ultimately, the second fragment will propose a third option: the *bizarria* of a fantastic collection in which the mundane ("chicken sandwiches") will coexist with the fantastic ("the glass eye").

Such stylistic is found in some of Ashbery's favorite artists, most characteristically perhaps in Joseph Cornell. Just as in Cornell's boxes, in the poet's pieces we watch an intriguing composition, whose map of internal relations and tensions is never to be fully described or captured. It is this collection that is Ashbery's most authentic self-divagation. The earlier images function here as a failure of the fully rational and realistic poetic autobiography; the ordinary report is an index of the autobiographical but also a preparation for a search in different, less realistic localities. Thus the carefully selected collection fulfills a double role: it constitutes the poem, allowing it to go on when the more realistic options fail, and are the only possible statement of authenticity. It is only here, Ashbery states, at the intersection of the dreamy and ordinary, that I can offer any kind of self-portrait. The museum of the bizarre found in the final lines can now be seen to throw a strangely illuminating light on the trivia that open the poem. It is from this perspective that we may return to the "dark towns" and hear them reverberate with poetic allusion. In the same manner, the difficulty of finding one's way in the most familiar surroundings ("I still can't figure out") becomes ripe with meaning if read as a comment on Ashbery's life-long poetic strategy of shunning the obvious, of the willful loss of bearings, and the exploration of uncertainty. In fact, if read in this way, the speaker's insistence that he "still can't figure out" how to move along the apparently easy and worn out routes testifies to Ashbery's retention of poetic strength. The earlier capacity to wonder has not lost any of its sharpness; the mundane world inhabited by my "real" self, the errand-following self, still stands as an awe inspiring phenomenon, a maze whose fascination lurks beneath the boredom of everydayness.

But, it is not only the cityscape that is thus saved from ennui; the life of the real self also receives a revitalizing perspective, an angle from which it is seen as just a possibility, a construction whose ordinariness and stability are only an illusion. The immersion in the mysterious modifies the life of the everyday, it brings life to it and is the poet's final gesture at self-creation. The self that finds itself amidst the bizarre furniture at the end of the poem is both composed and real; it does spell a triumph of poetic power, which, amazingly, Ashbery achieves by swerving away from Bloom's seriousness in the treatment of poetic anxieties. His "museum" is proposed as an accidental finding, an ironical self-portrait, which, however, glories in its imaginative freshness and power.

In such self-creative strategies, Ashbery departs both from Bloom's narrative of Romantic self-creation and from its Rortian corrections. The strict, straightforward, anxiety-free Rortian approaches discussed earlier may fail when applied to poems like "The Problem of Anxiety." Ashbery seems far from this more self-conscious model of self-creation. "Life Is a Dream", the poem I mentioned earlier, conveys an air of regret as it looks back on a life of more deliberate and calculated self-creation. It portrays such a life as a series of choices which are too exacting, eventually too narrow, doomed to end in "the vacant lot / next to the lumber yard, where they have rollcall."[24]

Ashbery's poems of the 1990's and after the year 2000 are not confessional self-scrutinies, or even romantic poems of quest for the self. They may be described, however, as aesthetic embodiments of the paradoxes of self-creation described by Shusterman, especially the paradox of self-creation as a mixture of conscious will with self-abandonment aimed at bringing spontaneous extra-personal forces into play. Shusterman reminds us of an aspect of genius that was obvious to the Romantics, and that is not present in sober philosophers like Rorty: genius is not fully transparent to itself; what is more, a large chunk of its energies is stored in an area that is not accessible to genius consciously.

9. Conclusion: Why Want Genius

To see Ashbery with the help of Shusterman's reading of Emersonian self-reliance as self-creation is to get a possible answer to the question of why talk of genius at all; after all, have we not wanted to abandon the very idea of genius as too stifled; a stale, badly Romantic, even reactionary idea? To read Ashbery in the context of the discourses of self-creation offered by Bloom, Rorty, and especially Shusterman is to rehabilitate genius. Genius becomes a name for a stance that ushers fresh energy into the realm of one's creation, one's life. Ashbery's poems are meditations on how we always fail to touch the essence of what we are, even though we may suspect and sense this essence daily, even though we sense which types of experience are nourishing and which deleterious to us. As such, they are special places which test the poet's, or reader's, capacity to remain in the most fruitful possible relation to this sense. In this way, apparently purely aesthetic creations are a truly spiritual exercise. Ashbery's poems want to retain autonomy from all critical strategies of classification; they want to remain alive on their own terms. In them, genius is the art of staying alive on one's own terms, without falling victim to the illusion of a world-annulling solipsism.

NOTES

1. Richard Rorty, *Philosophy as Cultural Politics* (Cambridge, UK: Cambridge University Press, 2007), p. 91.
2. Richard Rorty, "Redemption from Egotism: James and Proust as Spiritual Exercises," retrieved from Richard Rorty's Stanford website, 2002.
3. Richard Rorty, *Contingency, Irony, and Solidarity* (Cambridge: Cambridge University Press, 1989), p. 43.
4. Alexander Nehamas, *The Art of Living: Socratic Reflections from Plato to Foucault* (Berkeley: University of California Press, 1998), p. 4.
5. Richard Rorty, *Truth and Progress* (Cambridge: Cambridge University Press, 1998), p. 327.
6. Rorty, *Contingency*, p. 102.
7. Richard Shusterman, *Pragmatist Aesthetics: Living Beauty, Rethinking Art* (New York: Lanham: Rowman & Littlfield, 2000, 2nd ed.), p. 247.
8. Rorty, *Contingency*, p. 152.
9. Shusterman, *Pragmatist Aesthetics*, p. 249.
10. *Ibid.*, p. 253.
11. Vladimir Nabokov, "The Art of Literature and Common Sense," in *Lectures on Literature* (San Diego: Harcourt, 1980), p. 377.
12. *Ibid.*, p. 378.
13. Richard Rorty, "Introduction," in Vladimir Nabokov, *Pale Fire* (London: Everyman's Library, 1992), pp. xviii–xix.
14. Rorty, "Redemption from Egotism."
15. Harold Bloom, *The Anxiety of Influence: A Theory of Poetry* (London: Oxford University Press, 1973), pp. 131–132.
16. *Ibid.*, p.121.
17. Harold Bloom, *Figures of Capable Imagination* (New York: Seabury, 1976), p. 193.
18. Harold Bloom, *Kabbalah and Criticism* (New York: Continuum, 2005), p. 63.

19. Harold Bloom, "The Breaking of Form," in *Deconstruction and Criticism* (New York: Continuum, 1979), pp. 1–37.
20. John Ashbery, *Self-Portrait in a Convex Mirror* (New York: Penguin Books, 1975), p. 75.
21. Richard Shusterman, *Performing Live* (Ithaca: Cornell University Press, 2000), p. 216.
22. John Ashbery, *Your Name Here* (New York: Farrar, 2000), p. 59.
23. John Ashbery, *Can You Hear Bird?* (New York: The Noonday Press, 1995), p. 121.
24. John Ashbery, *Your Name Here*, p. 59.

Three

CHALLENGING THE TABOO
OF THE AUTOBIOGRAPHICAL

Wojciech Małecki

Pretend what we may, the whole man is at work within us
when we form our philosophical opinions.[1]
William James

Philosophy has equal reason to shun the autobiographical
since its claim is to speak, using Kant's predicates of the a
priori, with necessity and universality. Yet philosophers
have left us with a trail of images of themselves preparing
for philosophy or recovering from it. After the instances of
Augustine's forbidden pears and Rousseau's unconfessed
ribbon, we may stray from Descartes in his dressing gown
sitting before the fire, or Hume's sociably returning from
his closet to play backgammon, to Emerson walking across
a muddy common, or Thoreau lying on the ice, looking
down through a hole he has cut in it at the summer still on
the floor of the pond; or to Wittgenstein resting on his
spade, or Austin's shooting his neighbor's donkey, perhaps
by mistake, perhaps by accident.[2]
Stanley Cavell

The chief characteristic of this specifically human life,
whose appearance and disappearance constitute worldly events,
is that it is itself full of events which can be ultimately told as a story,
establish a biography; it is of this life, *bios*, as distinguished from mere *zōē*,
that Aristotle said that it 'somehow is a kind of praxis.'[3]
Hannah Arendt

What relations can there be between philosophy and autobiography? Are they
limited to such trivial facts as that philosophy can make autobiographical
discourse—just as any other thing, for that matter—the subject of its inquiries,
or that philosophers—just as members of any other profession—can and
sometimes do write autobiographies (some of which even a non-professional
public can revel in, as the example of Bertrand Russell clearly shows)? But
might these relations be more intimate? Can autobiography be considered a

legitimate form of philosophical discourse, for instance? This latter question is actually not as nonsensical as it might seem to some because, after all, if one were to consult the history of philosophy, one would have to admit that some of the most towering and formative texts in this discipline are either autobiographies *per se* or at least contain important autobiographical elements; take for instance, Augustine's *Confessions,* Boethius's *Consolation of Philosophy*, Montaigne's *Essays*, Nietzsche's *Ecce Homo*,[4] or even Descartes' *Meditations* (as Foucault reminds us: "we must not forget that Descartes wrote 'meditations'—and meditations are a practice of the self").[5] Yet on the other hand, in some quarters of the philosophical world the incorporation of the autobiographical, or more generally, the personal, into philosophical discourse seems to be a "taboo," as Richard Shusterman remarks.[6] Why is this so? Is such an approach justified? And if it is not, what can be done to counter it? In this paper, I am going to attempt to provide some provisional answers to these questions by studying how Shusterman challenges the aforementioned taboo. To be more exact, I am going to analyze not only his arguments regarding the importance of autobiography to (writing) philosophy, but also the employment of autobiography in his own philosophical writings.

But before I get to Shusterman's defense of philosophical autobiography, let me begin with what he understands both autobiography and philosophy to be. Although he in fact never provides any precise definition of autobiography, something which might seem reasonable given its reputation as "the slipperiest of literary genres,"[7] Shusterman at least discerns some features of it which he sees as especially salient and which are definitely worth mentioning here since they are related both to some obstacles to the very idea of philosophical autobiography, and to Shusterman's attempts at overcoming them. First of all, then, autobiography, contrary to what the prefix 'auto-' might suggest, cannot be merely personal for, on the power of the social theory of the self Shusterman inherits from pragmatists such as Dewey and Mead (and which he shares with other contemporary thinkers, for example, Charles Taylor[8]), not only do we always conceive of ourselves against the background of other human beings, but we are also constituted as more or less provisional nodes in the matrix of social relations in which *qua* humans we are inevitably entangled.[9] As we see, then, Shusterman's stance is situated at the opposite pole of the so-called "ideology of individualism"[10] which pervades some theoretical accounts of autobiography (in the words of Paul John Eakin, "The myth of autonomy [of the autobiographical self] dies hard and autobiography criticism has not yet fully addressed the extent to which the self is defined by—and lives in terms of—its relations with others")[11] On the other hand, however, it is important to note that this does not mean that he professes the popular philosophical *doxa* which discards the notion of the self altogether.[12]

The second important feature of all autobiography is its contextuality, by which Shusterman means that how we narrate our autobiography (and this "how" embraces here both what might be described as "form" as well as "content") is determined by the particular existential situation, or period of life, in which that act of narration takes place, and thus our autobiographical account of the past may easily change in time (not only in the sense that it will include more events, but that our interpretation of the same events will differ).[13] And one does not even have to evoke here the category of dramatic experiences which can transform one's perspective on one's whole life (and henceforth our autobiographical narrative), such as, say, witnessing a relative's or friend's tragic death. Indeed, such a transformation may occur gradually and be caused by factors that are almost impossible to discern (not only at the time of their operation but also *ex post facto*).[14]

Strictly related to this contextuality is autobiography's third important characteristic, namely its inevitable partiality (or cognitive intransparency) whose chief consequence is the impossibility for one's autobiography to yield an objectively true rendering of one's existence and its meaning.[15] In order to explain that point Shusterman, among other things, leans upon the narrative theory of the self (to which he subscribes just as many other contemporary philosophers do, other notable examples being Alasdair McIntyre and Daniel C. Dennett).[16]

In a nutshell, according to that conception, our self-understanding is determined by the larger narrative which we tell of ourselves, and given that such a narrative always stretches from the (remembered) past to our (projected) future, the self-understanding at a particular moment is shaped by both our memories and the visions of our future which we spin. Now it suffices only to evoke the trivial fact of the human inability to predict the future in an infallible, exact way to conclude that autobiographical writing always suffers from severe epistemic limitations and ambiguity. For instance, as Shusterman claims, "...when we are keenly aware of two rival futures we can vacillate radically in the meaning we give to present experience at a juncture where the two future contexts seem equally possible".[17] It is worth adding that the partiality of autobiography, according to Shusterman, stems not solely from its dependency on what we might call, borrowing a term from Husserl, a protentive aspect of human self-understanding, but from the general perspectival and selective nature of our understanding of the world, too.[18]

Autobiography, according to Shusterman, has also a definite "pragmatic" dimension; that is, it is destined to serve a specific goal (thought of which always guides us, consciously or not, when we are undertaking the task of self-narration), even if it be pure entertainment. In case of philosophical autobiography, which interests me here the most, the end is rather "self-knowledge," and can be further specified in the following way:

> Usually we want to know about dimensions of our self because of some problem that confronts us, philosophical or otherwise. We tell a story about ourselves in order to become clearer to ourselves so as to get clearer bearings with respect to present concerns and future choices of action. St.

Augustine decided to perform the autobiographical exercise of his *Confessions* partly, it seems, to come to grips with his choice of leaving the life of an acclaimed intellectual in Milan to become the Catholic bishop of a congregation in Africa, and partly to leave a testament to the memory of his parents and his own life (since he thought he had recently come close to dying from illness, though he went on to live over thirty years more).[19]

Finally, let me stress that while it is not an unambiguous matter whether all autobiography belongs to literature or not (Philippe Lejeune, for instance, the foremost French theoretician of autobiographical writing, has "reasonably," as he himself put it, refused to approach that question at all)[20] Shusterman, seems not to have doubts about giving a positive answer to it. This is probably because of the following specific implications which he draws from the narrative conception of the self:

> ...at any given moment when we write about our selves, we have to project (even if only by implicit presumption) not only a present context but also a presumed future trajectory of our current of life that then serves as the wider context in which the contexts of past and present are embedded. Since we never fully know the future, the implicit presumption of its direction involves a creative or *poetic* leap of the imagination, a *fictive* projection that may prove true but cannot now be known as such.[21]

Whether the term "poetic" bears anything more than a metonymical sense here, and whether the aforementioned projections can be subsumed under the category of fiction solely by virtue of their referring to the (unknown) future, remains a matter for further discussion for which there is no place here.

Instead, now that we know to some extent about Shusterman's take on autobiography, let us turn to his conception of philosophy. Unfortunately, any broader presentation of Shusterman's metaphilosophical views is impossible here, but even very brief, necessarily sketchy and simplified remarks on that subject will be useful for the purpose of this paper. Consider first a dual typology of philosophies which Shusterman makes a starting point of his book *Practicing Philosophy*. As he points out, one can distinguish between philosophy as *bios philosophicos*, i.e., the practice of perfecting the actual life of the philosopher; and philosophy as "theory," which "concerns the formulation or criticism of general, systematic views about the world."[22] Significantly, the relations between the two have not been unproblematic, which can be exemplified by the fact that some representatives of the former type of philosophy, such as Cicero, Seneca, and Montaigne, "...disparage[d] pure theorists as mere 'grammarians'... who 'teach us how to argue instead of how to live.'"[23] Even though such an evaluation might seem glaringly awkward today, one must remember that the tradition of *bios philosophicos*, as scholars such as Pierre Hadot constantly remind us,[24] was very potent in the times of Cicero.

Then, for instance, Socrates's defiant life and death was deemed not merely, as it is usually now, an attractive story with which one may amuse one's students, but rather an example to be emulated. It is exactly this tradition that Shusterman wants to revitalize in his *Practicing Philosophy* and other works,[25] and he does so by synthesizing the practical and the theoretical, the written and the performed, in a more comprehensive form of philosophical life.

Speaking of pragmatism and theory, there should be no doubt that specific conceptions that Shusterman, as a pragmatist, is bequeathed by William James and other classical American thinkers significantly color his version of *bios philosophicos* and give it a distinct, if not uncontroversial, theoretical foundation. As he explains in the beginning of his essay "The Urban Aesthetics of Absence" (to which I will later return as it constitutes one of Shusterman's most interesting attempts at philosophical autobiography):

> Pragmatism, as I practice it, is a philosophy of embodied, situated experience. Rather than relying on a priori principles or seeking necessary truths, the pragmatist works from experience, trying to clarify its meaning so that its present quality and its consequences for future experience might be improved.[26]

Given Shusterman's epistemological claims, which I have hinted at while discussing his conception of autobiography, it is understandable that he conceives experience (at least that available to human beings) as "contextual," (that is, defined by our subject-position). Yet at the same time he is quick to underscore that such a contextuality does not entail any form of experiential solipsism, and this is because there are various "homologies" to be found between our experiences and those of others, not to mention the fact that we cannot preclude (for that would be a transcendental claim for which there is no place in pragmatism) that such homologies may exist between our experience and the environment which surrounds us. "Nonetheless," he sums up, "a philosophy that argues from experience and recognizes its contextuality should be reflective enough to declare its own experiential situatedness,"[27] something which, in case of each individual philosopher, implies reflection on the details of his or her life.

Shusterman's blend of the ancient conception of *bios philosophicos* and pragmatism is also enriched by various insights he takes from the likes of Ludwig Wittgenstein, Michel Foucault, and even Confucius,[28] and culminates in the following definitions of philosophy as an art of living: "critically reflective and ameliorative self-care practiced through the disciplined pursuit of knowledge" and "a life practice of self-examination and self-creation in the quest to live better."[29] Unsurprisingly, if philosophy thus conceived is to be expressed through the medium of discourse, it might involve autobiographical narrative, or at least this is what Shusterman thinks. Indeed, he goes so far as to argue, in his *Practicing Philosophy*, that a "philosophical" (in the specific sense just discussed) work that failed to do so "would be incomplete, even dishonest."[30] Of course, many contemporary philosophers who indeed do not incorporate life-writing into their papers and books are not troubled by any such feelings of dishonesty, and this is simply because the conception of *bios philosophicos* is as alien to their professional identity as the idea that they, for instance, should wear chitons, himations and laurel wreaths while at work. One might point out that the devil, here, hides in the very word "professional," which only confirms Thoreau's well-known complaint, cited approvingly by Shusterman, that "There are nowadays professors of philosophy, but not philosophers."[31] But the very fact that philosophy is rather a job than a way of living, however crucial, does not, in itself, explain the "repression"[32] of the autobiographical, in some philosophical quarters,[33] and we must look for additional determinants here. The most obvious of these is that the profession of philosophy often relies on the ideals of "theory" understood as an objective, impersonal reflection on the most general traits of reality, formulated in maximally transparent, scientific discourse.[34] Such a theoretical attitude creates doubtless many obstacles to the autobiographical, yet, following Shusterman, I would like to focus only on a specific obstacle related to philosophy's celebration of the "necessary and universal" (and thus to its aversion to "contingency" and "personal subjectivity").

Shusterman finds it indeed striking that this aversion precludes the presence of personal testimony even in those philosophical texts which concern nothing less than personhood itself. As he explains, "inquiring into personal identity, [philosophy] seeks a necessary core," and tries to find it in things such as universal rationality, which is presumed to be shared by all human beings worthy of that name.[35] Thus it inevitably neglects or at least downplays the idiosyncrasies of individual lives (deeming them irrelevant epiphenomena), an approach which is even strengthened by a

> ...deeper presumption that if identity were a matter of contingency rather than ontological or rational necessity, then something deep and sublime would disappear from personhood, and self-dignity would be lost.[36]

Confronted with such a situation, Shusterman tries to demonstrate that probing into the necessary core of the self in order to avoid its contingency constitutes an impossible, since inherently inconsistent, task—and this is because if there can be any essential feature of the human self, it must be contingency itself. He does so by evoking the aforementioned theory of the social construction of the self, which has the contingent nature thereof as its natural corollary, assuming that all societies are nothing but products of historical processes that in turn, far from being guided by any necessary teleology, are rather defined by chance (which, of course, is a thesis surely not every philosopher might agree with). Moreover, points out Shusterman, even if one treated the social aspects of the self as mere appearances, or its external layers, and wanted to peel them off, as it were, in order to reach the self's deepest personal center (elevating it to the status of the essential or true self, untouched by contingency), one's attempt would be frustrated in the end. For, after all, he asks, haven't we learned from Freud that our most secret thoughts, desires, and fears which we hide from the rest of the world, have all been shaped by "peripities" of the history of our childhood?[37] These arguments prepare the ground for Shusterman's following twofold inference: (1) that given the just proven contingency of the self, philosophical discourse on the self needs to recognize the importance of this contingency (i.e., to "take [it] seriously") and (2) that "Inquiry into its [i.e., the self's] identity should *thus* allow an autobiographical moment long repressed in philosophy."[38] Now, since Shusterman's task here is primarily to refute "the charge that [autobiography] should have no place in philosophical discourse" which might be raised by philosophers who harbor a "deep-rooted prejudice for universality and necessity,"[39] it is relevant here to examine whether such philosophers (let us dub them, for the sake of convenience, "theorists") could find the above plausible.

First of all, in order for that to happen, "theorists" would obviously have to accept at least Shusterman's interpretation of Freudian psychoanalysis (if not also the thesis of the social construction of the self), something which might not prove possible. But even if it did, and even if they thus agreed with step (1), they would in all probability reject (2), for they simply would not be able to treat the imperative to "take seriously" the self's contingency as reason enough (or reason at all) to include the autobiographical in the philosophical discourse on the self. Indeed, the "theorists" would argue that in order to approach the problem of the contingency of the self with enough seriousness one needs to do so within the confines of properly abstract, impersonal discourse, and provide not narratives, but instead clear, concise, logically valid arguments that would decisively solve it. It is also worth noting here that even one of the most notorious philosophical enemies of "theory" and at the same time an advocate of narratives, Richard Rorty, when addressing the contingency of the self in his seminal book *Contingency, Irony, and Solidarity* (as well as in other places) declined to resort to (his own) autobiography, which, on the other hand, does not mean that he excluded the autobiographical from philosophy as such.[40] The example of Rorty surely does not settle anything decisively, yet the fact remains that there is no necessary inference from the philosophical recognition of the contingency of the self, to the recognition of autobiography as a valid form of philosophical discourse.

An analogous problem haunts Shusterman's argument which flows from his attachment to the narrative theory of the self and claims that "If we he help determine who we are by the stories we tell of ourselves, *then* one is *surely* entitled to theorize issues of the self in one's own voice and from one's own experience."[41] Again, the "theorists" could gladly agree that anyone who wants to theorize what it is like to be a self can refer to one's own experience, though on the condition that one does not limit oneself to it. (For if—the argument would go—one wants to theorize seriously, that is, put forward some justified claims concerning the general nature of the self, and this is what it means to theorize the self, after all, then in order to avoid false generalizations, one must consider the fact that such a nature embraces also personal experiences of others, which may in many respects be incompatible with one's own.) Yet the "theorists" would certainly treat the claim that the narrativity of the self entitles one to theorize it in one's "own voice" (and what Shusterman means by this phrase here is, roughly, "through the medium of autobiographical narrative") as a blatant *non-sequitur*, which one might put schematically as "if one wants to theorize x, and x has property y, then one's theoretical discourse is entitled to have property y, too," and which makes just as much sense as saying that if one wants to theorize racism one can do so in a racist way, or that if one wants to theorize falsity then one's theoretical discourse can be false. Actually, in order to secure the validity of both this reasoning, and the above discussed inference from (1) to (2) Shusterman needs to supply an additional premise, and he seems to be attempting to do just that when he says: "Further, if philosophy is a personal life-practice devoted to self-improvement through self-understanding, then certain details of one's life surely become relevant for analysis."[42] Yet, at least as far as his confrontation with the "theorists" is concerned, invoking this conception of philosophy hardly supports Shusterman's argumentation, for they by definition reject such an ideal and thus it, instead of justifying anything, is itself in need of justification here.

So much for Shusterman's theoretical defense of the idea of philosophical autobiography, which as we have seen, must be considered largely unsuccessful. Yet as we know, he challenges the "taboo" of the autobiographical in practice, too, by actually attempting philosophical autobiography, something which may indeed be a more efficient strategy to promote his idea, given that, as Shusterman himself concedes, "pragmatically, the proof of the pudding is in eating."[43] First, then, one can distinguish two groups of Shusterman's texts that relate to his biography:

a) Those which are explicitly and decisively autobiographical in character, including:
  - The philosophical short story "Human Nature at the Schlachtensee," which portrays an episode from Shusterman's stay in Berlin as a Fulbright Professor. In brief, Shusterman and his then-girlfriend (now wife), Erica Ando, while jogging together in a park by the lake Schlachtensee, at the outskirts of the city, discover a dead body, guarded by policemen, and even though the whole scene looks rather suspicious, the couple fail, despite their desire to do so, and partly because of the fear generated by their being aliens in a foreign country, to ask the policemen what has happened. As the narrative proceeds, the unsolved "mystery of the corpse" becomes a topic of the discussion at a party held by Shusterman's German friends, and, as a result of the latter being scholars in the humanities,

some in philosophy to boot, this generates a flurry of intricate interpretations of the event, which relate to Hegel's reading of *Antigone*,
feminism, and constructivist theories of environment, and ultimately
spur Shusterman to formulate some theoretical conclusions concerning human nature and the task of the philosopher.[44]

- The essay "Regarding Oneself and Seeing Double," written especially for a collection entitled *Philosopher's I: Personal Reflections
on Life in Philosophy*, which covers selected significant events and
periods in Shusterman's life (his assistance at the birth of his
daughter Talia, his teenage exposure to anti-Semitism, his service
in Israeli military intelligence), linking them to particular strains of
his philosophical writings.[45]

- The essay "Next Year in Jerusalem? Jewish Identity and the Myth
of Return," (originally published in the collection entitled *Jewish
Identity*, and then included in Shusterman's *Practicing Philosophy*), in which a certain strategy for Jewish existence is derived
from Shusterman's experiences as an American Jew who left his
home country as a teenager and then spent a large period of his life
in Israel, only to later resettle in America.[46]

b) Texts which, although not principally autobiographical in character, contain some important autobiographical elements (accounts of, or allusions
to, given events, etc.): for instance, the essay "Multiculturalism and the
Art of Living" (Shusterman's meeting of "a beauty of Japanese extrac-
tion" who "became the love of [his] life"[47]); "The Urban Aesthetics of
Absence" (his visit to a Berlin techno club; his service as a military intelligence officer in the Sinai); "Somaesthetics and the Revival of Aesthetics" (events from his academic travels[48]); "Pragmatism and East-Asian
Thought" (Shusterman's experience as a body therapist[49]); "Art and Philosophy" (his training in meditation at a Zen cloister in Japan[50]).

It is worth mentioning here that some of Shusterman's autobiographical
exercises invite a comparative analysis that could demonstrate their deep analogies *vis-à-vis* other philosophical autobiographies, particularly as far as the
rhetorical strategies and motifs utilized in them are concerned. One could try,
for instance, to demonstrate how Shusterman's autobiographical exercises are
inscribed into the tradition of philosophical self-purification and confessions of
guilt, as there are clear instances of such acts in his corpus.[51] But given Shusterman's identity as a pragmatist, instead of exploring these and other intertextual relations, I would like to concentrate rather on the pragmatic aspect of his
philosophic-autobiographical narratives. To begin with, he admits that most of
the aforementioned narratives were written in reaction to particular challenges
which life has posed to him and which prompted him to seek self-knowledge:

I can testify that my own (rather meager and hesitant) efforts in autobi-

ography were certainly motivated by the pragmatic interest of finding
out who I was or where I stood in order better to find out what I should
do or become. The final chapter of *Practicing Philosophy* focused on the
vexed question of Jewish identity, because, after a long period in Israel, I
had to resume life as a secular Jew in the diaspora. The autobiographical
philosophical reflections of *Performing Live* were likewise attempts to
come to grips with troubling existential questions: my loneliness and al-
ienation in Berlin, my confusions and anxieties as a binational and as a
partner in an interracial marriage.[52]

This "self-help" function of philosophical autobiography hardly demands further commentary, so let me turn to another, probably more interesting, though not necessarily more salient, one, which is related to Nietzsche's
famously bold dictum that "every philosophy" is but an "involuntary and
unconscious memoir."[53] Even though Shusterman, a keen reader of Nietzsche,
has qualms about accepting that claim in its entirety (perhaps because it
smacks of crude psychologism), he nevertheless is convinced that "the personal will always motivate us [philosophers] beneath the surface"[54] and that
hence there is a complex web of relations stretching between the events of
one's personal life and the content of one's philosophical ideas. This complexity makes it, of course, hard to determine which events have had impact
on which ideas (for lack of space, I omit here the question of how one's philosophical ideas and texts can influence one's life), especially that the nature of
such relations can differ from case to case; they can be those of convergence
or discord, for example. What Shusterman means here is, to grossly simplify
things, that for some philosophers philosophical writing may function as compensation for what they are lacking in their private existence, and thus constitute, in a certain sense, a negation, or reversal, of their biographies; while for
others, philosophy may be, so to speak, a continuation, or "mirroring," of their
lives.[55] However serious they might be, these difficulties in determining the
reverberations between a philosopher's life and his works, do not change the
fact—or so Shusterman believes—that in order to better understand a given
thinker's ideas at least some knowledge of his (auto)biography is needed. In
this light, one might perceive Shusterman's autobiographical remarks, which
highlight the rootedness of his specific insights in real-life experiences and are
scattered throughout his oeuvre, as a conscious strategy of securing the proper
understanding of these insights by his audience; something which would be all
the more appropriate given that, as he himself claims, echoing the words of
his philosophical father figure John Dewey, *most* of his ideas spring exactly
from such "experiences," and not from philosophical "books" he has read.
Shusterman explains, for instance, the dialectic of multiplicity and "reconstructed unities that embrace plurality and change," which pervades his philosophy, as a consequence of his polarized, vexed identity as an American
Jew, complicated by his being an ex-Israeli; while at the same time he attrib-

utes his critical approach toward the social world and the urge to improve it to the frustrations and anger which troubled him in his teenage years.[56] Of course, given the contextuality of autobiography, which I have mentioned before, one might wonder how strongly the particular context in which Shusterman weaves his narratives, a context which includes, among other things, his being a professional philosopher, inflects his account of these circumstances. In particular, it is hard to say whether they really were *causes* of his philosophical beliefs, or whether they have been (unwittingly) reinterpreted by him as such only *ex post facto*, in order to fit them into the particular narrative that defines him at the moment. Shusterman, however, is conscious of such problems and addresses them by stating that:

> Although this [that is, his philosophical autobiography] is an attractive explanatory speculation, I would not know how to verify it as a causal explanation in an empirically decisive way. Still, I am not convinced that factual or causal demonstration is always what we want from explanations. Certainly, aesthetic explanations, as Wittgenstein argued, are more often matters of redirecting perception till something perceptually 'clicks' than they are matters of determining empirical causes and conditions.[57]

Be that as it may, the aforementioned contrast between life-experiences and books as sources of philosophy allows me, in conclusion, to evoke a rather obvious, yet still quite useful, distinction between two types of philosophers. The first one embraces those thinkers whose biographies can be reduced, roughly, to the chronological list of the educational institutions they attended and of works they conceived—painting in effect the picture of an existence led among dusty library shelves, where the most exciting events are having an exchange with a mean colleague at a conference, or replying to an overly critical review, or something equally serious. On the other hand, there are philosophers whose lives deserve to be portrayed if not in action-movies then in dynamic, suspenseful dramas. People like Foucault, with his well-known "S/M, drugs, and politics'n'philosophy" attitude, which threw him into places as different as gay clubs in San Francisco and post-Islamic-revolution Iran. Or Wittgenstein, a genius of aristocratic descent constantly tormented by thoughts of suicide, unfit for the rigid structures of the academia, a voluntary hermit, and a soldier "decorated" for bravery.

The reason I am mentioning this distinction is that Shusterman belongs rather to the latter than the former type and, significantly for the topic of this paper, makes use of that fact in constructing his textual persona. Namely, what we learn from Shusterman's essays is that he, full of "adolescent energy,... extremism" and "a blazing anger" at what he then perceived as the hypocrisy of American society, left his home at the tender age of sixteen, and then, traveling through Europe, went to Israel, where not only was he adopted by his new family, and continued his education studying Philosophy and English, but also served in the country's Military Intelligence, which meant at that time, as it does now, participating in serious military conflicts, such as the Yom Kippur War, and involved risking one's life.[58] Significantly even when he exchanged the army for the academia, having obtained his Ph.D. at Oxford and getting tenured positions first in Israel and then in America, this did not put an end to his existence as "the Wandering Jew."[59] His essays thus portray his numerous travels, for instance, the long stay in Berlin which included "drinking deeply from the often dark wonders of this bewitching city," and exploring its "pleasures and morbid fascinations."[60] And we get a hint of what these explorations meant in practice in his essay on "The Urban Aesthetics of Absence" in which he describes his visit to an illegal, underground techno club with "degenerating plaster walls," filled with "the break beats and the loops blaring from the speakers" and with "the techno crowd."

Such passages certainly add to the attractiveness of Shusterman's auto-biographical narratives, yet it seems unlikely that, captivating as they might be, they could make someone skeptical of the idea of philosophical autobiog-raphy change her mind on that issue, even if they perhaps help Shusterman gain some adherents among his readers. I will not, however, speculate how often that happens, just as I will not attempt to adjudicate whether these narra-tives indeed make his ideas clearer to his general audience. What I would like to stress, nevertheless—if I am allowed to end this essay (which deals, after all, with personal aspects of philosophizing) on a personal note—is that they have definitely clarified at least some of these ideas to me.[61]

NOTES

1. William James, *The Will to Believe and Other Essays in Popular Philosophy* (Cam-bridge: Harvard University Press, 1979), p. 77.

2. Stanley Cavell, *A Pitch of Philosophy: Autobiographical Exercises* (Cambridge: Harvard University Press 1994), p. 3. Cf. Jacques Derrida, *Signéponge/Signsponge*, trans. Richard Rand (New York: Columbia University Press, 1984), p. 32.

3. Hannah Arendt, *The Human Condition* (Chicago: University of Chicago Press, 1958), p. 97.

4. See Cavell, *A Pitch of Philosophy*, p. 3.

5. Michel Foucault, "On the Genealogy of Ethics: An Overview of the Work in Pro-gress" in *The Foucault Reader*, ed. Paul Rabinow (New York: Pantheon Books, 1984), p. 371.

6. Richard Shusterman, *Practicing Philosophy: Pragmatism and the Philosophical Life* (New York and London: Routledge, 1997), p. 181.

7. Paul J. Eakin, *How Our Lives Become Stories: Making Selves* (Ithaca: Cornell Uni-versity Press, 1999), p. 2.

8. See, for example, Charles Taylor, *Philosophical Arguments* (Cambridge, Mass.: Harvard University Press, 1995). Cf. James Livingston, "The Strange Career of 'Social Self,'" *Radical History Review*, 2000:76 (2000), p. 53–79.

9. Richard Shusterman, "Regarding Oneself and Seeing Double: Fragments of Autobiography," in *The Philosophical I: Personal Reflections on Life in Philosophy*, ed. George Yancey (Lanham: Rowman and Littlefield, 2002), p. 2.

10. I borrow this term from Robert Smith; see his *Derrida and Autobiography* (Cambridge: Cambridge University Press 1995), p. 56.

11. Eakin, *How Our Lives Become Stories*, p. 43.

12. See Jean-Luc Nancy, "Introduction," in *Who Comes After the Subject?*, ed. Eduardo Cadava, Peter Connor, and Jean-Luc Nancy (New York and London: Routledge, 1991), p. 5; cf. "Eating Well, or the Calculation of the Subject: An Interview with Jacques Derrida," *ibid.*, pp. 96–119. Cf. Michael Sprinker "Fictions of the Self: The End of Autobiography," in *Autobiographical: Essays Theoretical and Critical*, ed. James Olney, (Princeton: Princeton University Press, 1980).

13. Shusterman, "Regarding Oneself...," p. 2.

14. Significantly, there is also some neurological evidence for the contextuality of memory, and thus of autobiography. See Israel Rosenfield, *The Invention of Memory: A New View of the Brain* (New York: Basic, 1988).

15. Shusterman, "Regarding Oneself...," p. 2–3.

16. See Shusterman, *Practicing Philosophy*, chap. 7; Richard Shusterman, *Pragmatist Aesthetics: Living Beauty, Rethinking Art* (New York: Rowman and Littlefield, 2000, 2nd ed.), chap. 9; Alasdair MacIntyre, *After Virtue* (London: Duckworth, 1984, 2nd ed.).

17. Shusterman, "Regarding Oneself...," p. 3.

18. One should add here that there are other arguments for the partiality of autobiography, see Smith, *Derrida and Autobiography*, pp. 67–68, and, in general, the texts he overviews in chap. 5 of that book: for instance. Michael Ryan, "Self-de(con)struction," *Diacritics*, 6:1 (Spring 1976), pp. 34–41. For Shusterman's views on the general perspectivalism of human experience see Shusterman, "Beneath Interpretation," in *Pragmatist Aesthetics*.

19. Shusterman, "Regarding Oneself...," p. 3.

20. See Philippe Lejeune, *Définir l'autobiographie*, a text presented at a congress on autobiography in Beijing, in 1999; I am using a Polish translation of it, by Regina Lubas-Bartoszyńska, published in Philippe Lejeune, *Wariacje na temat pewnego paktu: O autobiografii*, ed. Regina Lubas-Bartoszyńska (Kraków: Universitas, 2001), pp. 1–19.

21. Shusterman, "Regarding Oneself," p. 3.

22. Shusterman, *Practicing Philosophy*, p. 2.

23. *Ibid.* Cf. Richard Shusterman, "Philosophy as Literature and More Than Literature," in *The Blackwell Companion to Philosophy of Literature*, eds. Walter Jost and Garry Hagberg, (Malden, MA: Blackwell Publishers, 2010), p. 8.

24. Pierre Hadot, *Philosophy as a Way of Life*, trans. Michael Chase, (Oxford: Blackwell, 1995).

25. Cf. Julia Kristeva's gendered account of *bios philosophicos* (understood as a conception which integrates philosophical theory and life) which she formulates in her book on Hannah Arendt. Julia Kristeva, *Hannah Arendt: Life Is a Narrative*, trans. Frank Collins (Toronto-London: University of Toronto Press, 2001), p. 4.

26. Richard Shusterman, *Performing Live: Aesthetic Alternatives for the Ends of Art* (Ithaca: Cornell University Press, 2000), p. 96.

27. *Ibid.*

28. Shusterman, *Practicing Philosophy*, chap. 1; cf. Richard Shusterman, "Pragmatism and East-Asian Thought," *Metaphilosophy*, 35:1–2 (2004), pp. 13–42.
29. Shusterman, *Practicing Philosophy*, pp. 62, 179.
30. *Ibid.*, p. 179
31. Henry D. Thoreau, *The Portable Thoreau* (New York: Viking, 1969), p. 270. Ct. in Shusterman, *Practicing Philosophy*, p. 1. Cf. Shusterman, "Philosophy as Literature...," p. 8.
32. Shusterman, *Practicing Philosophy*, p. 182.
33. In fact, Shusterman seems to make a rather sweeping claim that the autobiographical has been "long repressed in philosophy" in general, even though he cites "Kierkegaard and Nietzsche" and "more recently ... Derrida and Cavell" as exceptions. *Ibid.*
34. "The taboo of the personal and contingent reflects philosophy's deep-rooted prejudice for universality and necessity." *Ibid.*, p. 181.
35. *Ibid.*
36. *Ibid.*
37. See *ibid.*, p. 182. Cf. the role of Freud's psychonalysis in another pragmatist account of the contingency of the self, namely that presented by Richard Rorty. Richard Rorty, *Contingency, Irony, and Solidarity* (Cambridge: Cambridge University Press, 1989), chap. 2.
38. Shusterman, *Practicing Philosophy*, p. 182 (emphasis added).
39. Note that Shusterman does not refer here explicitly to any concrete philosophers.
40. See Rorty, *Contingency, Irony, and Solidarity*. As far as Rorty's own attempts at philosophical biography are concerned see, for instance, his "Trotsky and the Wild Orchids," in *Philosophy and Social Hope* (London: Penguin Books, 1999), pp. 3–20.
41. Shusterman, *Practicing Philosophy*, p. 182 (emphasis added).
42. *Ibid.*
43. *Ibid.*, p. 9.
44. Richard Shusterman, "Human Nature at the Schlachtensee," in *Aesthetics in the Human Environment*, eds. Pauline von Bonsdorff and Arto Haapala (Lahti, Finland: International Institute of Applied Aesthetics, 1999), pp. 35–47.
45. See Shusterman, "Regarding Oneself...."
46. See Richard Shusterman, "Next Year in Jerusalem?: Postmodern Jewish Identity and the Myth of Return," in *Jewish Identity*, eds. David Theo Goldberg and Michael Krausz (Philadelphia: Temple University Press, 1993), pp. 291–308, cf. chap. 7 of Shusterman, *Practicing Philosophy*.
47. Shusterman, *Performing Live*, p. 183.
48. Richard Shusterman, "Somaesthetics and the Revival of Aesthetics," *Filozofski Vestnik*, 37:2 (2007), pp. 135–149.
49. See Richard Shusterman, "Pragmatism and East-Asian Thought," pp. 37–38.
50. See Richard Shusterman, "Art and Religion," *Journal of Aesthetic Education*, 42:3 (Fall 2008), pp. 12–15.
51. See, for example, Shusterman, "Regarding Oneself...." Cf. Shusterman, "Human Nature at the Schlachtensee," p. 47, and Paul de Man, *Allegories of Reading: Figural Language in Rousseau, Nietzsche, Rilke, and Proust* (New Haven: Yale University Press, 1979).
52. See, for example, Shusterman, "Regarding Oneself...," p. 4.

53. Friedrich Nietzsche, *Beyond Good and Evil: Prelude to a Philosophy of the Future,* trans. Walter Kaufmann (New York: Vintage, 1966), p. 13.

54. Shusterman, *Performing Live,* p. 200.

55. See Richard Shusterman, "Życie, sztuka i filozofia," in *O sztuce i życiu: Od Poetyki Hip-Hopu do Filozofii Somatycznej,* ed. and trans. Wojciech Małecki (Wrocław: Atla 2, 2007), pp. 25–26.

56. See Shusterman, "Regarding Oneself...." pp. 5–6, 12.

57. *Ibid.,* p. 7.

58. *Ibid.,* pp. 13–15, cf. Shusterman, *Performing Live,* p. 199.

59. Shusterman, *Performing Live,* p. 199.

60. *Ibid.* p. 96, Shusterman, *Practicing Philosophy,* p. xii,

61. This paper was written during my stay as a visiting research fellow at the John F. Kennedy Institut für Nordamerikastudien, Freie Universität Berlin, in April/May 2009. I am grateful to the Institute for providing me with an excellent research environment.

Four

"YOU MUST CHANGE YOUR LIFE": PRAGMATISM AND THE THERAPEUTIC FUNCTION OF ART

Dorota Koczanowicz

> Beauty is truth, truth beauty—that is all
> Ye know on earth, and all ye need to know.
> John Keats, "Ode on a Grecian Urn"[1]

> We cannot know his legendary head
> with eyes like ripening fruit. And yet his torso
> is still suffused with brilliance from inside,
> like a lamp, in which his gaze, now turned to low,
>
> gleams in all its power. Otherwise
> the curved breast could not dazzle you so, nor could
> a smile run through the placid hips and thighs
> to that dark center where procreation flared.
>
> Otherwise this stone would seem defaced
> beneath the translucent cascade of the shoulders
> and would not glisten like a wild beast's fur:
>
> would not, from all the borders of itself,
> burst like a star: for here there is no place
> that does not see you. You must change your life.
> Rainer Maria Rilke, "Archaic Torso of Apollo"[2]

John Keats reminds us of the ancient association between the values of beauty, the truth, and the good. Their connection provides us with a chance to overcome the chaos of everyday existence. As Leszek Koczanowicz has written:

Art uses the same strategy as science does: they replace singularity with universality and time-dependence with timelessness. If something is lost in this process, it is the warmth and emotion of the particular, concrete being, which is replaced by a cold, universal form. But this is an irrevocable feature of the triumph over time, which is likewise a triumph over death.[3]

Faith in the unlimited power of art goes back to the ancient world, but the power of this faith has diminished with the passage of time. Today it can be observed that there are ever increasing doubts and uncertainties among aestheticians and art theorists. Art itself willingly turns away from the concept of beauty; artists frequently work "around" beauty or indeed in opposition to it. Despite this trend, however, there continues to exist a seemingly inextinguishable sentiment for the traditional association, a sentiment realized both in the form of artworks themselves and in theoretical discussions.

The British novelist and philosopher Iris Murdoch, in her theoretical works as well as in her novels, and in contrast to many contemporary art theorists, frequently defended the cognitive role of art. In her work "Metaphysics as a Guide to Morals" she writes that artists, even abstract painters, "…long remained happily, more or less secretly, obsessed with the transcendent … this has been, one might say, the secret which inspires the artist."[4] To clarify her point, she draws attention to two phenomena. First, art (and especially painting) provides us with a possibility for "pure perception."

> Yes, something like pure perception. Really attending to great pictures, I think, is like enlightenment in Buddhism. It does really make one feel that the reality of the world appears as something one has not seen before. That suddenly you're confronted with color and forms, a kind of vital reality…. [T]his matter of the veil being removed is something which is done by painting in a very immediate way. One may say, well, music and poetry do it also. But what we're doing mainly in life is looking, seeing. It's the visual world which is with us all the time. And to have that makes a sort of doorway into what the world really is, to what philosophers call 'being,' that mysterious term. Something like reality opposed to the kind of pseudo-reality of fallen darkness which most of us are in most of the time.[5]

According to Murdoch the second dimension of the cognitive role of art, after perception, is art's ability to endow us with a kind of energy that can, in terms of Plato's famous simile, draw us out of the cave in which we spend our everyday lives.

> I don't believe in a literal God, or heaven, or life after death, but I believe in a religious feeling, which is what the Buddhists have—that the world, and our conduct in the world is capable of a movement to a higher state… I believe enjoyment of art is also connected with a sense of something better which is more thru and more good, but which is here given to us in a reflection or a shadow—which we may ourselves overcome.[6]

In this approach, art is to be considered an alternative to the scientific mode of cognition; one which can, like science, both organize and change our perception. Similarly to scientific cognition, artistic cognition permits us to transcend individual experience, and although it cannot be formulated in laws, yet by its means we can enter into a certain domain of universality. Of course, art is governed by intuition, not by the understanding, but it can give us insight into the essence of things. It remains to be asked what the basis of this intuition is, and here there may be, and historically have been, different kinds of answers. Murdoch, for example, in one of her novels asserts that love (Eros) is the force that permits Plato's prisoners to follow her out of the cave; that otherwise they see about them only the shadows—illusions and fantasies— that provide no basis for endowing life with meaning.

1. Art as Shelter. The Case of Dora and John

Dora, the heroine of Murdoch's 1958 novel *The Bell,* is a young woman who is unable to come to terms with herself in her relationship with her older, conservative husband, and who falls into deepening conflict with him and his environment. When we first meet Dora, we are given the difficulties of her situation in two dramatic sentences: "Dora Greenfield left her husband because she was afraid of him. She decided six months later to return to him for the same reason."[7] The conflict worsens because Dora, as it turns out, is unable to submit completely to, and follow, the strict regulations governing life at Imber Abbey, home of the lay brotherhood of which her husband Paul is an adherent.

Dora's refusal to conform leads to the unmasking of the seeming honesty of the community and the uncovering of concealed tensions within it. Unable to accept lies, hidden dislikes, secrets, and pain, she provokes a spontaneous reaction among a generally self-controlled and reserved group of people. At the same time, she forces them to confront both each other and themselves. This leads in the end to the break-up of the previously hermetic community, whose unity had in fact been based upon dishonesty and domination.

The moment of crisis in Dora's relations with her husband comes not during a fierce argument, but rather as the result of a concatenation of discontent on both sides and Dora's feeling of increasing isolation: "But now, driven by this fit of solipsistic melancholy one degree more desperate, she felt the need of an act...."[8] The young woman feels a need to take immediate action, and so on an impulse, with no clear plans, boards a bus bound for London. Guided by her intuition, she finds herself in the National Gallery and proceeds past paintings that she is already acquainted with. "Passing between them now, as through a well-loved grove, she felt a calm descending on her."[9] She knows them well, for she has been to the Gallery many times before. She feels that they belong to her, for she knows them as well as she knows her own face:

Vaguely, consoled by the presence of something welcoming and responding in the place, her footsteps took her to various shrines at which
she had worshipped so often before: the great light spaces of Italian pictures, more vast and southern than any real South, the angels of Botticel-
li, radiant as birds, ... the solemn world of Piero della Francesca....".[10]

Dora does not want to accept life as simply a succession of repeated actions. Her creative nature struggles to break free of the constraints of married
and community life, and this leads to conflicts and an increasing sense of
frustration. Contact with art is, as she has found in the past, a way of lifting
herself out of everyday existence, of renouncing it even if only for a few moments. When Dora feels that art is something that is actually a part of her, this
gives her a feeling of being liberated from all care. The burden of her husband's lack of understanding is lifted, for she finds understanding in her contact with painting. Relations with the "world of art" become for Dora more
real than her relations with the "real world."

It occurred to her that here at last was something real and perfect.... But
the pictures were something real outside herself, which spoke to her
kindly and yet in sovereign tones, something superior and good whose
presence destroyed the dreary trance-like solipsism of her earlier mood.[11]

Friedrich Schiller argued that it is only through beauty that man can make
his way to freedom. For Dora, freedom means the same as the feeling of inner
peace and clarity. To her, perhaps paradoxically, this feeling of freedom was not
needed in order to permit her finally to escape, but just the opposite, to allow her
to return to her responsibilities and the limits they impose. Thanks to her temporary retreat into art, she acquired a new perspective on her situation and was
thus able to clarify her thoughts and make firm decisions.

Iris Murdoch spoke more than once about her predilection for the artistic
and aesthetic tradition which is based on the unity of a famous triad: truth, beauty and the good. The case of Dora can be considered not only as a literary corre-
late of Murdoch's own views, but more broadly as a model illustration of the
relation to art proposed by those artists and theoreticians who yearn for the old
idea of art founded on a conception of beauty. One such conservative is the
American scholar Donald Kuspit. He proposes the following treatment of art:

...art is the privileged space of contemplation, and as such a reprieve and
sanctuary from the barbarism of the world—however much that may be
its subject matter—and thus a psychic space in which we can own ourselves and survive, that is, realize autonomy....[12]

Kuspit cannot stand avant-garde and postmodern art, holding that art
should be a kind of refuge for the wounded spirit of modern man, and not an

instrument of torture that simply exposes him further to the painful side of life. We all know things are bad, argues Kuspit, and the contemporary artist, rather than exacerbating our feeling of depression, should model himself or herself on the old masters and provide us with relief in the form of beautiful, high-quality art.

Must, however, the consolations of art be connected only with rigorous adherence to the traditional styles of the old masters? Might not contemporary art, avant-garde art, also possess a therapeutic potential? It seems to me that a retreat into "perfect beauty" need not be the only possibility—all the more, because beauty in its cold perfection can seem cruel as well. Charles Baudelaire, in "Le confiteor de l'artiste", writes: "The study of beauty is a duel in which the artist cries in terror before he is overcome."[13]

John, the young hero (and the author's alter ego) of John M. Coetzee's novel *Youth*, like Dora in *The Bell* finds himself at a crossroads in life, and like her seeks shelter in a London art gallery. One day he finds himself at the Tate. His first reaction upon encountering the work of Jackson Pollock might seem to serve as an illustration of Donald Kuspit's thesis, but, as the narrator describes it, he soon receives a different impression:

> In the next room, high up on a wall, sits a huge painting consisting of no more than an elongated black blob on a white field. *Homage to the Spanish Republic 24* by Robert Motherwell, says the label. He is transfixed. Menacing and mysterious, the black shape takes him over. A sound like the stroke of a gong goes out from it, leaving him shaken and weak-kneed. Where does its power come from, this amorphous shape that bears no resemblance to Spain or anything else, yet stirs up a well of dark feeling within him? It is not beautiful, yet it speaks like beauty, imperiously.[14]

Art galleries became for Murdoch's Dora, and in a certain sense also for Coetzee's John, places of confrontation with the self, with one's own conception of oneself and of others, and art a source of spiritual comfort—as in a poetic phrase which promises that on the light boat of art from the troubles of the world one will drift away. Dora does not solve her problems but turns away from them, retreating from life into art. While it is the work of the old masters that speaks most powerfully to Dora, John feels that power in the presence of the art of the avant-garde; but both of them protect themselves against an inhospitable reality by means of aesthetic experience.

Iris Murdoch is aware that her aesthetic conception is clearly out of favor, and that it has been replaced by views that not only sever the traditional association of art with truth, beauty and the good, but also assail these latter values in their own right. This school of criticism has found its plainest expression in the postulates of poststructuralism, but I believe that its roots go back to the moment when art was divorced from metaphysics.

Might a corrective be in order? Pragmatism demonstrates that, if the extremes are avoided, it is possible to find consolation in art, without either severing its connections to avant-garde creativity or excluding its relation to beauty. Indeed, perhaps an even more significant question than that of the rejection or acceptance of new phenomena in art is the more general one of the relation of art to life. In the cases of both Dora and John we may speak of a kind of flight from everyday problems into the world of art. This model of aesthetic experience, which assumes a temporary suspension of quotidian existence, results from deeply rooted tendencies towards fragmentation in our culture. Richard Shusterman notes that

> [a]rt's semblance is neither as innocent nor as morally effective as Schiller suggests. Beauty as semblance and art as imaginative play encourage the compartmentalization of the aesthetic as an escape from reality, an idea which helps legitimate the ugly brutality of the real, non-aesthetic world.[15]

It is just this, which Shusterman warns against, that Kuspit rates so highly. But if art is to have a meaningful place in culture, it would seem that we cannot, as Kuspit would have it, turn it into a decorative ornament, whose function is limited to the masking of life's defects. Behind Kuspit's outlook there lurks, in fact, a deep lack of faith in the power of art, that is, in an art which could have real influence upon a bad reality, an art capable of entering into dialogue with that reality, capable of critiquing it and bringing about change.

2. Experience of Art. The Art of Life

In his book *Art as Experience* John Dewey discussed the problem of the relationship between art and other spheres of human activity. In describing his outlook, he came out against the idea of conceiving art in isolation from the individual's everyday life. Such a conception of art, as alienated from the life around it, in effect pathologizes art, making of it something that is accessible only to a small group of connoisseurs. Writing of Dewey's view, Martrin Jay properly observes that "at root, it was the impoverished character of everyday experience that the elite concept of art developed as a kind of compensation."[16] But what does pragmatism offer as an alternative? Shusterman, following Dewey, criticizes the "decay" of culture and advocates the overcoming of artificial divisions. The merging of life and art may come about, according to pragmatists, through the redefinition of aesthetic experience. Also Thomas Alexander in his book on Dewey's aesthetics emphasizes:

> Because aesthetic experience is distinctively capable of grasping experience in general as a process of articulation or growth, it succeeds in providing the basis for overcoming the dualism which separates man from the world or from his fellow human beings.[17]

Dewey's thought, taken as a theoretical basis, serves to indicate the causes and consequences of the processes that led to the breaking up and compartmentalizing of reality, including our concept of fine art. It makes it possible to conceive the liberation of art from the "cloister of elitism" and the leveling of "painful" and "unhealthy" distinctions between art and life.

Aesthetic experience, as the most sublimated form of experience, integrates the external (objective) with the internal (subjective), and unites them in one totality, thereby obviating this general distinction. Thus of aesthetic experience Dewey writes that it is the original experience:

> In art as experience, actuality and possibility or ideality, the new and the old, objective material and personal response, the individual and the universal, surface and depth, sense and meaning, are integrated in an experience in which they are all transfigured from the significance that belongs to them when isolated in reflection.[18]

In the process of experiencing something a crucial role is played by the emotions, which function as a kind of adhesive connecting all the various elements of the experience. Feelings are the active forces that communicate order to experience. Dewey speaks of the function of emotion as follows: "It selects what is congruous and dyes what is selected with its color, thereby giving qualitative unity to materials externally disparate and dissimilar. It thus provides unity in and through varied parts of experience."[19]

The notion of art understood as a "condensation and improvement of ordinary human experience" carries with it, first, the conviction that there is an essential connection between art and life, and second, the assumption of an affinity between experience in general and aesthetic experience. Experience understood in this way is close to the idea of human self-fulfillment in the course of life and struggle, and constitutes art in an embryonic form. Equally in the life processes of the individual and of society as a whole, Dewey perceives a profound connection to aesthetic values and art. He does not treat aesthetic experience as something specific, something isolated from other forms of experience. Rather, in his theory of experience it is suggested that it should be possible to add an aesthetic dimension to every human activity as Krystyna Wilkoszewska has written:

> ...experience is not other than nature, it is nature, one of her innumerable forms. ... [H]armony between the energies of the organism and the energies of its environment becomes, in the pulsating rhythm of life, the germ of the aesthetic quality of experience. If a new order is achieved, participation in it has the character of fulfillment, similar to aesthetic sensation. Thus it is that every ordinary, everyday experience bears within it the chance of becoming an aesthetic experience....[20]

Even though Dewey, for obvious reasons, did not undertake a discussion of avant-garde and postmodern art, I think we can assume that he would not be necessarily hostile to it. Within his aesthetic theory one finds place for new forms of art, inasmuch as the integrating tendencies of aesthetic experience do not eliminate its dis-integrating factors.

> To achieve in the course of life a period of balance is at the same time to undertake a new relationship to one's surroundings, a relationship bearing the prospect of new potential adaptations, but ones which must be achieved through effort and struggle. A time of fulfillment is also a time of new beginning. Any attempt to maintain beyond its appointed time the satisfaction that comes with a period of fulfillment and harmony, is bound to mean a retreat from the world, which in turn means a lowering and decline of vitality.[21]

Though Dewey is describing ordinary life, his words apply no less to dynamic aesthetic experience, for it is the rhythm of ordinary life that serves as its embryo. The feeling of unity that is achieved through aesthetic exposure has only a momentary character and does not submit to extended contemplation. It is transitory, disintegrating in the moment of its culmination in order to form the start of a successive experience. As we read in *Pragmatist Aesthetics*: "Aesthetic experience shines as living beauty, not only because it is surrounded by the death of disorder and monotonous routine, but because its own sparkling career projects the process of its dying as it lives."[22] The dynamic unity of the Deweyan work of art seems to correspond to the active, stimulating *modus operandi* of contemporary, avant-garde art. As Shusterman puts it, "...for Dewey, the permanence of experienced unity is not only impossible, it is aesthetically undesirable; for art requires the challenge of tension and disruptive novelty and the rhythmic struggle of achievement and breakdown of order."[23]

Dewey's idea of beauty has more in common with the exalted unity of the modern work that raises formal and material resistance, than it does with the contemplative, harmonious nature of so-called classical art. The pragmatist theory of aesthetic experience does not allow the expressive value of art to be reduced to the role of being a provider of soothing, contemplative emotions. As Dewey aptly remarked, "[i]t is known that pressure creates energy, and a complete lack of opposition does not aid normal development."[24] We derive this energy from our life processes, which are at the same time the origins of art. Beauty is not a central category in Dewey's aesthetics; the aesthetic remains tied to life values, which in Dewey's axiology are not divisible into class or species.

The conception of art that appears in the writings of John Dewey is broadened and democratized. Art ceases to be identified with precious objects locked up in museum display cases, fetishes divorced from all context, and becomes the embodiment of a living aesthetic experience. As Shusterman writes: "Pragmatist aesthetics … construes the aesthetic in much wider terms so as to do greater justice to its practical and cognitive dimensions and to promote art's greater integration into the praxis of life."[25] Our museums are bursting with objects that were never intended by their creators to end up in museums. They were formed to give immediate satisfaction to the cultural or practical needs of concrete individuals. Religious artifacts and representations of deities, as well as objects for everyday use such as furniture, clothing and eating utensils, were all made to be part of a social life.

> Instead of being elevated to a niche apart, they belonged to display of prowess, the manifestation of group and clan membership of gods, feast-ing and fasting, fighting, hunting, and all the rhythmic crises that punc-tuate the stream of living.[26]

Both Dewey and Shusterman mean to carry out a reform of the concept of art, but the areas of art that they undertake to analyze are not the same. Dewey's project is the bolder one; Shusterman, while acknowledging the force of his predecessor's ambition, restricts the field of engagement. His aim is not, as Dewey's was, to completely alter the conceptual boundaries of art, but rather, in the first place, to defend the idea of popular culture as a valuable element of art taken as a whole, and in the second place, to extend the bounda-ries of the concept of art so that it may include "the ethical art of the for-mation of one's own life." Both these American pragmatists, with their inten-tion to democratize art, are involved in the dispute over the extent of the con-cept of art and they probably should be considered allies in this dispute of Martin Gayford and Iris Murdoch. Beauty, truth, and the good are considered by most contemporary scholars and critics to be formulae that are out of date, out of fashion and generally inapplicable these days; it would be difficult to find today even a lingering trace of the former certainty as to their unity. Gay-ford describes the situation as follows:

> Currently, of course, not only this connection [between beauty, truth, and the good—D.K.], but all the constituent concepts—truth, beauty, the good, and even art itself—are under furious attack. According to poststructuralist theory—the intellectual orthodoxy of our time—there exists nothing such as truth or value. And aesthetic experience is an ideological illusion, hence beauty, too, does not exist, and for art there remains only the task of ad-ministering the ritual 'challenge' or 'shock' to the body politic.[27]

Gayford is allied with Shusterman in defense of the notion of aesthetic experience, which still, despite reports of its death (along with those of the end of art), seems to be a source of immediate, exceptionally complete satis-faction. The difference between them lies only in this that Gayford does not have a pragmatic bent and delimits the ground for aesthetic experience in a much more conservative fashion. The Deweyan concept of aesthetic experience admits the concatenation of art and life, the introduction of the aesthetic element into all spheres of human activity, including actions devoted towards self-cognition and understanding one's relation with the world. In this conception, the boundary between cognition and beauty is crossed, as both categories are only aspects of the greater whole that constitutes human existence.

Since the most important characteristic of aesthetic experience, according to Dewey, is its ability to provide an immediate context of meaning to a situation, art becomes a gateway to the truth and at the same time a vital ingredient of every experience, which aspires to being considered full and complete. To me it seems possible to detect a similar tone in the thinking of Iris Murdoch. The kind of revelation of which Murdoch speaks as "pure perception" is the lot of both her character Dora and of Coetzee's John. Pragmatism, however, suggests a different solution; namely, the intimate connection of art with life. As the pragmatist scholar Thomas M. Alexander writes:

> The living moment, when perception is exercised at its fullest, is the origin of art. Art is experience directed toward the intelligent exploration of the senses of the world, and it takes as its theme the rich and varied possibilities of response which stimulate involvement and discovery.... Sense is the sense of meaning. Life prefigures art because art articulates or is a figuration of life.[28]

Therapy is supposed to lead to the resolution of difficult situations, generally to improve life. In the concluding line of "Ancient Torso of Apollo," Rainer Rilke wrote, "You must change your life" (*Du muss dein Leben ändern*). The point of reference for this change is the perfection of art. This perfection of which the poet speaks is not that of the finished work, for the statue of Apollo, which is the poem's occasion, is missing limbs and head; but it is the sheer power of art that permits the statue to "burst like a star" and to animate every damaged fragment and to see with unseeing eyes. Classically beautiful art can reveal its matchless perfection and be "the star to every wandering bark," but flaws, defects, and an obvious abandonment of harmonious form also have their virtues. Coetzee's hero John, impressed by the work of Robert Motherwell, testifies to the fact that the effectiveness and power of art obtain also among abstract and avant-garde works.

Within the framework of pragmatism, art occupies a distinct position. In accordance with the thinking of Dewey and Shusterman, the therapeutic function of art can be understood not only as individual contact with artworks, but also as a lifelong process of "caring" for every experience so as to bring it towards perfection. The criterion of such perfection is provided by art itself. Thus it is not a question of dividing reality into the sacrum of art and the profanum of life, but of the integration of both spheres in an aesthetic project that might pertain to every existent being.

The therapeutic function of art proposed by Irish Murdoch and Donald Kuspit depends above all on terminology. Art condenses and gives meaning to that which in our immediate experience is chaotic, unbounded and incomplete. Art, like myth, is (in the words of Erich Fromm) a forgotten language, the understanding of which allows us to comprehend ourselves, or in other words to realize what is going on in our psyche. We have believed since the time of Freud that such understanding, such ability to name, is the necessary and sole condition of therapy.

Pragmatism sets up against this conception an entirely different perspective. Art is not an intensified and crystallized picture of everyday ambivalence, and thus is not set in opposition to life, but rather is woven into the texture of everyday existence. At root, art is indistinguishable from life. But it constitutes that moment of quotidian experience that provides the latter with sense. It means that we are able to adopt another perspective on our existence.

The question remains, whether these two distinct perspectives can still meet in a single point. As Shusterman writes:

> Pragmatism can appreciate cultural objects 'for their own sake' (that is, for their experienced qualities and meanings) while also appreciating their instrumental uses, just as we can simultaneously relish a work for its cognitive and hedonistic effects.[29]

This statement suggests that it is possible to treat an art's challenge to our existence as a kind of "regulative idea." Pragmatism then would show the ways of fulfillment of this idea in experience of ordinary life.

NOTES

1. John Keats, "Ode on a Grecian Urn," in *The Poetical Works of John Keats* (London: William Smith,1841), p. 201.
2. Rainer Maria Rilke, "Archaic Torso of Apollo," in *The Selected Poetry of Rainer Maria Rilke*, trans. Stephen Mitchell (New York: Vintage, 1989), p. 61.
3. Leszek Koczanowicz, "Piękno i poznanie" [Beauty and Cognition], in *O nauce i sztuce* [On Science and Art], ed. Jan Mozrzymas (Wrocław: Wydawnictwo Uniwersytetu Wrocławskiego, 2004), p. 39.
4. Martin Gayford, "The Beautiful and the Good: Iris Murdoch on the Value of Art," *Modern Painters* (1986), p. 52.
5. *Ibid.*, p. 53.
6. *Ibid.*, p. 54.
7. Iris Murdoch, *The Bell* (New York: Penguin Books, 2001), p. 1.
8. *Ibid.*, p. 168.
9. *Ibid.*, p. 174.
10. *Ibid.*
11. *Ibid.*, p. 175.

12. Donald Kuspit, *The End of Art* (Cambridge: Cambridge University Press, 2005), p. 37.
13. "L'étude du beau est un duel où l'artiste crie de frayeur avant d'être vaincu." Charles Baudelaire, "Le confiteor de l'artiste," in *Les paradis artificiels / Le spleen de Paris* (Paris: Bokking International, 1995), p. 15 (trans. David Schauffler).
14. John M. Coetzee, *Youth* (Harmondsworth: Viking Press, 2002), p. 92.
15. Richard Shusterman, *Pragmatist Aesthetics. Living Beauty, Rethinking Art* (Cambridge: Blackwell, 1992), pp. 155–156.
16. Martin Jay, *Songs of Experience. Modern American and European Variations on Universal Theme* (Berkeley: University of California Press, 2005), p. 242.
17. Thomas M. Alexander, *John Dewey's Theory of Art, Experience and Nature: The Horizons of Feeling* (Albany: SUNY Press, 1987), p. 189.
18. John Dewey, *Art as Experience* (New York: Perigee Book, 1980), pp. 296–297.
19. *Ibid.*, p. 42.
20. Krystyna Wilkoszewska, "Estetyka pragmatyczna" [Pragmatist Aesthetics], in *Estetyki filozoficzne XX wieku* [Philosophical Aesthetics in the 20th Century], ed. Krystyna Wilkoszewska (Kraków: Universitas, 2000), p. 118.
21. Dewey, *Art as Experience*, p. 23.
22. Shusterman, *Pragmatist Aesthetics*, p. 33.
23. *Ibid.*, p. 32.
24. Dewey, *Art as Experience*, p. 75.
25. Richard Shusterman, "Popular Art and Education," *Studies in Philosophy and Education*, 13 (1995), p. 206.
26. Dewey, *Art as Experience*, pp. 6–7.
27. Gayford, "The Beautiful and the Good...," p. 50.
28. Alexander, *John Dewey's Theory of Art*, p. 197.
29. Richard Shusterman, *Surface and Depth. Dialectics of Criticism and Culture* (Ithaca: Cornell University Press, 2002), p. 206.

Part Two

EPISTEMOLOGY, METAPHYSICS, ETHICS, AND POLITICS

Five

PHILOSOPHY AND LIFE: PRAGMATISM, WITTGENSTEIN, AND METAPHYSICS

Sami Pihlström

1. Introduction

This essay discusses Richard Shusterman's pragmatist proposal to turn philosophy more relevant to human life. Obviously, this metaphilosophical project is connected with Shusterman's work on pragmatist aesthetics, with its emphasis on experience in all its richness, especially somatic experience,[1] but I will not specifically comment on his views on art, aesthetic experience, or "somaesthetics" here. My main focus will, rather, be on Shusterman's 1997 book, *Practicing Philosophy*,[2] especially its discussions of the "philosophical profiles" of Ludwig Wittgenstein and pragmatists like John Dewey. My main question—an open issue I invite Shusterman to reconsider, not a problem I could claim to solve here—concerns the relation between "philosophical life" and metaphysics.

The pragmatist and Wittgensteinian accounts of philosophical life might seem to be resolutely anti-metaphysical. Thus, arguing for philosophy as a life-practice, or practicing philosophy as a part of one's "real life" rather than as a purely theoretical activity, might seem to lead us out of the traditional metaphysical quest for a theory of ultimate reality, or Being qua Being. I agree that this traditional picture of metaphysics vitally needs correction. However, I do think that both pragmatist and Wittgensteinian accounts of philosophical life, properly developed, are also metaphysical. They are, however, metaphysical in the sense of offering a critical, practice-embedded approach to the basic structure(s) of reality insofar as it is humanly conceptualized and categorized—in short, a "human world."[3] Philosophical life is, then, life seen as such a fundamentally metaphysical "world-structuring" activity.

The metaphysical pursuit of not only understanding reality more deeply but of living a decent human life in this world of ethical challenges is itself fundamentally ethical. The examination of the prospects of philosophy as a practice of life enables me to defend the view that, from a pragmatist perspective, ethics and metaphysics are inextricably entangled. This entanglement is so deep that I would be prepared to view even Shusterman's pragmatist approaches to global issues of ethnicity, race, war, etc., as (potentially) metaphysically illuminating, too.[4] These topics cannot be discussed in this paper, however.

I will begin by sketching Shusterman's account of Wittgenstein's and the pragmatists' (especially Dewey's) views on the relation between philosophy and life. I will then try to explain why these views do not necessarily lead us out of the metaphysical predicament and why, on the contrary, the pragmatist should closely tie philosophical life and metaphysical problems together. Here I will take my lead from James rather than Dewey, though without forgetting the Wittgensteinian perspective. The issue that will be used as a litmus test for a pragmatically adequate view of philosophy and life is the problem of death, which Shusterman also discusses at some length. Here, in particular, the Jamesian perspective (connected with a Wittgensteinian one) may, as I have suggested elsewhere, offer richer pragmatic resources than the Deweyan one.[5] More generally, a pragmatically adequate philosophy of death and mortality cannot be practiced from a purely theoretical point of view—as seems to be the case with most of the current, particularly analytic, contributions to the field—but must be worked on precisely from the perspective of "practicing philosophy" as an "art of living" recommended by Shusterman.

2. Practicing Philosophy: Metaphysics and Life

In the introduction to *Practicing Philosophy*, Shusterman draws a distinction between philosophy as a theoretical activity and as an art of living. He argues that pragmatism represents a healthy return to the "practical perspective" already adopted by Hellenistic philosophers, and that this is a "revival of a tradition that saw theory as a useful instrument to a higher philosophical practice: the art of living wisely and well."[6] Thus, pragmatism enlarges the scope of philosophy and enhances its cultural impact, reflexively offering reasons— pragmatic reasons—for seeing pragmatism itself as something more than mere academic philosophy.[7] Neither the old Greeks nor nineteenth and twentieth century pragmatists abandoned theory, however; they just saw, and pragmatists should continue to see, theory as subordinated to practice, ultimately in the service of the good life. Accordingly, already Socrates, whom Shusterman perceptively calls a "proto-pragmatist," did not aim at "truth for truth's sake" in his search for wisdom but at an "ameliorative care of the self."[8] This "therapeutic" project is particularly clear in the Hellenistic schools, such as Epicureanism, Stoicism, and Skepticism.

According to Shusterman, the three modern "exemplars" he picks in the first chapter of *Practicing Philosophy*—Dewey, Wittgenstein, and Foucault— all shared the view that philosophy has the "existential task" of helping us "lead better lives by bettering ourselves through self-knowledge, self-criticism, and self-mastery"; therefore, philosophy, for these thinkers, was "a life-practice where theory derived its real meaning and value only in terms of the life in which it functioned, in the concrete pursuit of better living."[9] In addition to describing some philosophically relevant biographical details, he cites these philosophers' remarks on the "problem of life" (Wittgenstein), on rival philosophies as "different ways of construing life" (Dewey), and on philosophy as "an embodied life-practice in which the self is transfigured through experiment, discipline, and ordeal" (Foucault).[10] His chapter on the "philosophical profiles" of these three great thinkers then unfolds through considerations of philosophical living as aesthetic concern with beauty, as a somatic (bodily) practice, as self-transformation, growth, and search for integrity, as a heroic facing of death, and as an integration of personal transformation ("self-perfection") with the construction (and reconstruction) of a democratic society.

In addition to the three figures he discusses, Shusterman might have invoked the philosophical profile of William James—and he has devoted a more recent paper to James's views on somatic introspection and self-care. He writes:

> Recognizing that the quest for knowledge is always guided by interest, pragmatism can argue that heightened interest should generate better theory by promoting more penetrating, enduring attention, more subtle awareness, and keener sensitivity. Although some aspects of James's somatic philosophy are surely vulnerable to criticism, I believe his intense personal preoccupations with the body-mind nexus tended to enrich and sharpen rather than distort his philosophical vision. Worries about his own body-mind attunement prompted him to seek more than a purely theoretical, metaphysical, and speculative understanding of how physical life and mental life are related.[11]

The pragmatically therapeutic approach to philosophical problems, including the mind-body problem, thus aims at something "more" than metaphysical theory—something better or deeper, something that may require one's personal intimacy with the problems investigated, to the extent that they are, or may become, problems tormenting one's own life. This is also how Dewey, Wittgenstein, and Foucault viewed the problems they discussed.

The "more than metaphysics" pragmatism seeks is nevertheless (re)interpretable in terms of a more inclusive conception of metaphysics, which includes as its crucial element the ethical and therapeutic concern with the good (or always better) life. The basic idea of what I call "pragmatist metaphysics"[12] is that metaphysics examines the basic structures of the human world, not the world *an sich*; hence, it can be in the service of the good life, understood not as merely theoretical speculation but as an attempt to "structure" reality into a humanly habitable shape. Pragmatist metaphysics in this sense is "Kantian" rather than "Aristotelian," because the categories it postulates are not categories of reality as it (supposedly) is in itself, independently of our categorizations, but humanly constructed categories, arising from our various practical needs to "take" reality to be in a way or another. Examples of such a pragmatist (and Kantian) attitude to metaphysics can be found, for instance, in James's discussions of traditional metaphysical problems in the third and fourth lectures of *Pragmatism*.[13] The pragmatist metaphysician should share with Shusterman and his three heroes (Dewey, Wittgenstein, Foucault) "the ideal of critically self-reflective self-care as self-improvement through the disciplined pursuit of relevant knowledge,"[14] while continuing to hold on to the highest theoretical standards in the acquisition of such knowledge, and also understanding this ideal itself as metaphysical.

The practice of self-care and self-improvement, of Deweyan "growth," is metaphysical in the sense of aiming at a better understanding of one's own place, including one's potentialities, in the world's scheme of things, but it is also irreducibly ethical, because such understanding and its criteria always already depend on moral value commitments. The schemes through which we categorize reality are themselves valuationally loaded, and any human potentials our metaphysics may reveal are themselves potentially ethically relevant. There is no "ready-made" world we could view from a "God's-Eye View,"[15] instead, we are responsible for the schemes through which we represent reality and ourselves as its representers and cognizers.

Shusterman himself recognizes that there is a metaphysical element in pragmatism. For example, when discussing rap music, he notes that rap emphasizes "the temporally changing and malleable nature of the real," thus joining James, Dewey, and Goodman in maintaining "a very tenable metaphysical position," continuing the pragmatist tradition both in the "metaphysics of material, historical flux" and in the "noncompartmentalized aesthetics that highlights cognitive function and embodied process in the pursuit of productive practical reform."[16] Moreover, Dewey's naturalistic humanism, according to Shusterman, did not just dissolve but "answered" the metaphysical question about the reality of consciousness, knowledge, and value, and the epistemological one about how material reality could be known by minds.[17] The fact that these traditional questions were redescribed by Dewey in a way avoiding age-old dualisms and emphasizing continuity and "emergence" instead should not lead us to think that Dewey simply avoided such questions, thoroughly dismissed or dissolved them, or did not take them seriously as philosophical problems. He transformed them, pragmatically and critically— and we may say that Wittgenstein did something very similar to traditional metaphysical and semantic questions about the nature of meaning and understanding. Just as Wittgenstein found the essence of things to lie in "grammar,"[18] the pragmatist metaphysician treats questions of reality and existence in terms of the value-laden practice and the practice-embedded (conceivable) experiences through which the world is conceptualized and categorized by us.

This, more generally, is what pragmatist metaphysics is all about: transforming metaphysical questions from merely intellectual exercises disconnected from practice into genuine, humanly deep questions about how the world ought to be construed in order for us to be able to live in it. It is in this sense that metaphysics can be understood as examining the basic (or even fundamental, though always reinterpretable) categorial features of a "human world." The pragmatist need not, and should not, claim that we "make the world" *ex nihilo*; as even Nelson Goodman emphasized in his "irrealist" theory of "worldmaking," making is always "remaking."[19]

There is a tension here, however, right in the center of pragmatist metaphysics. Is the process-ontological "flux" Shusterman invokes—a concept used by many other process-philosophically oriented pragmatists as well, including Shusterman's one-time colleague Joseph Margolis[20]—supposed to yield a metaphysical theory of the world "in itself," of the basic and ultimate nature of reality, understood as processual and dynamic instead of any static collection of objects or states of affairs? Or is it, rather (once again), a humanly constructed concept categorizing the reality we live in from a world-engaging perspective of practices? If we opt for the latter, we may deny that any humanly constructed ontological concept, even the one of flux (process), can be used to categorize reality *an sich*. The world cannot be meaningfully claimed to be anything as seen from the imagined "God's-Eye View"; there is no such "absolute" way the world is. Thus, even the processuality and dynamic character of the world is not absolute but our way of conceptualizing our reality. Even process ontology, then, must be subordinated to pragmatism. It seems to me that the supposedly pragmatist metaphysician who starts from the ultimate and absolute character of a processual conception of reality betrays the pragmatist principle to ground each and every ontological characterization in human practices.

Even (pragmatic) realism itself, our need to postulate an objective reality we never constructed out of nothing, is a pragmatic need in the end based on our practices of engaging with the world. Pragmatist metaphysics is not radically constructivist but fully acknowledges this need, thus leading to a robust realism that nevertheless—analogously to the way in which empirical realism requires transcendental idealism in Kant—presupposes a more fundamental pragmatist account of the emergence of any ontological categorizations possible for us. We may realistically postulate the "flux"; we just have to keep in mind that this postulation, like our commitment to realism itself, is a pragmatically useful one, something we need in our lives. These reflections may take us quite far away from Shusterman's healthy naturalism. However, it would be an interesting task to connect his relatively brief remarks on the "metaphysics" of pragmatism (that is, the "flux") with a broader account of pragmatic realism and pragmatist metaphysics, transcendentally reinterpreted, because it seems to me that this metaphysical reappraisal of pragmatism may be fruitfully connected with the pursuit of philosophical life.

3. Philosophy, Life, and Death

Concretizing our general picture of the entanglement of ethical and metaphysical perspectives in pragmatism, we may emphasize the central importance of the problem of death to the pursuit of philosophy as an art of living—both classical, for instance, Hellenistic, and modern, for instance, pragmatist and

Wittgensteinian. Here, again, James is in my view the classical pragmatist who offers us the richest resources, even though Shusterman focuses on Dewey, along with Wittgenstein and Foucault.[21] Both Wittgensteinian and pragmatist insights into human mortality may be employed to criticize the currently popular analytic philosophy of death because of its overly theoretical stance whose insights into what it is actually like to live a mortal life, instead of just being able to discuss the criteria of death with high intellectual sophistication, may be relatively scarce.[22] Again, the truly important issue is not whether, say, one's survival of death as a disembodied mind or spirit is a coherent conceptual (or metaphysical) possibility, or whether we can find exact criteria for personal identity, enabling us to determine in any particular case whether a being is dead or alive, but how we should think about our own mortal existence—how we should live forward, "being toward death." These issues may be raised in a pragmatic spirit without excessive Heideggerian jargon. In any case, death, as a human problem, is something more than an exercise in conceptual analysis and argumentation. Its merely theoretical analysis deflates the problem from its central human—both metaphysical and ethical—importance.

Joining the tradition from Plato through Montaigne to Heidegger, which sees death as an ultimate issue in philosophy—or philosophy itself as a "practice of dying"—Shusterman's three heroes of philosophical life were all in their distinctive ways concerned with death (and even suicide), possibly with the exception of Dewey, who according to Shusterman unduly "neglected" the issue. We ought to, these thinkers maintained, somehow come to terms with death and mortality; the meaning and value of our existence depends on our being able to "master" death—or even to "enjoy" it in something like Foucault's sense. This does not mean that we should adopt a gloomy and pessimistic attitude to life, realizing that everything ends with death, but that we should—as existentialists like Jean-Paul Sartre have also taught us—perceive the value and importance of life in the finitude of our existence. Dewey's pragmatism is criticized by Shusterman because of his disturbing silence about death; his "neglect of this theme is a weakness," though he also seems to have held, more positively, that death should be "accepted" as a natural part of life.[23] The latter is, obviously, the naturalist attitude to death. Yet, it might also be admitted, even if (or especially if) one is a naturalist, that a fear of death belongs to our "human nature."

James's pragmatist approach to death, mortality, and immortality integrates ethical and metaphysical perspectives. James, though always focusing on concrete life, is not only a deep metaphysical thinker, but a thinker deeply concerned with mortality. This may be one key difference between James's and Dewey's pragmatisms. I believe that, when reading James's reflections on metaphysical problems, such as freedom and the reality of God, or in particular his reflections on the possibility of immortality,[24] we should take seriously his pragmatic way of approaching the very notions of reality and objecthood: "What we say about reality ... depends on the perspective into which we throw it."[25] When attempting to understand the world, including our own mortal existence, we are not just "readers" of the "cosmic novel" but its "very personages," involved in a reality "in the making," a reality whose structure is to a large extent up to us to construct and reconstruct, when we seek a "living understanding of [its] movement."[26] As James remarked, apparently influenced by Ralph Waldo Emerson (another American thinker concerned with re-integrating philosophical thought with life), "the trail of the human serpent is ... over everything."[27] There is a tension here, however, once again, because on the one hand it seems that death and mortality can themselves be pragmatically constructed and reconstructed as elements of the human world (whose metaphysical categorizations, as was just pointed out, are all human, valuationally and practically embedded), while on the other hand the finitude that results from our mortality may itself be required for us to be able to employ the pragmatic method, to turn our gaze toward future experiences that can only be significant to us if there is a finite number of them to expect.[28]

Deweyan pragmatism, while anti-metaphysical in important ways, may nevertheless be claimed to yield a metaphysics emphasizing the mystery of the natural world, requiring a kind of humility and recognition of our indebtedness to nature for everything there is and for everything we are, or can ever hope to be.[29] Jerome P. Soneson, applying Deweyan pragmatism and pluralism to theology, argues that such a "combined sense of mystery and indebtedness" characterizes the Deweyan "religious quality of experience," and that if this is appreciated, we may even view Dewey as "fundamentally a religious thinker."[30] The primary context for this understanding of Dewey is the "precariousness" or "instability" of existence—our insecurity and contingency—he emphasized not only in his writings on religion but especially in *Experience and Nature*.[31] Our natural life is potentially tragic, because we may always lose things we hold dear. This insecurity is part of nature, and thus of the human world our metaphysical reflections are concerned with. Yet, it is also connected with the notion of hope, whose pragmatist significance requires the kind of insecurity Deweyan naturalism emphasizes. As Soneson reflects:

> The tension between tragedy and hope, I want to argue, is the womb in which the religious function, as Dewey understands it, is nurtured and born. There is no need for the religious function apart from the tragedy of life. On the other hand, the religious function is not possible apart from the potential for growth that grounds the hope that circumstances can change for the better, that fulfillment or satisfaction—salvation, to use the more traditional term—is possible amid the tragedy of life.[32]

Deweyan pragmatically naturalist philosophy of religion by no means denies the reality—the full, painful reality—of evil and tragedy.[33] Moreover, a recognition of their reality is a kind of metaphysics—a metaphysics of the fundamental (though historically changeable) traits of human existence in a precarious natural world full of contingency, a world that is a source of tragic collapses as well as of liberating, enabling, energizing hope. This inevitable tension between hope and tragedy must be understood as coloring the "philosophical life" in its Deweyan forms.

Soneson is, I believe, right to point out that Dewey is a metaphysician in a "Kantian" sense. For both Dewey and Kant, "the task of metaphysics is to state the conditions for the possibility of knowledge,"[34] though for Dewey, such conditions are not apodictic a priori ones. Metaphysics "...reflect[s] upon what our talk about things implies about the kind of world or context in which we live".[35] It is roughly in this sense that we may view even Dewey's treatment of the religious aspects of experience as metaphysical in a quasi-Kantian manner. The dualism between metaphysics and the criticism of metaphysics (just like the one between religious and secular values, experiences, or ideals) collapses in Deweyan naturalist pragmatism—as it does in Wittgensteinian reflections on the ways in which "essence lies in grammar." The true pragmatist has no practical use for such sharp dichotomies, not even in theology.

Yet, arguably, Dewey might have paid more attention to death, evil, and suffering as both metaphysical, ethical, and religious or theological problems. To this extent Shusterman is correct, albeit de-emphasizing Dewey's concerns with a Kantian-like metaphysics of natural existence and the human world. Despite the devastating loss of two sons, Dewey maintained a generally optimistic (melioristic) attitude to life, while recognizing the reality of tragedy.[36] The question is whether his recognition of the tragic sense of life is deep enough. For instance, James's famous depiction of the "sick soul" in the *Varieties* may, in the end, be religiously more adequate. Even James's treatment of death, mortality, and immortality in "Human Immortality" may be philosophically more interesting than Dewey's almost thoroughly this-worldly and secular, naturalistic, way of philosophically facing death.[37]

Whether we adopt a Jamesian or a Deweyan pragmatist approach to the topic of mortality—or a Wittgensteinian one, as described by Shusterman—the important point here is that death is for us both a metaphysical and an ethical issue. In particular, we cannot help to be ethically concerned with the other person's mortal existence. This central role played by other human beings was not neglected by either James or Dewey, despite the differences in their views on death and mortality. In addition to these classical pragmatists, Emmanuel Levinas's ethics of otherness might lead us to appreciate above all the vulnerability and mortality of the other's face—with intriguing connections to Shusterman's way of emphasizing our bodily existence.[38] Death, for us, is never a purely intellectual or theoretical problem, but a pragmatic problem of life, of our own life and especially of our common life with the mortal others surrounding us. It is precisely for this reason that it is also, *pace* Levinas's idea of ethics as a "first philosophy" and Putnam's proposal (to some extent influenced by Levinas) to develop an "ethics without ontology," metaphysical.

4. Concluding Remarks

These thoughts are offered as (minor) challenges to Shusterman, not as final theories about anything—thus, they invite more pragmatist work in an open-minded, forward-looking spirit. Perhaps like Shusterman, I see pragmatism as a critical middle path, a *via media*, between a number of implausible extremes in various areas of philosophy, including realism and anti-realism (idealism, constructivism), naturalism and anti-naturalism, as well as individualist liberalism and more socially oriented communitarianism. Indeed, James himself described pragmatism as such a mediator in his famous typology of philosophical temperaments in the opening of *Pragmatism*.[39] Here I want to put forward pragmatism as a metaphilosophical middle path between the purely theoretical (or what James would have described as "intellectualist") and the too radically practical (that is, anti-intellectualist or anti-theoretical) conceptions of philosophy. According to the former, philosophy aims at a better theory of how things ultimately are, whereas the latter simply subordinates theory to practice and treats all theoretical pursuits as merely instrumental. The pragmatically most satisfactory choice, as usual, can be found between these extremes—and its adoption can, reflexively, be defended on pragmatic grounds. The pragmatic middle ground is the pragmatically best one to occupy, because it gives us better resources than its more extremist rivals for acknowledging both the importance of theoretical matters and the importance of daily human life—and the mutual interaction and entanglement of these two. Therefore, it is better equipped to lead us to as harmonious and "full" life as possible.

Yet, success here is never guaranteed. Just as pragmatist epistemology must be thoroughly fallibilist, recognizing and emphasizing the fallible and corrigible nature of any of our beliefs and theories, a pragmatist "philosophy of life," or any philosophical life pragmatically led, must acknowledge the fragility of our mortal existence. We may always fail not only in our cognitive inquiries (metaphysical ones included) but also in our attempts to live well. Our most comprehensive pragmatist account of what it means to live well must come to terms with this fragility.

A healthy development of this attitude requires a harmonious interplay between theoretical and practical pursuits of life. A too radically practical and anti-theoretical attitude to philosophy can be perceived not only in some (neo-)pragmatist literature but also in recent Wittgenstein scholarship. Increasingly, commentators tend to view Wittgenstein as a purely "therapeutic" thinker who seeks to liberate us from the dominance of philosophical theses, theories, and arguments.[40] It would be insane to deny that there is a very important therapeutic strand in Wittgenstein's thought, but it is seriously misleading to claim that there are no philosophical arguments—or, hence, their conclusions ("theses," "theories")—to be found in Wittgenstein at all. For instance, I am prepared to view the famous private language argument as a Kantian-like transcendental argument seeking to establish certain basic (though presumably historically relative and practice-embedded, thus mutable and reinterpretable) conditions for the very possibility of language, meaning, and understanding.[41] Yet, I definitely agree with Shusterman and others that Wittgenstein's arguments and elaborations, however theoretical they may get, seek to transform our lives. They seek to awaken our intellectual sensibilities to something that too easily remains unseen—to those things that are the most familiar ones and therefore escape our notice. This "existential wonder," however, is not detached from the metaphysical concern of structuring reality into a humanly understandable shape. The transformation that Wittgenstein, like the pragmatists, expects us to go through is both ethical and metaphysical, with the two profoundly entangled.[42] If successful—and, to repeat, its success is never guaranteed—this transformation will yield a sharpened understanding of our finite mortal lives.

I am not claiming that Shusterman reads either pragmatism or Wittgenstein with too anti-theoretical and anti-metaphysical eyes. It just seems to me that there is a slight threat in his position to thus misconstrue these classics. It is for this reason that I have felt it necessary to offer a reminder of the irreducibly metaphysical character of the most fundamental ethical and pragmatic-therapeutic "problems of life."[43]

NOTES

1. See Richard Shusterman, *Pragmatist Aesthetics: Living Beauty, Rethinking Art* (Oxford: Blackwell, 1992; as well as his more recent volume, *Body Consciousness: A Philosophy of Mindfulness and Somaesthetics* (Cambridge: Cambridge University Press, 2008).
2. Richard Shusterman, *Practicing Philosophy: Pragmatism and the Philosophical Life* (New York and London: Routledge, 1997).
3. I have tried to defend this general account of pragmatist metaphysics in a number of earlier (and forthcoming) publications, whose main ideas I will not here repeat. See Sami Pihlström, "Metaphysics with a Human Face: William James and the Prospects of Pragmatist Metaphysics," *William James Studies*, 2 (2007), online: http://williamjamesstudies.press.uiuc.edu; *"The Trail of the Human Serpent Is over Everything": Jamesian Perspectives on Mind, World, and Religion* (Lanham, MD: University Press of America [Rowman & Littlefield Publishing Group], 2008); "Pragmatism and the Ethical Grounds of Metaphysics," *Philosophical Topics*, 36:1 (2008); and *Pragmatist Metaphysics: An Essay on the Ethical Grounds of Ontology.* (London: Continuum, 2009).
4. See *The Range of Pragmatism and the Limits of Philosophy*, ed. Richard Shusterman (Malden: Blackwell, 2004), p. 11. In his "Introduction," Shusterman very pragmatistically, echoing William James, puts forward his collection not as a final answer to such problems but as "a program for more work" on the range of pragmatism and the limits of philosophy in relation to them.
5. See my discussion of James's views on death, mortality, and immortality in Pihlström, *"The Trail of the Human Serpent Is over Everything,"* ch. 3.

6. Shusterman, *Practicing Philosophy*, p. 5.
7. *Ibid.*, p. 8.
8. *Ibid.*, p. 17.
9. *Ibid.*, p. 21.
10. *Ibid.*, pp. 21–23.
11. Richard Shusterman, "William James, Somatic Introspection, and Care of the Self," *The Philosophical Forum*, 36 (2005), p. 422.
12. See the references given in note 3 above, especially my book, *Pragmatist Metaphysics*.
13. William James, *Pragmatism: A New Name for Some Old Ways of Thinking*, eds. Frederick H. Burkhardt, Fredson Bowers, and Ignas K. Skrupskelis (Cambridge: Harvard University Press, 1975). These problems are discussed in Pihlström, *"The Trail of the Human Serpent Is over Everything,"* ch. 3. See also my *Pragmatist Metaphysics*, ch. 5.
14. Shusterman, *Practicing Philosophy*, p. 61.
15. I am here employing some of the metaphors Putnam famously used to criticize metaphysical realism, without committing myself to any of his specific views (for instance, internal realism). See Hilary Putnam, *Realism with a Human Face*, ed. James Conant (Cambridge: Harvard University Press, 1990); and more recently, Hilary Putnam, *Ethics without Ontology* (Cambridge: Harvard University Press, 2004). I discuss Putnam's struggle with realism in several places, including my *Pragmatist Metaphysics*, chs. 2–3.
16. Shusterman, *Practicing Philosophy*, p. 145.
17. *Ibid.*, p. 159.
18. Ludwig Wittgenstein, *Philosophical Investigations*, trans. Gertrude E. M. Anscombe (Oxford: Basil Blackwell, 1958), I, §§ 371, 373.
19. See Nelson Goodman, *Ways of Worldmaking* (Indianapolis: Hackett, 1978).
20. See, for instance, Joseph Margolis, *The Flux of History and the Flux of Science* (Berkeley: University of California Press, 1993); Joseph Margolis, *Historied Thought, Constructed World* (Berkeley: University of California Press, 1995).
21. See Shusterman, *Practicing Philosophy*, pp. 42–50.
22. I am not saying that intellectual sophistication (about the criteria of death or about anything else) is irrelevant to living a mortal life; it just seems to me that analytic philosophical thanatology (if such a phrase is allowed) is stuck with conceptual problems whose resolution may not significantly help us in genuinely understanding what our mortal condition is like. For leading analytic perspectives on death, see Antony Flew, *The Logic of Mortality* (Oxford and New York: Blackwell, 1987); Fred Feldman, *Confrontations with the Reaper: A Philosophical Study of the Nature and Value of Death* (Oxford: Oxford University Press, 1992); *The Metaphysics of Death*, ed. John M. Fischer (Stanford: Stanford University Press, 1993); *Thinking Clearly about Death*, rev. ed. Jay F. Rosenberg (Indianapolis, IN: Hackett, 1998); as well as Geoffrey Scarrey, *Death* (Stocksfield: Acumen, 2007). For somewhat richer perspectives, including the Heideggerian one, see *Death and Philosophy*, eds. Jeff Malpas and Robert C. Solomon (London and New York: Routledge, 1998). For further discussion, see Sami Pihlström, "Mortality as a Philosophical-Anthropological Issue: Normativity, Thanatology, and 'Human Nature,'" *Human Affairs*, 17 (2007), pp. 54–70.
23. Shusterman, *Practicing Philosophy*, p. 48.

24. James's 1898 essay, "Human Immortality," is reprinted in William James, *Essays on Religion and Morality*, eds. Frederick H. Burkhardt, Fredson Bowers, and Ignas K. Skrupskelis (Cambridge, MA and London: Harvard University Press, 1982).

25. James, *Pragmatism*, p. 118.

26. William James, *A Pluralistic Universe* (1909), eds. Frederick H. Burkhardt, Fredson Bowers, and Ignas K. Skrupskelis (Cambridge, MA and London: Harvard University Press, 1977), pp. 27, 117–118.

27. James, *Pragmatism*, p. 37. For the recognition of the Emersonian background of this phrase, I am grateful to Dr. Heikki A. Kovalainen.

28. For further reflections along these lines, see Pihlström, *"The Trail of the Human Serpent Is over Everything,"* ch. 3.

29. One of the most insightful studies of Dewey in this regard, focusing on his concerns with value and religion, is Stephen C. Rockefeller, *John Dewey: Religious Faith and Democratic Humanism* (New York: Columbia University Press, 1991). Two key texts by Dewey in this context are undoubtedly *Experience and Nature* (1925, 2nd ed. 1929) and *A Common Faith* (1934), both republished in John Dewey, *The Collected Works of John Dewey 1882–1953*, vol. 37, ed. Jo Ann Boydston (Carbondale: Southern Illinois University Press, 1967–1987), *The Later Works*, vols 1 and 9, respectively.

30. Jerome P. Soneson, *Pragmatism and Pluralism: John Dewey's Significance for Theology* (Minneapolis: Fortress Press, 1993), pp. 90, 126–127.

31. See *ibid.*, p. 129.

32. *Ibid.*, p. 131.

33. See also Rockefeller, *John Dewey*, pp. 484–490. For a dispute over whether there is a place in Dewey for the "tragic sense of life," see Raymond D. Boisvert, "The Nemesis of Necessity: Tragedy's Challenge to Deweyan Pragmatism," in *Dewey Reconfigured: Essays on Deweyan Pragmatism*, eds. Casey Haskins and David I. Seiple (Albany: SUNY Press, 1999), pp. 151–168; Donald Morse, "Pragmatism and the Tragic Sense of Life," *Transactions of the Charles S. Peirce Society*, 37 (2001), pp. 556–572; Raymond D. Boisvert, "Updating Dewey: A Reply to Morse," *Transactions of the Charles S. Peirce Society* 37 (2001), pp. 573–583; and Naoko Saito, "Pragmatism and the Tragic Sense: Deweyan Growth in an Age of Nihilism," *Journal of Philosophy of Education*, 36 (2002), pp. 247–263. On the reality of evil in James, see Pihlström, *"The Trail of the Human Serpent Is over Everything,"* ch. 4.

34. Soneson, *Pragmatism and Pluralism*, pp. 166–167.

35. *Ibid.*, p. 167.

36. See Rockefeller, *John Dewey*, ch. 5; cf. Shusterman, *Practicing Philosophy*, p. 48.

37. For these writings by James, see William James, *The Varieties of Religious Experience: A Study in Human Nature* (1902), eds. Frederick H. Burkhardt, Fredson Bowers, and Ignas K. Skrupskelis (Cambridge, MA and London: Harvard University Press, 1985); and James, *Essays on Religion and Morality*.

38. See, for instance, the reflections on death in Emmanuel Levinas, *Entre Nous: Thinking-of-the-Other*, trans. Michael B. Smith and Barbara Harshav (London and New York: Continuum, 2006). Comparisons between Levinas and the pragmatists remain scarce, though I have tried to point out some important similarities in my above-cited works, especially *"The Trail of the Human Serpent Is over Everything"* and *Pragmatist Metaphysics*.

39. See James, *Pragmatism*, Lecture I.

40. I have in mind, of course, the recently influential and much-debated paradigm called "New Wittgensteinianism." See *The New Wittgenstein*, eds. Alice Crary and Rupert Read (London and New York: Routledge, 2000). For a balanced attempt at a recognition of the key insights of this interpretive standpoint connected with the acknowledgment that we cannot give up metaphysical pursuits for good, see Thomas Wallgren, *Transformative Philosophy: Socrates, Wittgenstein, and the Democratic Spirit of Philosophy* (Lanham, MD: Lexington Books, 2006), especially ch. 5.

41. For my reasons of thinking that Wittgenstein successfully combines pragmatist and transcendental approaches to philosophical problems, see Pihlström, *Naturalizing the Transcendental*, ch. 2.

42. In addition to Shusterman's writings on Wittgenstein, and Wallgren's book cited above, see Gordon C. F. Bearn, *Waking to Wonder: Wittgenstein's Existential Investigations* (Albany: SUNY Press, 1997).

43. I am grateful to Wojciech Malecki for his kind invitation to contribute this article to this collection of essays on Richard Shusterman's philosophy, as well as to Professor Shusterman himself for a couple of conversations on pragmatism we had years ago in Helsinki. I also gratefully acknowledge several discussions of the relations between philosophy and life (often in a pragmatist context) with my Finnish friends and colleagues, especially Heikki A. Kovalainen, Olli-Pekka Moisio, and Henrik Rydenfelt.

Six

FAITH AND THE LIMITS OF FALLIBILISM

Adam Chmielewski

It is a well known fact that Richard Shusterman has been exposed to such a variety of experiences that they might easily enrich not one, but several lives. An American Jew who fled his home in Philadelphia to Europe, and then to Israel, where he became accepted by the Polish-Jewish Nisker (subsequently Nir) family and virtually adopted by them; as an Israeli citizen, he married a Jewish woman and fought in the Israeli army. After military service he spent several years in Oxford, England, studying aesthetics; upon his return to America he became engaged to a Japanese woman and he subsequently spent long spells of time moving among various places in the world, most notably France, Japan and Germany. Unquestionably, Richard Shusterman's personal itineraries epitomize a cosmopolitan postmodern identity.

For all I know, he felt only once that his multilayered identity became problematic for him. Here is an extended quotation from a conversation we had more than a decade ago:

> [While in Oxford] I had these two identities [American and Israeli ones] and was in trouble when people asked the question: 'Where are you from?' In the beginning I would say 'America' because I thought that would be the easiest and natural thing to do, since we were going to be speaking in English and since I was always told that being an intelligence officer meant also that you should never say: (a) that you're an intelligence officer; (b) even that you come from Israel, because I was in a very classified unit. So I had my military training to tell me 'always say that you're an American.' Also once I got special leave to visit my parents while I was in the army and always your briefing from the security people was: don't admit you're an Israeli; always use your American passport. So it was natural for me to say: 'I'm American.' But then the next question would be: 'Where did you study?'—'Jerusalem'; 'Where did you do your M.A.?'—'Jerusalem'; 'Where did you do your B.A.?' —'Jerusalem.' And 'Have you just finished?'—'No, I just got out of the army'; 'Vietnam?'—'No, Israel.' It just became a burden. [I]t just was counter-productive and uneconomical conversationally to say: 'I'm from America' when the next [answers] were going to be in effect denying it. So that was the first time that this kind of dualism or contextual

problem came up because, when I was in Israel, the fact that I came from America was never a problem. People would say: 'Oh, you're an Israeli who comes from America. Lots of people are like that.' When I was in America the whole thing would never come up because I was an American who had been in Israel. The problem arose only in the context of neutral ground where you have to identify yourself as coming from some place. So the problem actually arose, and so I more or less defined myself in Oxford as an Israeli.[1]

I am fully aware of the risks involved in calling Richard Shusterman a cosmopolitan: he is, after all, of Jewish descent, whereas I was born into a nation that is known in the world more for its anti-Semitism than for anything else; I am also aware that the term "cosmopolitanism" has always been an essential part of anti-Semitic rhetoric of all brands, used as a condemnatory accusation thrown at the Jews. I am aware of this risk, and am willing to take it—for a purpose. For I would like to take this opportunity to address an aspect of the problem of religion in the contemporary world, an issue which is rapidly gaining in urgency. I am additionally motivated by Richard Shusterman's paper in which he decided to take an issue with the timbre of the sermon of Cardinal Josef Ratzinger given shortly before his elevation to the office of the Pope of the Catholic Church.

In this speech the future Pope condemned, as he had done many a time prior to this occasion, the "dictatorship of relativism" which, in his interpretation, denies the existence of one and incontestable truth; in this way relativism undermines the fundamental and absolute truth of the Creed of the Church which is known "for certain," since the knowledge of it comes from the divine revelation given to us by our loving friend, God.

Cardinal Ratzinger's pronouncements in this speech did not come as a surprise to people familiar with his activities during his chairmanship of the Congregation of the Doctrine of Faith. His election to the papal throne has elicited many unfavorable comments. For example, Andrew Sullivan, a writer for the *Atlantic Monthly*, wrote that

> [i]t would be hard to overstate the radicalism of this decision. It's not simply a continuation of John Paul II. It's a full-scale attack on the reformist wing of the church.... The space for dissidence, previously tiny, is now extinct. And the attack on individual political freedom is just beginning. [Ratzinger] raised the stakes even further by his extraordinarily bold homily at the beginning of the conclave, where he all but declared a war on modernity, liberalism (meaning modern liberal democracy of all stripes) and freedom of thought and conscience.[2]

Similarly Philipp Gessler, a journalist of *Die Tageszeitung*, a German newspaper now widely popular in Poland, has commented:

What can we now expect from the reactionary churchman? His last sermon before the conclave, denouncing the 'dictatorship of relativism,' shows where things will lead: Ratzinger will try to seal the bulkheads of the Holy Roman Church from the modern world—without the charisma and the humanity that characterized John Paul II. No good news for women, homosexuals, and Aids patients, to name just a few. Shortly after his election, Ratzinger, who calls himself Benedict XVI, announced to the faithful at St. Peters Square: 'I am only a simple, humble worker in the Lord's vineyard.' Simple he is not, humble hardly—and if there's one thing the intellectual is not, it's a worker.[3]

Even if there were some attempts to dispel the image of Ratzinger's "unleashing God's divisions in a Blitzkrieg against Western democracy," they remained rather unconvincing, especially after Benedict XVI has declared that those of the Mexican parliamentarians who voted in favor of the legality of abortion have excommunicated themselves out of the Catholic community, as well as when in 2004 he refused communion to the American presidential candidate John Kerry for his being pro-choice. These acts, which took place soon after his election, may be supported by references to earlier ones, most notably by his famous declaration *Dominus Iesus*, in which he claimed that it is only the Catholic Church that has as its disposal the fullest range of the salvational means, thus branding other religious faiths inferior in this respect.

The unfavourable picture of Cardinal Ratzinger/Benedict XVI has been somewhat dispelled by his appearance in a debate with Jürgen Habermas in the Bavarian Katholische Akademie; the debate was compared to the past meetings between Luther and Zwingli, or between Cassirer and Heidegger. The two intellectuals were talking on the "Pre-political moral foundations of the liberal state," a topic introduced to the political and philosophical debates by Ernst-Wolfgang Böckenforde.

In the debate, Habermas claimed[4] that the democratic process generates its own grounds of justification and does not need to be based on a prepolitical religious grounding. He also defended his concept of "constitutional patriotism," much welcomed by the majority of the Germans for whom, in the aftermath of the Second World War, the idea of constitutional patriotism is just about the only concept to gather them together and to preserve their own pride, which cannot be sustained anymore by references to their history and ethnicity. Yet even if he did not go so far as to adopt the Thomist view of the subjection of the civil law to the law of the Church and to natural law, and eventually to the law of God, and even if he did not abandon his belief in the moral autonomy of the liberal state, he claimed that religion is no longer a threat to the liberal state, but a source of remedy to the challenges of technology and consumerist uprootedness that gradually overwhelms ever larger strata of people across the world. He argued that the liberal state should "treat with care all cultural sources on which the normative consciousness and solidarity of citizens draws." Religion is chief among these sources: "In sacred writings and religious traditions, intuitions of sin and redemption, of deliverance from a life experienced as unholy, have been articulated, subtly spelt out and kept alive through interpretation over millennia."[5] Although he said that the civic ties cannot be based on religious ties, one should treat the latter delicately and to recognize them as important for one's struggle against the alienating forces of modernity.

Just as Habermas surprised the audience by his generosity toward religion, Ratzinger, similarly, included in his speech not only some words of appreciation of the divine light of rationality and its role "in controlling the pathologies of religion," but also of modern multicultural state. He stressed, against Habermas, that popular vote cannot bestow true legitimacy on the constitution, because majorities can easily be mistaken or immoral, and it is for this reason that it is necessary to acknowledge a transcendent standard of justice, grounded in the natural law. He acknowledged that the concept itself was not of religious origin, and argued that it should be restored to its original cosmopolitan breadth. He asserted that the discussion of natural law "...must today be conceived and pursued interculturally. For Christians, it would have to do with the creation and the creator. In the Indian world, this might correspond to the concept of 'Dharma,' the inner lawfulness of being; in the Chinese tradition to the idea of the ordinances of heaven."[6] Natural law theory presupposes a concept of nature which is not specifically Christian, is theistic or metaphysical in character, and which as such provides a superhuman rational ground for human action and should remain our guide. Even if natural law has been interpreted in view of the unfortunate evolutionary theory which claims for itself scientific status, Ratzinger, to remedy this, recommended that we subject science to a critical assessment by philosophy which is able to keep open "...a view of the whole, of the broader dimensions of human reality, of which only partial aspects can ever be revealed in science."[7]

Despite irreconcilable differences between the chief exponent of the secular Enlightenment and the watchdog of the Catholic faith, the fact that the debate took place in the first place demonstrated that the Cardinal was willing to face the arguments of an another worldview. Yet the debate turned out to be rather disappointing to all those who hoped to hear from Habermas a definitive argument in defense of the neutrality of the state. As Edward Skidelsky has noted, the debate was a "strange spectacle of philosopher and cardinal bending over backwards to accommodate each other"; it seemed, though, that it was Habermas who did a larger share of the bending.

It is thus understandable that Richard Shusterman, along many others, has been upset about the gist of the speech delivered by Cardinal Ratzinger shortly before his election to the papal office in 2004. Shusterman stresses that the Cardinal attempted to excite the fear of the relativist menace which not only does not accept but vigorously denies the unique, universal and unquestionable truth of this form of Christianity of which the Roman Catholic Church claims to be the repository. Stating that Cardinal Ratzinger has been looking for philosophical help in the wrong quarters, Richard Shusterman advises the Pope to take a favorable view of the kind of fallibilism as defined and advocated by Charles Sanders Peirce.

Against Ratzinger's unyielding view of the truth and certainty of revealed faith, which Shusterman interprets as a case of fundamentalism, the latter questions the idea of "the fixity of adult faith" formulated by the Cardinal. Instead he points out that fallibilism,

> ...by acknowledging that human knowledge is imperfect and thus can always be improved, ... has the advantage of allowing for unending progress and posing no fixed limit to inquiry and to its meliorative ethical and cognitive satisfactions. Far from an unprincipled skepticism or relativism, it wholeheartedly believes that the productive stability of established knowledge is not undermined by its lack of absolute infallibility. Effective faith in knowledge does not require faith in its infallible fixity. Combining this working faith with the merits of openness and progress, fallibilism also has the virtue of humility, which seems central to all religious traditions. The fallibilist believer can even be absolutely certain in her faith in God while acknowledging that her understanding of God is fallible, insufficient, and improvable, thus prompting valuable efforts to deepen such understanding by drawing closer to God or perhaps even seeking a mystical communion.[8]

Another thing that is central in Shusterman's argument with the Cardinal is the doctrinal dualism which has received a powerful expression in the speech. Shusterman wishes to

> ...indicate how the fallibilist attitude is better suited for promoting spiritual development, deepening religious faith, and advancing ethical knowledge, because it avoids the tensions between growth and truth, dynamism and fixity, that divisively torture the Cardinal's text and point to dangers of spiritual stagnation and oppressive intolerance.[9]

Again, the fallibilist approach is supposed to enable to avoid "the dualistic discord" that permeates the disputed text.

I sympathize with Shusterman's argument that, by allowing in a fallibilist manner a wider margin of freedom in deepening of one's understanding of faith, or indeed anything, which would necessarily be based on a trustful recognition of individual powers of ratiocination, may be much more conducive to the strength of one's faith than an unbending instruction as to what and how one is supposed to believe. For the same reasons I also do believe that a trustful recognition of diverse individualities and their divergent rational capabilities may be more conducive to the unity of a community than attempts to impose it without regard and respect to individual wills.

Despite that I would like to argue that Shusterman's instructions addressed to Cardinal Ratzinger, firstly, run counter the exclusivist nature of the religion he represents, and in fact of all Judaistic religions, of which Christianity is undoubtedly a specimen; secondly, are incompatible with the nature of the edificatory and instructive tasks in view of which the Cardinal, as well as the Pope, whose most urgent duty is to preserve the unity of Christianity, is bound to speak to the faithful. Thus, even if I sympathize with Shusterman's fallibilism, I think that an attempt to instruct the head of the Catholic Church as to more effective means of achieving the mature faith that he desires to instill into the wayward, the doubting and the dissenting, is rather misplaced.

Shusterman's argument is based on a distinction between faith and the understanding of the object (and contents) of one's faith. The argument may be expressed as saying that we may be certain in our faith, yet at the same time, the true nature of the object of our faith may elude our understanding. In this way indeed the fallibilist stance toward our understanding of God may be seen as compatible with unfailing belief in Him. One might think that this distinction is fully compatible, on the one hand, with the Christian doctrine which is based on the acceptance of the mysterious, and thus intractable nature of God, and, on the other, with the unbending demand to believe in Him.

Despite the cogency of the distinction between faith and the understanding of its object, as well as that between the mystery of the object of one's belief and the firmness of one's belief in it, it is well known that, for extratheological and extra-epistemological reasons, by adopting in the 19th century the dogma of papal infallibility, the Catholic Church irrevocably deprived itself of the possibility of employing the distinction in practice.

Progressivism in interpretation of the true faith, alluded to by Shusterman, has been officially condemned many times by the Church. To take just one example of many: in 1857 the heresy of the Viennese priest and theologian Anthon Günther was condemned because he argued that the dogmas of the Catholic faith should be reinterpreted anew and adapted to the rising intellectual standards of the Viennese educated bourgeoisie and intelligentsia. The writings of Günther were officially condemned in a *breve* of Pius IX's *Eximiam tuam* addressed to the Archbishop of Köln, von Geissel, and the condemnation was repeated in the *Syllabus Errorum* in 1864; his followers, known as the Günterians, were dispersed and/or ejected from the Church. Actually the Güntherian heresy, which was in fact much less radical than other theological innovations inspired by Kantian and Hegelian philosophy, was one of many reasons for the First Vatican Council to adopt the dogma of papal infallibility.

But there are deeper reasons that stand in the way of adopting the fallibilist/progressive attitude within the Catholic Church. The incompatibility of such an attitude with most religions, especially the Judaistic ones, stems from their exclusivist nature.

It is in the nature of religion that it provides its believers with a strong sense of collective identity; as a rule, it is an identity defined in exclusionary terms, which respond to, and cater to, the intricacies of the constitution of humans more effectively than the inclusivity that characterizes some Eastern religions, especially Buddhism, to which Shusterman also refers in his polemic.

As Martha Nussbaum has pointed out, the exclusionary proclivities of humans may be traced back to the nature of our bodily constitution which gradually becomes sublimated into the symbols and categories of culture and of religion. She writes:

> Humans also typically need a group of humans to bound themselves against, who come to symbolize the disgusting and who, therefore, insulate the community even further from its own animality. Thus, every society ascribes disgust properties—bad smell, stickiness, sliminess, foulness, decay—to some group of persons, who are therefore found disgusting and shunned, and who in this way further insulate the dominant group from what they fear facing in themselves. In many European societies Jews have played that role: they have been characterized as disgusting in those physical ways, and they have been represented symbolically as vermin who had those same properties. In the traditional Hindu caste hierarchy, *dalits*, formerly called 'untouchables,' played a related role: through their contact with waste products they were regarded as themselves contaminated, thus not to be touched by the pure person; their very existence in the community shielded the pure from the decay and stench of their own animality.[10]

I believe that most religions, especially those with Judaistic roots, cannot, without risking the firmness of their identity, give up the idea of the exclusiveness of the truth they profess. The argument may be strengthened by reference to the striking developments that followed a recent public lecture on civil and religious law by Dr. Rowan Williams, Archbishop of Canterbury. In his speech he has said that introduction of some aspects of Sharia law into the British legal system is "unavoidable."[11] Addressing about a thousand listeners at the Great Hall of the Royal Courts of Justice, he argued that giving Islamic law official status in the United Kingdom would be conducive to a greater social cohesion because some Muslims did not relate to the present British legal system. Williams said that introducing some elements of Sharia would mean that Muslims would no longer have to choose between two systems in which they have to live now; the religious one, which they have brought with them to Britain, and the British one which they have found there. To quote from his speech:

> If what we want socially is a pattern of relations in which a plurality of diverse and overlapping affiliations work for a common good, and in which groups of serious and profound conviction are not systematically

faced with the stark alternatives of cultural loyalty or state loyalty, [introduction of some elements of Sharia] seems unavoidable.[12]

In an admirable fallibilist manner he compared the situation to religious schools, where "communal loyalties" were brought into direct contact with the wider society, leading to mutual questioning and mutual influence towards change, without compromising the "distinctiveness of the essential elements of those communal loyalties." He also said it was a "matter of fact" that Sharia law was already being practiced in Britain. "It's not as if we're bringing in an alien and rival system; we already have in this country a number of situations in which the internal law of religious communities is recognized by the law of the land.... There is a place for finding what would be a constructive accommodation with some aspects of Muslim law as we already do with some kinds of aspects of other religious law."[13]

There are many ways to try to understand the approach adopted by the Archbishop. One may refer to Europe's past when Christian Europe extended both collective and individual recognition to the Jews, but this was a consistently negative recognition. The religious factor played a predominant role in this attitude of Christians toward Jews. It is true that in 1247 Pope Innocent IV cleared the Jews of accusations of ritual murders of Christian children[14]; yet very few other popes, until John Paul II, were subsequently willing to do the same; in the intervening eight centuries the papacy has successfully educated European populations in anti-Semitism. This consistent anti-Semitism eventually led to the persecution and extermination of Jews in Europe, especially in Polish territories, where before the Second World War Jews were more numerous than anywhere else in Europe (10 per cent of the whole population) because they escaped from vicious pogroms in neighboring Russia, a country in which the infamous and libelous *Protocols of the Elders of Zion* originated.

It is worth mentioning in this context the fact that Polish Catholic consciences have recently been greatly upset by a book by Jan T. Gross, *Fear: Anti-Semitism in Poland After Auschwitz* in which he describes in detail the killings of Jews by Poles after the Second World War. The killings took place immediately after those very few survivors from the German extermination camps (of the original 3 million Jews in Poland before the war, there survived about 80,000) decided to come back to their homes in various places in Poland. To their great dismay they were not met with relief and joy that they had managed to survive, but with extreme hostility which led to pogroms and incidents in which at least 2000 Jews were killed. It may be hard to believe the painful truth that, as a consequence, Polish Jews were escaping from Poland to Germany because in crushed post-war Germany they felt much safer than in their Polish homeland. Gross's elaborate, also psychological and economic, explanation of this gruesome phenomenon points unmistakably to the religious factor which played a crucial role in the justification of the killing of Holocaust survivors in Polish eyes. Also, as the reaction of the Polish Catholic episcopate expressed in the debate following the publication of this book testifies, most Catholics in Poland still have a problem finding fault in themselves, citing, in a non-fallibilist manner, their faith as unerring. [15]

To speak generally, the Jews were for centuries "the Other" by reference to whom Christian Europe defined and preserved its identity. Gradually, they became "the Alien" to be gotten rid of. At present, the role of the European Others, and increasingly that of Aliens, is bestowed upon the Muslims. From this point of view the Anglican Archbishop's appeal is in sharp contrast with the position of the Catholic Church, adopted toward the European "Others" or "Aliens" of the past. For example, the Archbishop's view is in striking contrast with political theologian Carl Schmitt's claim that even if Christ told his followers to love their enemies (in the sense of *inimicos*), no Christian ever thought to surrender Christian Europe to the Turks or Saracens in the name of loving them, because they, in virtue of their religion, forever remained enemies—in the sense of *hostis*,[16] that is, public enemies. In other words, one may interpret the words of the Archbishop as a genuine acknowledgment of the past mistakes and sins once committed by Christianity, and as a call for legal measures which would make it impossible for them to be committed again. The Archbishop may be seen as calling upon post-religious Europe to recognize its past guilt, and not to treat the Muslims as it treated the Jews.

In fear that Europeans might now commit the same mistake they committed in the past against the Jews, he seems to have joined the multiculturalist ranks of those who call for collective recognition of the Muslims in Europe. The statements coming from the head of the Anglican Church can be seen as an innovative attempt to adopt, within a religion, a position that is quite close to Shusterman's fallibilism.

The Archbishop's call may also be understood against the background of the post-war consequences of European anti-Semitism. For after the Jewish survivors found it impossible to live among the ashes of their dead in Europe they, supported by many enlightened Europeans (Zionism was, after all, much welcomed by many Europeans), went to live in Palestine. One presumes that the Polish-Jewish family of the Niskers was among their number. As a result, however, it was the Middle Eastern Muslims who paid for the consequences of European anti-Semitism. There are now at least 1.5 million Muslims living in refugee camps in Lebanon, Jordan and Syria, suffering humiliation and misery, with very little to do except to conspire against America, because it is America, not Europe, who is picking up the tab for the protection of the state of Israel, established on territories from which the Palestinian Muslims were expelled. Europe does not seem to be willing to understand its own past role in the creation of the Middle Eastern mess and instead is trying to offset the harm suffered by the Muslims that followed the establishment of Israel in 1948 by, on the one hand, paying meager sums to the Muslim Palestine authorities, and, on the other, welcoming immigrant Muslims in Europe. We may add to this also the past and present consequences of the French involvement in Algeria.

Yet in the uproar that ensued from the Archbishop of Canterbury's sermon, post-religious Europe has plainly demonstrated that it is not willing to go so far in the recognition of present-day European Aliens as the Archbishop would like. Many called for the resignation of the Archbishop and proposed that he go to a university where he might freely kick around such ideas instead of leading the established Church of England. His remarks also met with a staunch defense of the existing system of law by Prime Minister Gordon Brown, who said that British law will remain based on British values and that Sharia law would present no justification for acting counter to national law. "Our general position is that Sharia law cannot be used as a justification for committing breaches of English law, nor should the principles of Sharia law be included in a civil court for resolving contractual disputes."[17]

In a more serious attempt to understand and to interpret this rather unusual position by the head of the Church, Frank Furedi pointed out that

> what is truly significant about the Archbishop's statement is not his apparently liberal tilt towards respecting the customs of a competing faith. Although the focus of Williams' speech was on the place of Sharia law in Britain, its main purpose was to argue for the re-legitimation of the role of religion in British society. As head of the Anglican Church, Dr. Williams is painfully aware of the diminishing significance and influence of his institution. In Britain, there are now more Christians practicing Catholicism than Anglicanism. Islam appears to motivate and inspire people in ways that many ordinary Anglicans find difficult to comprehend. The Church of England is haunted by dissension over sexual and lifestyle issues and continually struggles to uphold its international authority over the world's 77 million Anglicans.[18]

What makes the Archbishop's view particularly questionable, even absurd, is that in his apparent search for a method to accommodate the Muslim minority in Europe and thus allegedly to preserve the religious peace, he is calling for the subjugation of the political to the religious, even if it is not the religion he is supposed and expected to represent and defend. For in a strange case of *coincidentia oppositorum* the practical and legal measures based on a fallibilist, pluralist and allegedly tolerant approach would not be much different from similar measures grounded in the dogmatic and anti-tolerant approach that defined the position of the Catholic Church, which for centuries wished, if not to preserve its superior position over and above the civic law, then at least to remain in a strict alliance between the Altar and the Throne: the dominant position of an institutionalized religion versus the state, in the past justified by unyielding claims of its subjection to natural and God's law, will be re-established by means of fallibilist arguments as developed by the Archbishop. Furedi concludes that the Archbishop

...is not simply demanding more recognition for Sharia but for all forms of religious law. He may well be motivated by a genuine desire to promote tolerance for Islam—but he is far more concerned with maintaining and, if possible, enhancing the status of religion more broadly in a secular society. That he has sought to realize this aim by piggybacking on the forward movement of a competing religion is symptomatic of the malaise afflicting his church. Far from being a courageous statement, Williams' speech hides behind Sharia law and fails to spell out its real agenda.[19]

Muslims are in Europe because Europe needs cheaper labor, just like, say, Hispanic people are being imported into the US for the same reasons. Yet this has its own consequences which reach way beyond the economy: in its post-modern respect for the communally shaped identities, Europe has extended a collective recognition to the Muslims rather than individual recognition to each of them, something she failed to do in the past for the Jews. Yet if anyone hoped that this politics would enable society to avoid the ghettoization of Muslims, they were evidently wrong. For instead of a genuine liberal individual recognition awarded to each of them, the politics of collective recognition led to a ghettoization of them in various places in Europe, and to their collective humiliation. It is no wonder that some of the ghettos are becoming nests of terrorism within Europe, as well as transition centers for the incoming jihadists from the Middle East, like the one in Hamburg that gave shelter to and recruited the perpetrators of the 9/11 attack on New York City, or in London and Madrid which were sites of several terrorist attempts, some of them murderously successful.

Europe still lives in the shock that followed the murder of Theo Van Gogh by a Muslim, as well as the treatment of Ayaan Hirsi Ali by the Dutch authorities. The debate on the limits of tolerance in Europe began with Ian Buruma's book *Murder in Amsterdam* in which he explains the implications of the killing of Van Gogh by an Islamic extremist named Mohammed Bouyeri. As Francis Fukuyama stressed, these facts, among others, led to

a long and overdue recognition that the old version of multiculturalism [the Dutch] practiced was dangerous and counterproductive. Liberal tolerance was interpreted as respect not for the rights of individuals, but of groups, some of whom were themselves intolerant (by, for example, dictating whom their daughters could befriend or marry). Out of a misplaced sense of respect for other cultures, Muslims minorities were left to regulate their own behavior, an attitude which dovetailed with traditional European corporatist approaches to social organization. In Holland, where the state supports separate Catholic, Protestant and socialist schools, it was easy enough to add a Muslim 'pillar' that quickly turned into a ghetto disconnected from the surrounding society. New policies to reduce the separateness of the Muslim community, like laws discouraging the importation of brides from the Middle East, have been put in place in the Netherlands.

The Dutch and British police have been given new powers to monitor, detain and expel inflammatory clerics. But the much more difficult problem remains of fashioning a national identity that will connect citizens of all religions and ethnicities in a common democratic culture, as the American creed has served to unite new immigrants to the United States.[20]

I do not pretend to have all the answers to the problem of religion in a modern liberal and democratic state. Yet I think that a lesson that Europe is learning, again, from its experience with the radicalism and exclusivism of religions, will have to hark back to the speech of the French member of parliament Stanislas Clermont-Tonnerre in 1789, which reads now as a strange letter from the past and as a direct response to the claims of the Archbishop of Canterbury, as well as to the claims of Cardinal Ratzinger. Clermont-Tonnerre said then that "we must refuse everything to the Jews as a nation and accord everything to Jews as individuals. We must withdraw recognition from their judges; they should only have our judges. We must refuse legal protection to the maintenance of the so-called laws of their Judaic organization; they should not be allowed to form in the state either a political body or an order. They must be citizens individually. But, some will say to me, they do not want to be citizens. Well then! If they do not want to be citizens, they should say so, and then, we should banish them. It is repugnant to have in the state an association of non-citizens, and a nation within the nation."[21]

The state based on religious laws has proven itself to be incapable of preserving the peace and tolerance between citizens professing different religions. As it is unreasonable to expect a fallibilist humility and moderation from religions, it is the task of the state to ensure a framework in which individuals may be able to live in peace whatever religion they profess. It seems that the solution will have to be based on two distinctions simultaneously: one, between positive and negative recognition, and the other, between individual and collective recognition. Accordingly, the liberal state's policies toward religion are to stem from the juncture of these two distinctions: the state is to extend its negative recognition to those forms of groupings of its citizens which have proven themselves incapable of observing the principles of toleration of others, and, simultaneously, a positive recognition to the civic right of all as individuals. This solution naturally involves a presumption of the validity of a third distinction, the one between the private and the public. Even though the distinction between the private and the public is permanently undermined by the fact that all private is political and, from an agonistic view of the political, it cannot be defined precisely once and for all, it nevertheless points to a political measure which has to follow from an awareness that a legitimate state cannot become a safe haven for all religions professed by its citizens if it does not transcend all their incompatible claims to incontestable truth. This cannot be achieved by a state that proclaims it own complete fallibility—and helplessness—versus religions.

NOTES

1. An English version of this interview appears at www.chmielewski.uni.wroc.pl; for the Polish version see: "Życie, sztuka i filozofia," in Richard Shusterman, *O sztuce i życiu: Od poetyki hip-hopu do filozofii somatycznej*, ed. and trans. Wojciech Małecki (Wrocław: Atla 2, 2007).
2. Andrew Sullivan, "Still in Shock," *Atlantic Monthly* (Tuesday, April 19, 2005), accessed 29 October 2010. http://sullivanarchives.theatlantic.com/index.php.dish inc-archives.2005_04_01_dish_archive.html.
3. Philipp Gessler, "Oh My God! Ratzinger the New Pope," *Die Tageszeitung* (April 20, 2005).
4. See, for instance, Edward Skidelsky, "Habermas Versus the Pope," *The Prospect Magazine* (November 2005), issue 116. http://www.prospectmagazine.co.uk/2005/11/habermasvsthepope. Below I follow Skidelsky's account of the debate.
5. *Ibid.*
6. Cited in Adrian Pabst, "Debate Beyond Secular Reason" (part 2), *TELOSscope* (November 9, 2006). http://www.telospress.com/main/index.php?main_page=news_article&article_id=171.
7. Cited in Skidelsky, "Habermas Versus the Pope."
8. Richard Shusterman, "Fallibilism and Faith," *Common Knowledge*, 13: 2–3, p. 381.
9. *Ibid.*, p. 380.
10. Martha C. Nussbaum, "The Body of the Nation," *Boston Review* (summer 2004). http://bostonreview.net/BR29.3/nussbaum.html.
11. Cited in Riazat Butt, "Archbishop Backs Sharia Law for British Muslims," *The Guardian* (February 7, 2008) http://www.guardian.co.uk/uk/2008/feb/07/religion.world.
12. Cited in Kim Murphy, "Britain's Diversity Debate," *Los Angeles Times*, (February 09, 2008). http://articles.latimes.com/2008/feb/09/world/fg-britain9?pg=2.
13. *Ibid.*
14. Cf. David L. Kertzer, *The Popes Against the Jews: The Vatican's Role in the Rise of Modern Anti-Semitism* (New York: Knopf, 2001), in which he documented the doctrinal and institutional anti-Semitism of the popes, especially in the 19th century.
15. See Jan T. Gross, *Fear: Anti-Semitism in Poland After Auschwitz* (New York: Random House, 2006).
16. Carl Schmitt, *The Concept of the Political* (New Jersey: Rutgers University Press, New Brunswick, 1976), pp. 28–29.
17. Cited in Jean Eaglesham "Archbishop in Sharia Law Row," FT.com (February 7, 2008). http://www.ft.com/cms/s/0/01702bcc-d5b5-11dc-8b56-000779fd2ac.html #axzzlGko6ETKn
18. Frank Furedi, "Hiding Behind the Veil of Sharia Law," *Spiked* (Monday, February 11, 2008).
19. *Ibid.*
20. Francis Fukuyama, "A Year of Living Dangerously. Remember Theo van Gogh, and Shudder for the Future," *Wall Street Journal* (November 2, 2005).
21. Stanislas Clermont-Tonnere, *On the Subject of Admitting Non-Catholics, Comedians and Jews to All Privileges of Citizens, According to the Declaration of Rights*, (London: 1790), pp. 13–14.

Seven

EROTIC PRAGMATISM:
SHUSTERMAN'S DEWEYAN ADVANCES

Don Morse

Richard Shusterman's work can be seen as a unique contribution to the recent development in philosophy known as "The Embodiment Movement," a movement of thought that includes such thinkers as Mark Johnson, George Lakoff, Eugene Gendlin, James J. Gibson, and others. The main thrust of this movement, despite important differences of details, is the idea that dualism is problematic, and that we are now able to coherently and accurately think of the mind as part of, not simply our brains and bodies, but also of our "embodiment" as such, that is, of our situated engagement with the world. Shusterman's contribution to this tradition consists, among other things, in his emphasis on "somaesthetics," and, more particularly, "reflective somaesthetic consciousness," in which our increased attentive focus on our embodiment can enrich our lives and lead us to "enchanting intensities of experience" that "can ... be achieved in everyday living."[1]

To help make their case, thinkers in the Embodiment tradition often go back to the American pragmatist John Dewey, who also advocated a position that is quite similar to theirs, but one that is often more fully worked out and rounded out in its details. Shusterman, in fact, goes back to Dewey in such a way as to consider him, after a long list of somaestheticians who come up short, as finally "redeeming somatic reflection."[2] One reason for this return to Dewey by these thinkers is that Dewey makes it very clear what is so problematic about dualism. When mind is separated from the body, according to Dewey, the world exists without the benefit of thought. The world then runs its course without thinking, as a blind, habitual mechanism, without the benefits of intelligent appraisal and value. Thought, in turn, is then detached from any grounding, and becomes wayward, reclusive, withdrawn, and unrealistic. In political terms, the action of the world goes its way without thoughtful individual control, while individuals, unable to help shape what the world becomes, participate in self-withdrawal and get lost in entertainment or the restless search for meaning.[3]

Dewey's efforts to overcome dualism, and to return thought to action, involve an account of "body-mind" that shows their organic union.[4] Instead of speaking of minds and bodies, we should speak of "the living creature," a creature that must win "the support of the environment" and is always in "connection" and "interaction" with events.[5] Some of these interactions are very com-

plex and purposeful—humans are able to develop habits of inspection and response, modes of awareness, in relation to problems they encounter in the environment. For Dewey, thought evolved as a response to the natural and social
worlds, as a mechanism for responding to their predicaments. Moreover, like
Shusterman, Dewey also seems to advocate reflective somaesthetics, since he
everywhere makes so much of intelligent action, insisting that we need to learn
how to attend to our own embodiment in situations more clearly and carefully in
order to enhance our experience and intensify the meanings in our lives.

It is quite natural, therefore, for Shusterman to turn to Dewey as he does,
since Dewey was a theorist who first thoroughly worked out the details of an
embodiment position and indeed the details of a compelling somaesthetic
philosophy, which aims to improve everyday embodied living. However,
Shusterman finds one major flaw in Dewey's account that has important implications for the direction of his own work. "Dewey's theorizing of the
body," Shusterman finds, "sadly neglects the erotic."[6] With this important
statement, Shusterman announces a way by which he will try to advance beyond Dewey's philosophy to his own unique embodiment position.

In this essay, I examine Shusterman's claim that Dewey's view of the
body overlooks the erotic, and I draw out the implications of this lack for Shusterman's philosophy. I show how Shusterman tries to overcome this lack in his
own work, and how this effort amounts to a fundamental aspect of his own
somaesthetic position. I then examine the extent to which this new, erotic form
of pragmatism is an advance over Dewey's own version of somaesthetics. As
we will see, by emphasizing the erotic where Dewey does not, Shusterman is
able to extend Dewey's organism-interaction model of the self to include as
what we are, and should minister to, ever wider aspects of the non-self, including, as the ultimate conclusion of this extension, "an uplifting sense of cosmic
unity," according to which I embrace as part of myself the entire cosmos.[7] The
erotic dimension to bodily experience, as we will see, in which we go out towards others, allows Shusterman to expand and transform Dewey's organism-
environment model of what constitutes human experience to include much more
than Dewey himself can include, namely the entire ordered universe in its infinite extent. Shusterman is drawn to Dewey, yet tries to go beyond him by evoking "cosmic unity."[8] Whether these advances toward Dewey amount to advances beyond Dewey is a question I address in the final sections of the paper.

1. Dewey's Lack of the Erotic and its Implications for Shusterman's Work

What Shusterman affirms about Dewey's work is the "body-mind" account of
human experience, in which there is connection, not separation, between our
bodies as live organisms and the mind as a unique human endowment. Such a
view, in fact, underlies and informs any account of somaesthetic consciousness, for were there a separation (in kind) between body and mind, it would

forever remain unclear how we could become aware of our bodies and their felt, aesthetic components such as somaesthetics implies.

Shusterman is explicit about this aspect of Dewey's work from which he draws, saying that it is the account of the "body-mind" complex that suits somaesthetics so well. Going beyond James, according to Shusterman,

> Dewey plied a more consistent nondualistic naturalism. Instead of speaking of body and mind as two different, separable things whose reciprocal influences could be traced and correlated, Dewey insisted on treating them as a fundamental unit ... Dewey willingly flouted conventional usage by lexicographically asserting their oneness through such locutions as 'body-mind' and 'mind-body.'[9]

Shusterman goes on to say, in a footnote to this passage, that he himself intends to use the phrase "sentient soma" in the same way that Dewey intends to use "body-mind," that is, "to highlight the fundamental body-mind union in human experience."[10]

More important, however, is the fact that Shusterman sees this model of experience as forming the basis of an account of somaesthetics, and particularly the "aesthetic" dimensions of someaesthetics. Dewey, too, like Shusterman today, did not simply want to give a theoretical account of body-mind (the details of which need not detain us here), but also wanted to give the notion some practical meaning and upshot, specifically in terms of mining the body-mind field of experience for rich, aesthetic possibilities, as revealed by reflection upon the body. This later point is why Shusterman praises Dewey so highly, namely for having seen quite clearly the potential of body-mind for the discipline of reflective aesthetic enrichment. Whereas Merleau-Ponty, for example, had eschewed reflective aspects of bodily improvement, as Shusterman sees it,[11] Dewey embraced the effort wholeheartedly, even turning to the work of F. M. Alexander, a renowned body therapist, in order to underscore the vital importance of reflective someaesthetics, that is, in order to underscore the ultimately practical nature of reflection upon the soma.[12]

It is precisely here, however, in Dewey's utilization of, and theorizing about, "The Alexander Technique," that Shusterman finds, not only Dewey's great promise for somaesthetics, but also the basis for its lack, its lack of the erotic and passionate. Shusterman notes that it was part of Dewey's character to be dispassionate. According to Shusterman, who cites Dewey's own words here, Dewey possessed an "avowed 'temperament' for making 'logical consistency ... a dominant consideration.'"[13] Shusterman also brings up Dewey's near-affair with "the young Polish writer," Anzia Yezierska, and observes that the whole (failed) enterprise, in which Dewey did not act on his feelings for Yezierska, underscores "Dewey's personal tendency to strictly control his passions."[14] To confirm this account of the episode, namely that Dewey ardently yearned for Yezierska, yet put his feelings "in check," Shusterman quotes one of

Dewey's poems, ostensibly about the Polish writer.[15] Basically, at the end of the poem, Dewey says: "Renounce, renounce…All things must be given up."[16]

Dewey seems driven by the very difficult effort to rationally control his desires, on Shusterman's reading of this poem. Renunciation, it seems, was a key trait of his character.

But now, more importantly, this trait seems also to come out in Dewey's philosophy, as Shusterman sees it, especially in Dewey's reflections upon, and practice with, the Alexander Technique. What Dewey found compelling about this technique for somaesthetic reflection, according to Shusterman, is that it focused on the body and how to improve its performances. More specifically, Alexander's technique allowed one to become aware of and inhibit some bad habit that is causing us pain and discomfort, such as a certain posture of ours, for example. Dewey praised the technique for just this potential, but in doing so he seems to make a mistake, going to excess in his praise of Alexander's privileging of reason over the body in a way that problematizes his own embodied approach. As Shusterman points out, Alexander privileges reason over habit, much more than Dewey himself would normally allow; Alexander downplays and criticizes the role of the emotions and the arts; and he promotes a racist understanding of the world by claiming that some races lack the self-control of others.[17] Through it all, Dewey publicly praised Alexander's work, and "disappointingly fails to distance himself from Alexander's excessive claims."[18]

Such a failure on Dewey's part is not accidental, however. To be sure, this failure does not square with Dewey's philosophy, which overtly rejects traditional accounts of reason, emphasizes the role of the emotions and the arts for human experience, and promotes democratic forms of life, not racist ones. As Shusterman notes here, "Dewey clearly did not share Alexander's radical racism. His political engagement as one of the founders of the National Association for the Advancement of Colored People in 1909 showed an admirable commitment to African Americans."[19] And Dewey did privately express some reservations about Alexander, namely that Alexander wrongly eschewed "scientific testing."[20] Even though he published articles praising Alexander's efforts, Dewey's own work clearly contained differences with it, and Dewey was not happy with everything in Alexander's work.

And yet there is something problematic still about Dewey's open, public embrace of so many ideas that seemed to run counter to his own—something problematic and not quite accidental. There must have been something of the old conception of reason (a transcendent, detached reason versus engaged intelligence) at work in Dewey's own mind if he could so persistently fall for Alexander's conception, according to which reason would inhibit and control—and, indeed, eventually take total control over—our habits. In terms of racism, too, Shusterman notes that, although Dewey did help found the NAACP, he nonetheless also

> …did not give race much philosophical attention… [and] some of Dewey's writings display a sharp division between the mind of civilized and

'savage peoples' that today might be regarded as racist, even though he attributed the difference not to native gifts but to the 'backward institutions' of so-called savage society.[21]

The problem at work in Dewey's philosophy can be summed up by saying, in essence, that Dewey lacks a proper feeling for the erotic. If we define the erotic as a longing for something outside of oneself or a going-out-toward-another, than we can understand why, for Shusterman, these several problems with Dewey's account might be explained by saying that "Dewey's theorizing of the body ... sadly neglects the erotic."[22] I should note that Shusterman, as far as I can tell, does not directly link up these two ideas—namely, Dewey's failure in going too far in embracing Alexander and Dewey's lack of the erotic (except for in his claim that Dewey tried to constrain his passions). However, I believe that the two ideas are fundamentally linked in Shusterman's text, even if he does not explicitly relate them to one another. For Shusterman goes on to say, after he presents the problems that exist with the fact that Dewey embraces too much of Alexander's work, that a fuller account of somaesthetics, one going beyond that of the Alexander-Dewey type, would more or less embrace something like the erotic, as I have defined it.

Let me be more specific. In summing up the results of his critique of Alexander-Dewey, Shusterman says that "there is ... a larger lesson to be learned here—the self's essential dependence on environmental others."[23] The failure in question is a failure to recognize one's dependence on others than oneself, a failure to see one's connections to a wider world than one's narrow self-conception. "Alexander's perfectionist rhetoric about '*Man's Supreme Inheritance*' of 'reasoning intelligence' suggests an extremely proud and narrow individualism fueled by a haughtily hubristic humanist faith."[24]

A deeper appreciation for the erotic, however, would lead us to see that we always live outside of our narrow individuality, indeed that we live outside of the human, in contact with a world of other people, animals, and the natural environment. The lesson to be learned from Shusterman's critique of Alexander, and Dewey's problematic embrace of him, is that "...we still essentially and dependently belong to a much wider natural and social world that continues to shape the individuals we are (including our reasoning consciousness) in ways beyond the control of our will and consciousness."[25]

Here we arrive at the core idea. Dewey himself, to be sure, embraced and even pioneered the idea of the organism interacting with its environment as the fundamental starting point of experience. But he did not draw out the full implications of this view, and even turned away from them toward a more traditional stance in his embrace of Alexander. Had Dewey drawn out the full implications of his own conception of experience, he would have seen that the erotic is what ultimately underlies this conception. "The upshot for somatic philosophy is that one's body (like one's mind) incorporates its surroundings.... Our bodies (like our thoughts) are thus paradoxically always more and less than our own."[26] We have here an essential feature of human experience, namely that it consists of "a dynamic, symbiotic individual that is essentially engaging with and relating to others."[27] This essential feature in turn implies an ethics: that we should possess a "greater appreciation for the environmental others (human and nonhuman) that help define and sustain" us.[28]

> We are ... charged with caring for and harmonizing the environmental affordances of our embodied selves.... Such a cosmic model of somatic self-cultivation is expressed in the Confucian ideal of forming one body 'with Heaven and Earth and all things.'[29]

The core idea of this cosmic model is that, embracing the erotic as an essential trait of human experience, we go beyond Dewey's narrow conception of experience as the organism interacting with the environment and ultimately recognize the "cosmic unity" that such a conception implies.[30] We recognize ourselves as part of the world; we recognize the world and ourselves as part of the same thing, a thing and all its creatures about which, therefore, we should be concerned as we would be concerned for ourselves. With this fuller conception of somaesthetics at their disposal, with the advancement of erotic pragmatism, Alexander and Dewey would have been able to avoid the problematic privileging of rational self-control over passion that they in fact succumbed to, and they would have strayed much further away from a problematic conception of things than they managed to do. In the end, they lacked the all-encompassing, passionate gesture of concern for the wider world.

2.   Deweyan Advances?

Does Shusterman's movement toward and then away from and beyond Dewey amount to an advance over Dewey? Should we adopt an erotic pragmatism over and above Deweyan pragmatism? There are some who argue that Dewey's work always contained an erotic conception that explained and made possible all his central ideas. Thomas Alexander, for one, has argued that Dewey explicitly embraces otherness; this desire and urge for otherness is built into his very conception, as part of what it is. Referring to Dewey's method, Alexander writes: "Positively it enjoins: Begin and end all reflections with an awareness of the world that transcends thought. Approach that world with humility and with an open mind: have a receptive awe of and curiosity in the world. Strive to see the world in the individual and the individual in the world."[31] Because Dewey's method emphasizes a return to experience, it entails openness to what is, to what shows up in the world, much as Shusterman's own philosophy does.

Alexander, in fact, has called attention to the role that the concept of *"ecology"* plays in Dewey's philosophy.[32] Dewey's philosophy of experience,

since it centers on the notion of "*transaction*," or the mutual interaction between the live creature and its environment, goes some way toward giving us

> ...an evolutionary metaphysics that replaces the Greek ideal-knower
> with that of a creative ecosystem in which change, plurality, possibility,
> and mutual interdependence replace the canonical concepts of substance,
> timelessness, logical identity, self-sufficiency, and completion. Such a
> position might be called 'ecological emergentism.'[33]

We have a position here quite similar to Shusterman's own, namely the
position that there is a unity between ourselves and the environment, although
Alexander seems to be saying that this position is already in part Dewey's own,
whereas Shusterman seems to say that it is only implied by Dewey's work and
thinks that Dewey himself failed to develop it and to live up to it sufficiently.

Alexander admits, however, that in presenting his own philosophy,
Dewey only gives us "the rudiments of an evolutionary metaphysics" with an
ecological insight.[34] As Alexander puts it:

> Of all twentieth-century philosophies, the thought of John Dewey offers
> the most promise for an ecologically wise naturalism that also addresses
> the plurality of cultures. Dewey's own thought, however, was enmeshed
> in a number of assumptions that prevented these aspects of his thought
> from developing as far as they might.[35]

Like Shusterman, Alexander also appears to say that we need to go beyond Dewey and recognize more emphatically and consistently than Dewey
himself did the ecological, or even erotic-based, nature of human experience.
Alexander notes his "...own efforts to think 'beyond Dewey' under the humanistic thematic of what I call 'The Human Eros.' This is primarily a claim
that human beings by nature seek to experience the world as a fulfillment of
meaning and value."[36] In the end, then, both Alexander and Shusterman agree:
Dewey's work needs to be supplemented with greater attention to our bond with
the world, with things and people outside of ourselves. Moreover, both state
clearly that this connection entails "care," as Alexander says, or a "caring for"
the environment, as Shusterman puts it, which we must also embrace.[37] And
interestingly, they both go back to ancient Asian wisdom to find resources for
supplementing Dewey's basic gestures: Shusterman by referencing the Confucian notion of "forming one body 'with Heaven and Earth and all things,'"[38]
Alexander by returning to Buddhism and saying that, "[i]n reflecting on the
possibility of an ecological wisdom, the Buddhist worldview certainly presents
itself as an impressive alternative [to Western philosophies]."[39]
So it seems that Shusterman is correct, or at least that he would be correct
according to the thought of Alexander. Dewey did not go far enough in developing what Alexander has called "'The Human Eros,'" or the urge to find

meaning and value in the world beyond only our human selves.[40] Dewey focused too narrowly on a specific living creature interacting with its environment and not fully enough on what this interaction implied: a rich, multifaceted, indeed a cosmic, caring bond with the rest of the universe.

Indeed, I would add that Dewey explicitly turns away from such a cosmic conception, as can be seen, for example, in his debate with Bertrand Russell, as recounted by Tom Burke.[41] It must be noted, first, however, that Dewey did perceive quite clearly this wider notion of experience. As Dewey puts it in *Essays in Experimental Logic,*

> [c]onsciousness … is only a very small and shifting portion of experience. The scope and content of the focused apparency [sic] have immediate dynamic connections with portions of experience not at the time obvious. The word which I have just written is momentarily focal; around it there shade off into vagueness my typewriter, the desk, the room, the building, the campus, the town, and so on. *In* the experience, and in it in such a way as to *qualify* even what is shiningly apparent, are all the physical features of the environment extending into space no one can say how far, and all the habits and interests extending backward and forward in time, of the organism which uses the typewriter and which notes the written form of the word only as a temporary focus in a vast and changing scene.[42]

Dewey here explicitly asserts what Shusterman and Alexander claim that he knows, namely the situated nature of human experience in a much wider world. And yet, in his response to Russell, who complained about the vagueness of this conception, Dewey withdrew his former conception and limited it off in the way that Shusterman notes.

According to Tom Burke, Russell believed that Dewey's "notion of *situations* … commits Dewey to … some sort of holism," which is problematic because it is so massively sweeping.[43] It seemed that Dewey's talk of organism-environment interaction, otherwise spoken of as a situation, could be so vast as to include everything, with any given thing blending into the remotest points of the cosmos. Dewey's reply to Russell, according to Burke, is to explain that what Dewey means by a situation is not everything, not an event that includes all events, but rather a definitely circumscribed event, one characterized by certain specifiable limits. The limits come from the fact that situations become problematic; their problematic nature defines them as just the situations that they are and not some other situation. Burke describes the idea as follows: "Simply put, such boundedness is entailed by Dewey's characterization of situations as concrete fields of organism/environment 'life functions' subject to, and directed away from, breakdowns."[44]

But if this is correct, and a situation is bound by its consisting of "concrete fields" of interaction, then Shusterman and Alexander may not be correct in supposing, in their conception of what I am calling "erotic pragmatism," that, to use Shusterman's words, we are "forming one body 'with Heaven and Earth and all things.'"[45] To make that claim would expose pragmatism to Russell's charge after all, namely that if a situation is so large as to include everything, then we are not really talking about anything when we talk about a situation, at least nothing specific and definite, and so we cannot really mean anything definite when we talk about lived, embodied experience as well.

It seems that Dewey may have been correct, after all, to have restricted his notion of experience (or situations) instead of opening it up to include Shusterman's "cosmic unity."[46] Perhaps pragmatism *must* avoid an erotic dimension in order to render itself coherent and focused. It needs boundaries, limits like those provided by a living creature interacting with just its own restricted environment, in order to provide a basis of embodied experience that is crucial to its conception. It seems that there can be no erotic version of pragmatism, in which the living creature reaches out to, and includes within itself, the entire cosmos beyond itself.

And yet Shusterman and Alexander might well reply that there can be no ultimate boundaries really, because, as the Dewey quote above expresses it, "[i]n the experience, and in it in such a way as to *qualify* even what is shiningly apparent, are all the physical features of the environment extending into space no one can say how far."[47] We cannot say how far the content of the situation extends, for the features of the environment that help constitute the situation include a long, vague list of ever widening aspects of things: "The word which I have just written is momentarily focal; around it there shade off into vagueness my typewriter, the desk, the room, the building, the campus, the town, and so on."[48] In addition, situations necessarily include others, as Shusterman insists, specifically "environmental others (human and nonhuman)."[49] Situations include these others because they include the environment, which includes more than only my body and my thought. Indeed, as we saw, for Shusterman, my body and my thought are always more than only mine.[50] For they are constituted by the environment, which includes others, others who therefore help me make me what I am. Or, as Alexander might put it, adding perhaps another dimension to the claim, there is such a thing as "The Human Eros," which is that "human beings by nature seek to experience the world as a fulfillment of meaning and value," that is, we necessarily seek by our own make up to find meaning and value, not just inside ourselves, but in the larger, wider world around us.[51]

If we look closer at these claims for erotic pragmatism, however (first by Shusterman, then by Alexander), these claims for moving beyond Dewey to embrace erotic pragmatism, we begin to detect a problem. One problem is that Shusterman himself insists that our embodied situatedness is bounded by the problematic nature of situations, the fact that, as Burke says, they are characterized by "breakdowns."[52] As Shusterman explains, speaking about our habits in situations, which guide and motivate our interactions,

...we rely on them until they prove problematic in experience—whether
through failures in performance, errors in judgment, feelings of confusion, physical discomfort and pain .... At that point, we should examine
more closely our unreflective behavior. But to discern exactly which
habits are misguiding us, which precise dimension of a habit needs correction, and which sort of correction is called for requires rigorous practical work in critical somaesthetic self-consciousness.[53]

Several things are interesting about this passage, which expresses some
of Shusterman's core ideas. The first is that, as with Dewey in his reply to
Russell, we see that here, too, the problematic nature of experience will be our
guide in what we experience. Moreover, when that problematic quality to the
experience occurs, and we need to examine our habits, what we need is to
examine "which precise dimension of a habit needs correction." In other
words, there seems to be a "precise dimension" to each problematic experience.[54] In addition, there is such a precise dimension to each problematic
experience that to attend to it requires, not a grasp of the whole, but rather a
"rigorous," focused, reflective effort trying to discern the exact contours of the
situation experienced as a problem. The situation is characterized by a problem, it seems, which contains a precise dimension, with exact, specific features, and which requires difficult reflective work in order to read the exact
situation aright and know how to respond precisely to it and its needs.

It seems that here Shusterman is insisting on the same thing that Dewey
insisted on, namely the bounded nature of the situation by its "breakdowns."[55]
And yet, at the same time, Shusterman also wants to insist that somaesthetics
"promises the richest and deepest palate of experiential fulfillments because it
can draw on the profusion of cosmic resources, including an uplifting sense of
cosmic unity."[56] In other words, he also insists that we exist as a single body
connected to all things.[57] But these two claims insisted on would seem to be
opposed: that situations are bounded and that situations are unbounded. Evidently, there is some tension here in the conception of erotic pragmatism,
which is perhaps why Dewey himself insisted, in his response to Russell, that
we must restrict the situation, after all, so that at least we can focus on the
situation as problematic, and have it contain exact contours. It seems we have
to make a choice: either situations are bounded by their problematic nature or
they are unbounded and form a single body with everything in them. It is
difficult to see how we can embrace both claims simultaneously.

To be sure, one could try to say that the situation is bounded by a central
location, the existing site of some actual problem, but that the situation is also
at the same time unbounded by all the rest of the world into which it inevitably blends. But I think this response really amounts to the claim that the situation is unbounded; for in that case, if one were to analyze the contents of the
central location, and say what makes it the site of a problem (that is, say what
makes it the bounded situation that it is), then one would have to include, as

what makes it up, all of its actual and potential relations to the world around it that sustain it. If we allow the unbounded situation to exist at the gates, as it were, of the problem, just outside the door, then this is equivalent to allowing it to constitute the problem, since we would claim that the situation as such, although bounded, even so must inevitably blend into the things outside of itself in order to be the exact kind of situation it is (since there is an inevitable blending of it into the vaster cosmos on this account), and so again we would have to include the whole unbounded cosmos as part of the situation. We would then be left with Russell's challenge all over again. It may not be perfectly clear how, precisely, to measure the contours of a situation, but it does seem to be a problem to say about a situation that it is both bounded and unbounded at the same time. To be bounded, with its own precise central location requiring our attention, the situation would have to exclude everything irrelevant to its special predicament, or else it would never get the exact contours of a specific problem, while to be unbounded, it would have to include all of this other material. It seems that, by the nature of the case, we are forced into choosing one version of a situation over another, whether we conceive of it as bounded or unbounded. It is not fully clear, in any case, how we can have both.

If we turn to Alexander's similar insistence on the unbounded Eros of situations, we also find that there seems to be a tension in his account, but from another direction. Let us return to Alexander's passage about Eros. He writes: "'The Human Eros'. This is primarily a claim that human beings by nature seek to experience the world as a fulfillment of meaning and value."[58] Notice that, according to Alexander, human beings "by nature" seek this type of experience. But to speak of human beings doing something "by nature" is to essentialize human beings; it is to claim that they have a nature, an essence, according to which they must act. But to claim this is to depart from pragmatism, which has always been about evolution, change, and the lack of fixed essences.[59] It is okay, of course, to depart from pragmatism if one likes, but there does seem to be a tension in saying that this conception is pragmatic, and that Dewey's philosophy already contained this conception but needs to emphasize it more, as Alexander claims.[60] Dewey was an anti-essentialist, one might say, and Alexander may be problematically trying to essentialize his work.

3. Conclusion

So what shall we say about the prospects for an erotic pragmatism? My own sense is that, given the reflections above, we can see that Shusterman may be right to conclude that (at some points in his career) Dewey lacked the erotic dimension to his philosophy, but we should also add that having too much of the erotic dimension in one's philosophy could be a philosophical liability. Granted that Dewey may have lacked the erotic element in his personal life, as Shusterman has documented,[61] and granted that, if true, this would have been a tragic moral failing on his part, even so, Dewey may have also had purely philosophical grounds for making sure his philosophy lacked too much of the erotic, that is, for making sure it lacked an utterly cosmic dimension.

For, as the discussion above about the nature of erotic pragmatism should make clear, there is some tension in its conception (and Dewey's own account of pragmatism avoids this tension by bounding the situation). More specifically, it is not yet clear whether, in any conception of erotic pragmatism, embodied situations, which form the core element of the conception, are bounded or unbounded. A fundamental trait of erotic pragmatism has yet to be worked out, which is why I might rather refer to this philosophy as a "pregnant pragmatism"—there are some promising ideas here, yet they are still in development, still needing to be brought forth and made fully coherent. A similar point could be made about Alexander's claim that pragmatism (that is, a form of anti-essentialism) could well be coupled with a conception of "the Human Eros" (that is, a form of essentialism). There are tensions in the erotic pragmatist position that need to be resolved before one can comfortably jettison Dewey's own version of pragmatism in favor of an erotic pragmatism.

Whether this means that those who endorse the Deweyan conception must fall prey to his, at times, problematic backsliding into dispassionate rational self-control and the inadvertent exclusion of others, I think remains an open question. But I do not think, personally, that it must mean this. Deweyan pragmatism, after all, is deeply committed to the social nature of human existence. It is also incredibly open to growth, to expanding the meaning of ourselves and the range of our sympathies. My sense is that Deweyan pragmatism can and would (and should) accommodate ever wider and deeper ethical relations to others, namely through the expansion of what counts as a (bounded) problematic situation at any given time and place to include others and the helping of all the others within it, indeed, a necessarily rich, extensive, and diverse inclusion of others, but that it can do this without thereby having to include the entire vast cosmos (and thus falling prey to Russell's charge that, in effect, it includes nothing, because it includes so incredibly much). Dewey's tragic moral failing, if he had one, may not, after all, have infected his philosophy. For these reasons, reasons of the possible sufficiency of Dewey's philosophy itself, and because of the need for erotic pragmatism to clarify more precisely what it means by embodied experience (is it bounded or unbounded?), I do not think that one must go beyond Deweyan pragmatism to a new, erotic form of pragmatist philosophy instead.

Even so, the effort at elaborating an erotic pragmatism does offer us crucial insights. Richard Shusterman has helped to make embodiment a vital topic, showing us where human meaning and value come from and how we might enrich them. And Thomas Alexander has shown us the potential importance of having an ecological understanding of experience. By exploring the depths of the erotic, and bringing this exploration into contact with pragmatism, otherwise regarded by some as so drearily instrumental, these thinkers of the erotic have posed a significant challenge to pragmatism to expand its basic unit of meaning, that is, to enlarge the pragmatist conception of self to include ever widening groups of differences within itself. Shusterman, in particular, by creating a new discipline of critical somaesthetics, has called upon us most urgently to focus on our bodies and their meanings, meanings which must always include more than ourselves.

To make the most of these insights, however, there is more work to be done. Proponents of erotic pragmatism must clarify the nature of this pragmatism more fully before one can feel comfortable in saying that such pragmatism goes beyond Dewey's pragmatism and should be embraced instead of his version.

NOTES

1. Richard Shusterman, *Body Consciousness: A Philosophy of Mindfulness and Som-aesthetics* (Cambridge: Cambridge University Press, 2008), pp.1, 196, 216.
2. *Ibid.*, p. 180.
3. John Dewey, *The Essential Dewey, vol. 1: Pragmatism, Education, Democracy*, eds. Larry A. Hickman and Thomas M. Alexander (Bloomington and Indianapolis: Indiana University Press, 1998), p. 302ff.
4. John Dewey, *Experience and Nature* (Chicago and La Salle: Open Court, 1997), pp. 226ff.
5. Dewey, *The Essential Dewey*, pp. 50, 48, 147. For the claim that follows about thought, for Dewey, arising from natural and social conditions, see *ibid.*, pp. 127ff. The relation to social conditions is implied in the term "conduct" that Dewey uses on p. 128 and, indeed, is found throughout Dewey's work, but see, for example, *ibid.*, p. 296. For the claim that Dewey's work calls us back to an everyday aesthetic dimension, see *ibid.*, pp. 395ff.
6. Shusterman, *Body Consciousness*, p. 12.
7. *Ibid.*, p. 216.
8. *Ibid.*, p. 216.
9. *Ibid.*, p. 184.
10. *Ibid.*, p. 184, n. 7.
11. *Ibid.*, p. 50.
12. *Ibid.*, p. 189ff.
13. *Ibid.*, p. 182.
14. *Ibid.*, pp. 210–211, n. 37.
15. *Ibid.*, pp. 210–211, n. 37.
16. *Ibid.*, p. 211, n. 37.
17. *Ibid.*, pp. 203–210.
18. *Ibid.*, pp. 210 .
19. *Ibid.*, p. 210, n. 36.
20. *Ibid.*, p. 203, p. 203, n. 27.
21. *Ibid.*, p. 210, n. 36.
22. *Ibid.*, p. 12.
23. *Ibid.*, p. 213.
24. *Ibid.*
25. *Ibid.*
26. *Ibid.*, p. 214.
27. *Ibid.*

28. *Ibid.*, pp. 214–215.
29. *Ibid.*, p. 215.
30. *Ibid.*, p. 216.
31. Thomas Alexander, "Dewey's Denotative-Empirical Method: A Thread Through the Labyrinth," *Journal of Speculative Philosophy*, New Series, 18:3 (2004), p. 254.
32. Thomas Alexander, "The Aesthetics of Reality: The Development of Dewey's Ecological Theory of Experience," in *Dewey's Logical Theory: New Studies and Interpretations*, eds. F. Thomas Burke, D. Micah Hester, and Robert B. Talisse (Nashville, Vanderbilt University Press, 2002), p. 21.
33. *Ibid.*, p. 21.
34. *Ibid.*
35. Thomas M. Alexander, "Between Being and Emptiness: Toward an Eco-Ontology of Inhabitation," in *In Dewey's Wake: Unfinished Work of Pragmatic Reconstruction*, ed. William J. Gavin (Albany: State University of New York Press, 2003), p. 132.
36. *Ibid.*, p. 133.
37. *Ibid.*, pp. 137; Shusterman, *Body Consciousness*, p. 215.
38. Shusterman, *Body Consciousness*, p. 215.
39. Alexander, "Between Being and Emptiness," p. 140.
40. *Ibid.*, p. 133.
41. Tom Burke, *Dewey's New Logic: A Reply to Russell* (Chicago and London: The University of Chicago Press, 1998), p. 32ff; especially pp. 45–46.
42. John Dewey, *Essays in Experimental Logic* (New York: Dover Publications, 2004), p. 4.
43. Burke, *Dewey's New Logic*, p. 32.
44. *Ibid.*, p. 44.
45. Shusterman, *Body Consciousness*, p. 215.
46. *Ibid.*, p. 216.
47. Dewey, *Essays in Experimental Logic*, p. 4.
48. *Ibid.*, p. 4.
49. Shusterman, *Body Consciousness*, p. 214.
50. *Ibid.*, p. 214.
51. Alexander, "Between Being and Emptiness," p. 133.
52. Burke, *Dewey's New Logic*, p. 44.
53. Shusterman, *Body Consciousness*, p. 212.
54. *Ibid.*, p. 212.
55. Burke, *Dewey's New Logic*, p. 44.
56. Shusterman, *Body Consciousness*, p. 216.
57. *Ibid.*, p. 215.
58. Alexander, "Between Being and Emptiness," p. 133.
59. See, for instance, Dewey, *Essays in Experimental Logic*, pp. 39–45.
60. Alexander, "Between Being and Emptiness," pp. 132–133.
61. Shusterman, *Body Consciousness*, p. 210ff.

Eight

SHUSTERMAN AND THE PARADOXES OF SUPERHUMAN SELF-STYLING

Jerold J. Abrams

One thing is needful. —To 'give style' to one's
character—a great and rare art!
Friedrich Nietzsche, *The Gay Science*[1]

Self-stylization is original, distinctive, and demanding
precisely because we must cease to be our ordinary
selves so as to become our higher selves.
Richard Shusterman,
"Genius and the Paradoxes of Self-Styling"[2]

1. Self-Styling and the Future

Richard Shusterman in "Genius and the Paradoxes of Self-Styling" develops a
rich view of the philosophical promise and perils of self-styling. The central
idea of self-styling is that while the individual is unconsciously shaped by
contingent forces of evolution and culture, the individual becomes aware of
that process with maturity, and, by taking an objective perspective on the self,
one can shape one's habits toward an ideal of one's own. Each individual
possesses a unique character (or genius) with specific gifts that arise from the
dynamic interplay of evolution and cultural shaping. The ideal of self-styling
is the realization of one's particular genius through the perfection and enjoy-
ment of one's unique gifts in a completed character form. One perfects one's
genius by self-transformation and expresses that genius in given social forms
like sport, art, science, and philosophy. Such a project as Shusterman's differs
from others that focus more on literary rather than somatic self-styling. For
example, Richard Rorty and Alexander Nehamas also develop projects of self-
styling, which are both influenced by Nietzsche; and Rorty, like Shusterman,
is also a pragmatist.[3] But Nehamas and Rorty focus more on developing one's
literary voice, whereas Shusterman develops a more embodied view of self-
styling known as "somaesthetics," which encompasses literary self-styling but
focuses greater attention on the somatic form. Shusterman writes:

Somaesthetics can be provisionally defined, as the critical meliorative study of one's experience and use of one's body as a locus of sensory-aesthetic appreciation (aesthesis) and creative self-fashioning. It is therefore also devoted to the knowledge, discourses, and disciplines that structure such somatic care or can improve it.[4]

Because Shusterman's project focuses on somatic self-styling, his view lends itself to analysis of how the body can be restyled in more radical form.

Over its long history, the project of self-transformation has been confined to shaping the individual within general biological species limits: for example, the body can be trained to run and swim only so fast. But within this century we are faced with a further possibility for self-styling: namely, genetic engineering and nanotechnology may begin to alter the very form of the individual and the species. With these technologies, self-styling may begin to take on its most radical form to date, and the potential for the forms of human genius, should such self-styling succeed, would be greatly enhanced. This new project of self-styling is known today by various names such as superhumanism, posthumanism, transhumanism, betterhumanism, ex-humanism, hyperhumanism, neohumanism, and Humanity Plus (or H+). We will use superhumanism, but, in general, all of these names refer to the same thing: they refer to a future state of humanity enhanced by genetic engineering and nanotechnology that transcends humanity's relatively fixed natural limits on lifespan, planetary location, and cognition.

A common philosophical approach in this discussion conceives superhumanism as an extension of Nietzschean self-transformation, but ultimately resulting in a distorted form of humanity. For example, Francis Fukuyama and Leon Kass (who have both served on past President George W. Bush's bioethics council) equate superhumanism with Nietzschean self-transformation and warn against future species distortion.[5] Similarly, Jürgen Habermas in *The Future of Human Nature* refers to would-be superhuman beings as "self-styled Nietzscheans, indulging in fantasies," and makes the same claim that superhumanism will distort humanity.[6] The description of superhumanism as a form of self-styling is correct. But we should be careful about claims of any final picture of superhumanism. Kass and Fukuyama both argue that super-humanity will result in a future like the one Aldous Huxley depicts in *Brave New World*, a class-based society of engineered subhuman beings many of whom possess high levels of calculation, but no spirit or creativity, and no common human feeling. Against this view, superhuman beings will not have human lifespans or human limits on cognition like the individuals in the novel. It is tempting to think that we know for certain what superhumanity will be like or look like, perhaps particularly for those who wish to halt any experimentation on the human form. But no final picture of superhumanity can adequately be given because too much remains indeterminate with the transition beyond the biological human form. Yet despite our inability to formulate a final picture of superhumanity, we can perhaps formulate a reasonable picture of the transition from humanity to superhumanity as a transition from human self-styling to superhuman self-styling, and thereby extend by analogy the paradoxes of present self-styling to future self-styling.

2. Paradoxes of Self-Styling

In "Genius and the Paradoxes of Self-Styling" Shusterman uncovers "a series of deeply fascinating paradoxes":

> That the power of individual style lies not in its individuality but in its more-than-individual force; that the secret of acquiring style is that we must be true to ourselves yet also transform ourselves into something different; that the genius of self-styling demands the patient discipline of perfectionist striving yet can come only by letting go, through leaps of self-abandon.[7]

First, individual style requires non-individual guidance by others. Second, individual style requires one to become another yet remain oneself. Third, individual style requires intense self-control through self-abandon in which self-control all but disappears.

Proceeding with the first paradox, one must focus one's energies on realizing one's own unique capacities. But one's own capacities are not entirely one's own. Rather they belong to the species as a whole and the means to realize them are always already deeply social. Genius emerges in the individual and must be shaped in and by the individual. But the species possesses the individual genius and claims it for the species as a whole. A genius does not own his powers as someone owns land: rather the powers of the species reflect through the individual, who is possessed by the power of genius. To attain genius as an individual one must open oneself to guidance by the will and genius of the species as it is reflected within the individual. "For geniuses are not masters of genius," writes Shusterman, "but its servants, envoys, or instruments. Its spontaneity bespeaks a more-than-human energy beneath the individual's conscious will and beyond his powers of control."[8] As one realizes one's genius one channels the cognitive and creative powers of the species and expresses them within and to the species in a community which recognizes genius in projects of self-styling. Genius emerges only in relation to others, with them, against them, for them, and beyond them. Mozart's music, for example, is music in history, made in relation to other musical forms, like baroque, and made for other people. The language the self-styled genius speaks, then, is never wholly (or even mainly) his or her own, but is always already socially distributed and formative of the individual at the somatic and linguistic level. The "I" of the self-styled self is always already the intersubjective "we" of the species (in Hegel's sense), the genius of which can only be realized in the paradoxical relation of individuals who are at once "I" and "we," and who reveal in their genius the paradoxical relation of their individuality and their social collectivity, thereby revealing, in Hegel's terms, the "'I' that is 'We' and 'We' that is 'I.'"[9]

Facing this first paradox, one simultaneously faces a second paradox: namely, becoming other in order to become oneself and to remain oneself. According to Shusterman, "...the secret of acquiring style is that we must be true to ourselves yet also transform ourselves into something different."[10] On the one hand, one possesses a self-identity; on the other hand, one becomes a new individual who has yet to exist. How does one transform oneself into a new individual while remaining true to one's own identity? Or, as Shusterman asks, "How do we reconcile the notion of original style as honest self-expression with that of artful self-transformation?"[11] Answering this question relies partly on considering the alternative: namely, failing to become oneself in another. We are all familiar with the gifted individual who does not belong in a chosen social role: the individual's inner genius struggles to appear and does ultimately find a way to express itself in limited form. But one's social role and training appear as artifice laid over natural gifts rather than the means to the expression of a natural end. One has missed one's calling. Shusterman agrees with Nietzsche on this problem: "There exists no more repulsive and desolate creature than the man who has evaded his genius and now looks furtively to left and right, behind him and all around him."[12] Others can see how someone's talents and thwarted genius would thrive in another possible world, but one has styled oneself to become another and that other is not one's own. Just as the merits of realizing one's genius are never solely one's own, so, too, the tragic failure to realize one's genius belongs to the species as well. The individual's loss is our loss too.

Shusterman's solution to this paradox lies in the capacity of the individual to become another in a direction distinctly one's own: "The paradox of 'how to become what one is'—of both being true to your self yet becoming another, higher self—could then be resolved by artfully transforming yourself in your own way in terms of your already existing givens and potential."[13] The truly self-styled genius perfects one's unique capacities in another version of oneself who arises as a possibility for that particular individual. Of course, that does not mean that only one individual should be a mathematician or a musician—many will have a genius for mathematics or music—but one's own particular realization of the species genius of music (or mathematics) will consist in works and experiences that are uniquely one's own. Shusterman writes:

> In short, one must build on one's already existing self—its talents, potential, most promising inclinations, but one must not rest content with them. One can only get to one's higher self through the starting point of one's present self. If one has no real talent for music but only for mathematics, one should seek one's higher self not as a musician but as a mathematician.[14]

One becomes what one is by becoming another who is latent within the individual self.

As one faces these two paradoxes at once, one also faces a third related and potentially even more difficult paradox as one attempts to become what one is by not becoming anything in particular at all. In fact, a necessary condition for actualizing one's individual genius is the throwing off of any ideal or final form for the self. According to Shusterman, "…the genius of self-styling demands the patient discipline of perfectionist striving yet can come only by letting go, through leaps of self-abandon." While one can only become oneself by becoming another by adhering closely to one's previous self, one can only truly achieve one's ideal form by not adhering to a notion of oneself or any ideal at all. This paradoxical relation can also be found (in some form) in Nietzsche, as Shusterman points out.

> But for all this trumpeting of willed effort and self-motivated striving, have we not heard the tones of spontaneous, involuntary self-abandon reverberating just as strong? Rather than self-regarding, the genius, says Nietzsche, 'squanders himself, that is his greatness. The instinct of self-preservation is suspended.' To grow toward greatness and create oneself means to 'live dangerously' and 'lose oneself occasionally, if one wants to learn something from things different from oneself,' and thus enrich oneself.[15]

We find the point in Nietzsche's *Beyond Good and Evil*: "…the genuine philosopher … lives 'unphilosophically' and 'unwisely,' above all *imprudently* … he risks *himself* constantly, he plays the wicked game."[16] The same point also appears in *Human, All Too Human*: "Once one has found oneself one must understand how from time to time to *lose* oneself—and then how to find oneself again: supposing, that is, that one is a thinker. For to the thinker it is disadvantageous to be tied to one person all the time."[17] The idea here is that, at least on occasion—for one can hardly abandon oneself at all times of the day—one must put off altogether the focus on goals to engage in experiments of the imagination and body that involve a certain level of willful self-abandon.

But how can one perform at once the dual tasks of transforming the individual self toward a goal and abandoning that self to experiences that lack goal-oriented thinking or behavior? "How," asks Shusterman, "do we reconcile the paradox that we must push and discipline ourselves for genius but still need to 'let go' and abandon ourselves finally to achieve it?"[18] As a testament to the interrelatedness of these three paradoxes, the solution to this third paradox is to be found partly in the first paradox. One abandons oneself within self-styling not by living a life of willful self-destruction, but by submitting oneself to the will and genius of the species. "The trick, it seems," writes Shusterman, "is to direct our earnest efforts to the point where spontaneous, involuntary, more-than-personal forces can fruitfully be brought into play."[19]

By releasing oneself from one's ego, one may allow the mind/body to serve as an individuated prism through which the gifts and powers and genius of the species may pass. Yet, when one allows those gifts to pass through, they will inevitably bear the stamp of one's own particular form. "So genius means surrendering personal will, pride, and ego to something higher than the self, something that nonetheless gives the self its true distinction beyond any self-ish peculiarity."[20] The alteration of the senses and the imagination and even the temporary experience of madness can serve self-styling to break up habit-uated thoughts and to stimulate the creative imagination and to explore the depths of the spirit in pursuit of greater understanding of oneself.

3. The Superhuman Ideal

Central to Shusterman's picture is the value of discovering one's most funda-mental limits, struggling with them, and ultimately overcoming them. "Here is a task for both careful industry and dangerous abandon," writes Shusterman, "for intently pushing on to the limit, and going still further by then letting go."[21] Given this view of self-styling, a question arises about the limits of self-enhancement (particularly in light of emerging technologies of self-enhancement). If self-styling aims at pushing on to the limit and then trans-cending that limit by letting go of the various contingent fixations of our na-ture, then can there be an ultimate limit on self-styling, and can we even make sense of it in this discussion?

This question actually arises already (in germinal form) within the history of the philosophy of self-styling with Ralph Waldo Emerson, who also plays a central role in Shusterman's "Genius and the Paradoxes of Self-Styling." In "The Over-Soul" Emerson develops a view of the virtually superhuman genius.

> The soul's advances are not made by gradation, such as can be repre-sented by motion in a straight line, but rather by ascension of state, such as can be represented by metamorphosis,—from the egg to the worm, from the worm to the fly. The growths of genius are of a certain *total* character, that does not advance the elect individual first over John, then Adam, then Richard, and give to each the pain of discovered inferiority, but by every throe of growth the man expands there where he works, passing, at each pulsation, classes, populations, of men. With each divine impulse the mind rends the thin rinds of the visible and finite, and comes out into eternity, and inspires and expires its air.[22]

For Emerson the development of genius is not gradual but dramatic and even explosive. Genius develops by metamorphosis and transcends the gen-eral population of humanity. Nietzsche follows Emerson and develops a view of the metamorphosis of genius in the species into a superhuman form, which Nietzsche calls the overman.[23] This overman represents "the ideal of a human, superhuman well-being and benevolence that will often appear *inhuman*."[24] Nietzsche also suggests that humanity might be only a developmental stage on the way to a new kind of species: "What is great in man is that he is a bridge and not an end."[25]

Neither Emerson nor Nietzsche envisions his ideal as an outcome of technological self-shaping, which means that either they do not adequately articulate the means to the end of the superhuman, or that the end remains human (and not superhuman). We do find, however, a philosophy of the superhuman ideal achieved by technological means in American pragmatism, beginning with the work of Charles S. Peirce, which builds on Emerson's view of species transformation. At the heart of pragmatism are two basic ideas: evolution and technology. Shusterman makes this point in *Surface and Depth*.

> As both Dewey and Peirce remarked, pragmatism is inspired by Darwin's idea of evolution. The world, including the world of human thought, develops over time, and such development is contingent rather than necessary. The universe is not only plastic but variant, the product of chance probabilities. Human thought and action are evolutionary responses to the world, and they play a central part in reshaping the world.[26]

Over millions of years the species evolves and develops a highly technological mind, which Dewey in *Experience and Nature* calls "the tool of tools."[27] This tool of tools arises from natural selection and later becomes the means in all self-directed species shaping. The pragmatists recognized that science and technology over the course of the long run would transform the somatic and cognitive form of the species and eventually give rise to a different kind of species form. "Since Galileo," writes Peirce, "the progress of science has been accelerated more; and the question cannot be suppressed: 'What are we to anticipate in this respect?' ... I incline toward guessing that another and more intelligent race may supplant us to advantage, though this is the merest dream."[28] According to Peirce, these new superhuman beings would have new cognitive faculties superior to human faculties, but the development of these new faculties would not appear all at once. Rather humanity would progressively alter its cognitive form by developing new faculties. "Would not the human race," writes Peirce, "supposing that it could survive the shock at all, be pretty sure to develop a new form of intuition in which the things that now appear near would appear far?"[29] These faculties would in turn generate new experiences different in degree and kind from humanity's own, for example, in aesthetics and morals: "Esthetic good and evil are closely akin to pleasure and pain. They are what would be pleasure or pain to the fully developed superman."[30] Peirce does not develop this view at any great length. His view of the superhuman remains fragmentary. But his view provides an outline of a superhuman future, which, in recent years, science and technology has begun to fill in, especially with the development of genetic engineering and nanotechnology.

4. Technology and the Superhuman

The project of animal genetic engineering has been well underway since the cloning of the sheep Dolly by Ian Wilmut (announced in 1997); and few will doubt that this project may ultimately affect and even alter the form of humanity over the course of the long run. Less well known is the project of nanotechnology, which has also been well underway for quite some time. In fact, the theoretical foundations of nanotechnology emerge as early as 1959 with physicist Richard Feynman's paper, "There's Plenty of Room at the Bottom." "The principles of physics, as far as I can see," writes Feynman, "do not speak against the possibility of maneuvering things atom by atom."[31] According to Feynman, microscale robots may reorganize the atoms of organic and artificial forms and thereby alter those forms. Since Feynman, others have also taken up this project of nanotechnology. Prominent among them, Eric Drexler in *Engines of Creation: The Coming Era of Nanotechnology* envisions wide-ranging human control of the structure of matter: "Because assemblers [nanobots] will let us place atoms in almost any reasonable arrangement ... they will let us build almost anything that the laws of nature allow to exist."[32] Drexler elaborates this view in *Unbounding the Future: The Nanotechnology Revolution*: "The human race is approaching the great historical transition to thorough, inexpensive control of the structure of matter, with all that implies for medicine, the environment, and our way of life. What happens before and during that transition will shape its direction, and with it the future."[33]

This great transition in technological power is sometimes called "the singularity" and some think it will emerge within the twenty-first century. The artificial intelligence theorist Ray Kurzweil recognizes that many doubt this picture of explosive technological growth as too much too soon, especially given the relatively even pace of technology so far. But this "intuitive view," as Kurzweil calls it, mistakes the nonlinear nature of technological growth, which can, for example, be seen in the explosive growth of the Internet. According to Kurzweil's Law of Accelerating Returns, nanotechnology also will soon move into an explosive phase. The reason for this explosive growth phase will be the compounding of technological evolution. Because tools improve, they improve the ability to make other better tools faster, and other better and smaller tools even faster, and so on: "...each stage of evolution builds on the last stage, so the rate of progress of an evolutionary process increases at least exponentially over time."[34] Already we can see the pattern of complexity development within Moore's Law, which holds that computers double in complexity and power about every year. "Typically," writes Kurzweil, "we find that the doubling time for different measures—price-performance, bandwidth, capacity—of the capability of information technology is about one year."[35] Within the next three decades, this movement of compounding development will begin to take off in an explosive manner: "Exponential growth is seductive," writes Kurzweil, "starting out slowly and virtually unnoticeably, but beyond the knee of the curve it turns explosive and profoundly transformative."[36]

An example may clarify this view of the explosion of technology. Once the species learns how to enhance the structure of cognition with nanotechnology, then the species will possess artificially enhanced capacities of cognition. But once the species possesses artificially enhanced cognitive capacities, the species will then be better able to inquire into how cognition can further be enhanced. This increased understanding will then enable the further enhancement of the structure of cognition, and so on. What begins with one direct cognitive transformation soon compounds as cognition enters an ever-accelerating developmental cycle of enhancement. As the architecture of cognition and the body becomes increasingly artificial, humanity eventually will move beyond the primitive biological form in which consciousness is currently suspended, as Kurzweil points out in *The Singularity is Near*.

> As the nonbiological portion of our thinking begins to predominate by the end of the 2030s, we will be able to move beyond the basic architecture of the brain's neural regions. Brain implants based on massively distributed intelligent nanobots will greatly expand our memories and otherwise vastly improve all of our sensory, pattern-recognition, and cognitive abilities.[37]

For those who accept that superhumanity may emerge in at least some form (however minimal) within the next century, one commonly voiced concern regards egalitarianism. Perhaps only the wealthy will be able to engineer their germlines to enhance their future families, or enhance themselves with nanotechnology. Perhaps too a new class division will arise between the engineered and the unengineered (as Fukuyama and Kass suggest). This picture remains a possibility, but we should be careful about an assumption that equates technological resources of the past and present with technological resources of the future. Superhuman technologies may turn out to be widely available and inexpensive and enable potentially the universal transformation of the species. Drexler develops this view.

> The basic argument for low-cost production is this: Molecular manufacturing will be able to make almost anything with little labor, land, or maintenance, with high productivity, and with modest requirements for materials and energy. Its products will themselves be extremely productive, as energy producers, as materials collectors, and as manufacturing equipment. There has never been a technology with this combination of characteristics, so historical analogies must be used with care. Perhaps

the best analogy is this: Molecular manufacturing will do for matter processing what the computer has done for information processing.[38]

Kurzweil develops a similar view: "Because of the ongoing exponential
growth of price-performance, all of these technologies quickly become so
inexpensive as to become almost free."[39] Drexler and Kurzweil think of superhuman technologies not on the analogy of limited resources like coal and
oil and wood and land, but more on an analogy of access to the internet, which
is widely available and becoming increasingly available over time.

Another problem commonly raised is that superlongevity will lead to
overpopulation. Individuals will live longer and new artificial beings will also
be created who will eventually be able to copy themselves. As the growth of
technology explodes, the number of individuals will also explode. But like the
problem of egalitarianism, the problem of overpopulation may not be so problematic either. Already humanity arguably overpopulates the planet, and some
solution will ultimately be required. This solution may emerge in the form of
superhumanity because superhuman beings will not be confined to this planet.
In fact, from the perspective of superhumanity, the solar system is quite un-
derpopulated. Today billions populate the planet, but in the future trillions
may populate the solar system. This transition in the population is central to
the definition of the superhuman condition, which Nick Bostrom articulates in
"The Future of Humanity."

- Population of greater than one trillion persons
- Life expectancy greater than 500 years
- Large fraction of the population has cognitive capacities more than
  two standard deviations above the current human maximum
- Near-complete control over the sensory input, for the majority of
  people for most of the time
- Human psychological suffering becoming rare occurrence
- Any change in magnitude or profundity comparable to that of one of
  the above.[40]

For those who oppose this future of humanity, there is one standard type
of argument known as "relinquishment," which means halting inquiry into
high technology in order to halt the movement into superhumanity. The condition for halting the movement into superhumanity is the global relinquishment
of research into genetics, nanotechnology, and robotics. Global relinquishment entails a world government capable of enforcing strict and total surveillance of all inquiry into high technology. Creating a world government for
total surveillance and halting high technology in the short run is unlikely if not
practically impossible (as many point out). So, perhaps we should assume that
inquiry will continue to go on and technology will continue to alter the human

form into the future, at least in some form. I think we should probably assume, too, that no final and fixed picture of the future of the species, once it becomes superhuman, can be given (at least in the short run). The reason for this assumption is that superhuman enhancement will increase the diversity and plasticity and creativity of the human form. If we accept this general view of an open future of human transformation, then perhaps the discussion may be shifted to the transition from humanity to superhumanity. In particular, I think the same paradoxes Shusterman discusses in human self-styling may also beset the transition to superhuman self-styling.

5. Paradoxes of Superhuman Self-Styling

Once again, I think Shusterman's view seems quite open to this kind of extension of somaesthetics to superhumanism. "No longer an already attained presence," writes Shusterman, "the self becomes a path of development toward a higher ideal, and what we normally call our present selves are but completed fractions of our developmental trajectory that opens toward a superior future." Shusterman also writes that "the self's originality consists not of a fixed, ever present essence but of one's new, open-ended path of development toward higher self-achievement."[41] In superhuman self-styling, as in human self-styling, the body is "but a completed fraction" on the way to a "superior future." GNR technologies offer precisely the "developmental trajectory" and the "open-ended path" toward higher self-achievement. Given the continuity of self-transformation into the future, the same paradoxes should apply to the transition to superhumanity.

Of course, the paradoxes of human and human-to-superhuman self-styling will differ with respect to time and possibility. All self-styling is directed toward an open future at an imagined end, but superhuman self-styling is directed toward an open future that may never come. And typically the ends of human self-styling are already in view so that somaesthetic practice results in the attainment of the end. One cannot, however, practice being superhuman (not anyway in any concrete sense). So while the paradoxes of superhuman self-styling can be conceptualized in the present, they can only be lived in the future. But if superhuman self-styling does emerge, then the paradoxes of self-styling should become increasingly vivid as we approach the post-biological condition.

How then might the three paradoxes reappear in the future context of superhumanism? Recall Shusterman's first paradox: "the power of individual style lies not in its individuality but in its more-than-individual force." Approaching the superhuman condition, the individual will reshape and eventually replace the body: the biological substrate will be replaced by a silicon substrate that is stronger and more flexible and more adaptable beyond the surface of the earth. The human body is made of protein and protein breaks down too quickly and is not very viable beyond the surface of the planet. The robotics theorist Hans Moravec makes this point in *Mind Children: The Future of*

Robot and Human Intelligence: "Away from earth, protein is not an ideal material. It is stable only in a narrow temperature and pressure range, is very sensitive to radiation, and rules out many construction techniques and components."[42] The transformation beyond the protein substrate may appear to some to be too individualistic. Enhancing one's body beyond the biological integrity of the species may seem a self-absorbed project without a sense of human solidarity. But again we must keep in mind that the essence of self-transformation (in the pursuit of genius and self-realization) lies in "its more-than-individual force." The capacities of mind that the individual pursues are capacities the individual does not claim only for the self, but recognizes as distributed throughout the species. The individual seeks to realize the genius of the species by lifting contingent biological limits on mind and body to achieve an ideal that is at once individual and potentially species-wide. The ideal is individual because individuals choose to transform themselves toward particular forms. But these particular forms will also be forms in relation to other personal forms, which also aim to enhance the original cognitive and creative capacities that arise with the emergence of humanity in evolution. The ideal is potentially species-wide because (as in human self-styling) in superhuman self-styling, individual self-creation is only possible within a community of members who recognize the form of life of self-styling.

Shusterman's third paradox of self-styling will also arise within super-humanism: namely, "...that the genius of self-styling demands the patient discipline of perfectionist striving yet can come only by letting go, through leaps of self-abandon." The idea of self-abandon arises in superhumanism in at least two ways. First, the idea of self-abandon appears rather strikingly as soon as one considers the possibility of actually abandoning the biological body for an entirely new form, without knowing what exactly one will be. In abandoning the biological body, one also abandons many human activities, especially distinctly biological activities (like eating and drinking) that give life some of its meaning—again, without knowing what this will be like. There is no question (and we should not be careless in suggesting otherwise) that this loss is significant. Transforming humanity will come at the cost of redefining much of human experience. To suggest that dangers and a loss of sense of humanity might not accompany superhumanism is simply naive.

In contrast to this view, some argue that technological self-transformation will distort human gifts rather than realizing them. For example, Michael Sandel in *The Case Against Perfection* writes: "The problem with eugenics and genetic engineering is that they represent the one-sided triumph of willfulness over giftedness, of domination over reverence, of molding over beholding. ... What should be lost if biotechnology dissolved our sense of giftedness?"[43] While some technology is necessary for gift realization, too much distorts the human form: human gifts will be corrupted and many social forms will simply dissolve. "In opposing genetic enhancement," writes Sandel, "I have argued against the one-sided triumph of mastery over reverence, and have urged that we reclaim an appreciation of life as a gift."[44] I agree that some human forms will dissolve (for example, particular sports), but the gifts and capacities themselves need not dissolve. Indeed they may be far better realized in new bodies and in new social forms. Especially those gifts that are intrinsically instrumental (as a pragmatist conceives them), like cognition, creativity, and self-mastery, can only be developed by means of continuous self-transformation. Perhaps we may incorporate part of Sandel's point by recognizing that one may indeed distort one's own self-relation to one's gifts (or one's own experience of those gifts) if one self-transforms through superhumanism in a direction not pre-given by one's own unique gifts and capacities. As one becomes a superhuman other, one can only maintain the integrity of one's own form by pursuing the actualization of one's unique genius.

Shusterman's third paradox of self-styling will also arise within superhumanism: namely, "...that the genius of self-styling demands the patient discipline of perfectionist striving yet can come only by letting go, through leaps of self-abandon." The idea of self-abandon arises in superhumanism in at least two ways. First, the idea of self-abandon appears rather strikingly as soon as one considers the possibility of actually abandoning the biological body for an entirely new form, without knowing what exactly one will be. In abandoning the biological body, one also abandons many human activities, especially distinctly biological activities (like eating and drinking) that give life some of its meaning – again, without knowing what this will be like. There is no question (and we should not be careless in suggesting otherwise) that this loss is significant. Transforming humanity will come at the cost of redefining much of human experience. To suggest that dangers and a loss of sense of humanity might not accompany superhumanism is simply naive.

On the other hand, failing to transform humanity will result in the perpetuation of many of those biological dimensions of humanity that not only thwart genius and even basic cognitive development but can also distort human experience in general, for example, physical illness, cognitive disorders, unhappiness, shortness of life, and certainly death itself. In "Idea for a Universal History with a Cosmopolitan Purpose" Kant argues that only distant future generations can hope to actualize the cognitive capacities of the species, and that present individuals must fail partly for lack of longevity. The best one can do is to realize a small portion of one's gifts and then pass them on to the next generation genetically and by means of the educational shaping of the species.[45] But, Kant also thinks, if one could live hundreds of years, then perhaps one could much more fully realize one's genius. In his *Anthropology from a Pragmatic Point of View* Kant considers this perspective: "What a mass of knowledge, what discoveries of new methods would now be on hand if an Archimedes, a Newton, or a Lavoisier with their industry and talent would have been favored by Nature with hundreds of years of continuous life without the loss of vital power!"[46]

We mentioned that the idea of self-abandon arises in superhumanism in two ways. The first way is by abandoning the biological structure of the self. The second way is by abandoning oneself to the greater-than-individual genius of the species. Recall how Shusterman puts the problem: "How do we reconcile the paradox that we must push and discipline ourselves for genius but still need to 'let go' and abandon ourselves to finally achieve?" The solution, once again, is that we must "direct our earnest efforts to the point where the spontaneous, involuntary, more-than-personal forces can fruitfully be brought into play." This same solution may be seen within superhuman self-styling as well. If one pursues genius as one simultaneously and quite radically lets oneself go by means of somatic and cognitive transformation, this very letting go should be conceived as a means to perfecting the capacities of the species as a whole in a supra-individual form. To abandon oneself in superhuman self-styling is to abandon one's individual project to the experimental spirit of the species, which seeks to attain its own forms of genius within the individual and within the collective. It is also to abandon oneself to a project of self-transformation by means of technology that has been evolving for several centuries within the Enlightenment. The basic Enlightenment idea of scientific and technological progress toward the liberation of humanity from the bonds of nature toward the perfection of the mind has played an important role in the rise of the superhuman idea.

Of course, some will, rather dangerously, let themselves go without guidance by the species as a whole, and may very well encounter cognitive distortion or even somatic destruction—just as some encounter distortion or destruction in experimentally abandoning themselves in human self-styling. For example, athletics can damage one's body and even one's mind. The pursuit of artistic or cognitive genius can distort one's social relations: more than one genius has sacrificed social and cognitive stability in the pursuit of great works. So too with superhumanism, the transformation will be difficult, experimental, and certainly dangerous. And only with time and practice will the species adapt to its new forms of being.

6. Staying Human in a Superhuman World

In addition to Shusterman's three main paradoxes, a fourth paradox for self-styling arises which is unique to superhumanism. One who becomes superhuman must remain human while leaving humanity behind. The biological form of the species will be left behind, but the intersubjective social form must be maintained. The view that we can safely transcend this intersubjective normative architecture in superhumanism is misguided, as Shusterman himself points out in *Body Consciousness:*

> Despite our evolutionary progress of rational transcendence (including the technological advancements that some regard as rendering us

posthuman cyborgs), we will essentially and dependently belong to a much wider natural and social world that continues to shape the individuals we are (including our reasoning consciousness) in ways beyond the control of our will and consciousness.[47]

Many accidents of biological evolution will be removed with artifice, but the normative intersubjective architecture of the mind (which is dialogically mediated) must be maintained, if only as the condition for the possibility of any further superhuman self-transformation. For without this social integrity, the mind will not be capable of inquiring within a community of intersubjective beings into the future, and the individual will not be able to deliberate with other beings about its own self-transformation in relation to these other beings. If human beings become superhuman beings who do not recognize themselves in each other (and in humanity itself), because they have transformed themselves in too diverse and radical a way, they will not be able to form essential communicative bonds. Because the mind is somatically embodied and socially and historically distributed, superhuman beings must maintain continuity of consciousness with their own human past and with the past of the species—and they must maintain some continuity of somatic form. In the simplest terms, the basic look and experience of the face and the body will be essential to the community of superhuman beings because their historically extended minds will recognize each other and themselves in this form. The basic experience of having a body and being a body among other beings will remain a condition for continued intersubjective development. Becoming superhuman and remaining human, leaving the body and maintaining the body, changing the mind and maintaining the mind, will remain paradoxical relations for humanity as it faces its most difficult stage of development.

NOTES

1. Friedrich Nietzsche, *The Gay Science*, ed. Bernard Williams, trans. Josefine Nauckhoff (Cambridge: Cambridge University Press, 2001), pp. 163–164.
2. Richard Shusterman, "Genius and the Paradox of Self-Styling," in *Performing Live: Aesthetic Alternatives for the Ends of Art* (Ithaca: Cornell University Press, 2000), p. 212.
3. See Richard Rorty, *Contingency, Irony, and Solidarity* (Cambridge, Mass.: Cambridge University Press, 1995); and Alexander Nehamas, *Nietzsche: Life as Literature* (Cambridge: Harvard University Press, 1985), and Alexander Nehamas, *The Art of Living: Socratic Reflections from Plato to Foucault* (Berkeley: University of California Press, 2000).
4. Richard Shusterman, *Body Consciousness: A Philosophy of Mindfulness and Somaesthetics* (Cambridge: Cambridge University Press, 2008), p. 19.
5. Francis Fukuyama, *Our Posthuman Future: Consequences of the Biotechnology Revolution* (New York: Farrar, Straus and Giroux, 2002); and Leon Kass, *Life,*

Liberty and the Defense of Dignity: The Challenge for Bioethics (San Francisco: Encounter Books, 2002).

6. Jürgen Habermas, *The Future of Human Nature,* trans. Hella Beister and William Rehg (New York: Polity, 2003), p. 22.
7. Shusterman, "Genius and the Paradox of Self-Styling," p. 203.
8. *Ibid.,* p. 208.
9. G.W.F. Hegel, *Phenomenology of Spirit,* trans. Arnold V. Miller (Oxford: Oxford University Press, 1977), p. 110.
10. Shusterman, "Genius and the Paradox of Self-Styling," p. 203.
11. *Ibid.,* p. 213.
12. *Ibid.,* p. 204.
13. *Ibid.,* p. 214.
14. *Ibid.,* p. 214.
15. *Ibid.,* pp. 215–216.
16. Nietzsche, *Beyond Good and Evil,* p. 125.
17. Friedrich Nietzsche, *Human, All Too Human: A Book for Free Spirits,* trans. Reginald J. Hollingdale (Cambridge: Cambridge University Press, 1996), p. 387.
18. Shusterman, "Genius and the Paradox of Self-Styling," p. 216.
19. *Ibid.*
20. *Ibid.*
21. *Ibid.*
22. Ralph W. Emerson, *The Complete Writings of Ralph Waldo Emerson,* vol. 1 (New York: Wm. H. Wise & Co., 1929), p. 208.
23. Friedrich Nietzsche, *Thus Spoke Zarathustra,* trans. Walter Kaufmann (New York: The Modern Library, 1995), p. 12.
24. Nietzsche, *The Gay Science,* p. 247.
25. Nietzsche, *Thus Spoke Zarathustra,* p. 15.
26. Richard Shusterman, *Surface and Depth: Dialectics of Criticism and Culture* (Ithaca: Cornell University Press, 2002), p. 192.
27. John Dewey, *Experience and Nature,* in *John Dewey: The Later Works, 1925–1953,* vol. 1: 1925, ed. Jo Ann Boydston, assoc. textual editors Patricia Baysinger and Barbara Levine (Carbondale, IL: Southern Illinois University Press, 1988), p. 146.
28. Charles S. Peirce, "An Essay Toward Improving Our Reasoning in Security and in Uberty," in *The Essential Peirce,* vol. 2, ed. the Peirce Edition Project (Bloomington: Indiana University Press, 1998), p. 466.
29. Charles S. Peirce, *Collected Papers of Charles Sanders Peirce,* eds. Charles Hartshorne and Paul Weiss (Cambridge: Harvard University Press, 1965), p. 60.
30. Charles S. Peirce, "The Basis of Pragmaticism in the Normative Sciences," *in The Essential Peirce,* p. 379.
31. Richard P. Feynman, "There's Plenty of Room at the Bottom," presented December 29, 1959 to the American Physical Society at Caltech; also in *Engineering and Science* (1960), www.zyvex.com/nanotech/feynman.html.
32. Eric Drexler, *Engines of Creation: The Coming Era of Nanotechnology* (New York: Anchor Books, 1986), p. 14.
33. K. Eric Drexler, Chris Peterson, and Gayle Pergamit, *Unbounding the Future: The Nanotechnology Revolution* (New York: William Morrow and Co., Inc., 1991), p. 279.
34. Ray Kurzweil, *The Singularity is Near: When Humans Transcend Biology* (New York: Viking, 2005), p. 41.

35. *Ibid.*, p. 56.
36. *Ibid.*, p. 10.
37. *Ibid.*, p. 317.
38. Drexler, et al. *Unbounding the Future*, pp. 168–169.
39. Kurzweil, *The Singularity is Near*, p. 469.
40. Nick Bostrom, "The Future of Humanity" (2007), p. 19, www.nickbostrom.com.
41. Shusterman, "Genius and the Paradox of Self-Styling," p. 212.
42. Hans Moravec, *Mind Children: The Future of Robot and Human Intelligence* (Cambridge: Harvard University Press, 1988), p. 108.
43. Michael Sandel, *The Case Against Perfection: Ethics in the Age of Genetic Engineering* (Cambridge: Belknap Press of Harvard University Press, 2007), p. 85.
44. *Ibid.*, p. 101.
45. Immanuel Kant, "Idea for a Universal History with a Cosmopolitan Purpose," in *Kant: Political Writings,* ed. Hans Reiss, trans. Hugh B. Nisbet (Cambridge: Cambridge University Press, 1995).
46. Immanuel Kant, *Anthropology from a Pragmatic Point of View*, trans. Victor Lyle Dowdell, rev. and ed. Hans H. Rudnick (Carbondale: Southern Illinois University Press, 1978), p. 243.
47. Shusterman, *Body Consciousness,* pp. 213–214.

Part Three

SOMAESTHETICS

Nine

"BODY TROUBLE"?
SOMAESTHETICS AND FEMINISM

Monika Bokiniec

I have decided to focus my attention on one aspect of Richard Shusterman's philosophy, which is perhaps marginal for his work in general, but which I found especially interesting, namely his reading of *The Second Sex* by Simone de Beauvoir from the point of view of somaesthetics.[1] Commenting on de Beauvoir's philosophy, Shusterman indeed touched on one of the most baffling and ambiguous topics in feminist thought, namely the attitude towards the body.

At first sight, combining somaesthetics and feminism might seem to be a hazardous venture. And not because de Beauvoir never used this term, since Shusterman explains how this objection is irrelevant, as the way of thinking proposed by somaesthetics has been present in philosophical thinking for centuries, even though not by that name and largely marginalized. What is more,

> [a]s authentic living is a prime goal of existentialist ethics, one might expect Beauvoir to urge heightened attention to somatic experience, which evokes a more authentic recognition of human ambiguity, and even to recognize that such heightened body consciousness could be a useful tool for woman's liberation.[2]

What somaesthetics and feminism have in common is the fact that both fields postulate a close link between theory and practice. Also, both feminism and somaesthetics are oriented towards projective thinking, that is, towards stimulating actual, positive change. A difference may lie in the following direction: feminist projects are usually directed towards group interests, while somaesthetics concentrates on individual practices and benefits for the individual, social benefits being somewhat secondary. What is problematic is the question whether such a distinction can be made within pragmatically-oriented theories at all, but what I meant here was simply to show a different focus of those two approaches, conditioned, of course, by different assumptions. Most feminists would see the improvement of the social environment as the basis for improving an individual (woman's) life, while in somaesthetics the improvement and empowerment of individuals is a basis for creating a healthier society in general.

The body is an important topic for both. In Shusterman's somaesthetic project the attitude to the body needs revalorization in general, whereas in feminism the case is a little more problematic. Somaesthetics and at least some feminist projects have a common aim to re-orientate the philosophical focus from the abstract body as either a cultural construct or a degraded aspect of the human being (and as such, not worth in-depth philosophical attention), toward the actual body and the way it may positively influence our ability to realize a good life, including in the mental sphere.

It was noted by prominent women philosophers that women were naturalized and nature feminized, as a fact. It is worth mentioning that de Beauvoir was herself a kind of victim of symbolic association of all products of women's activity with the physiological sphere. Susan Bordo describes the reactions to publication of the English translation of *The Second Sex* in the following words:

> *Time* even headlined the review [of *The Second Sex*] with the birth announcement: 'Weight: 2 ¾ Lbs,' in one brilliant, if unconscious, stroke associating the book with the materiality of the body, the heavy immanence that is woman …, and woman's 'natural' role of child bearer. And so de Beauvoir, that most unnatural of creatures, a woman philosopher, was put in her rightful place.[3]

However, there is an essential disagreement within feminism over the project of dealing with this fact: some feminist projects advocate the theoretical dissociation of women from nature and the physical sphere of their existence; others propose to reinforce this connection and reverse the hierarchy of the physical and psychological spheres. Sherry Ortner sees the basis for this process of naturalization of women in the actual physiological composition of women:

> It is simply a fact that proportionately more of woman's body space, for a greater percentage of her lifetime, and at some—sometimes great— cost to her personal health, strength, and general stability, is taken up by natural processes surrounding the reproduction of the species.[4]

This simple physiological fact resulted in "the coding of femininity with corporality" (in Elizabeth Grosz's words[5]) and has served as a justification of the social, political and economical oppression of women.

In her essay "Woman as Body" Elizabeth Spelman

describes a phenomenon which may serve here as a background for Shusterman's proposition and will perhaps help to emphasize the contribution that the somaesthetic project may make to feminism. Spelman stresses the intimate connection that exists between the philosophical attitude towards the body and that towards women. It is, of course, due to the fact that the philosopher's attitude towards the body influences this person's epistemological, anthropological, and ethical concepts.[6] Most prominent philosophical traditions (with few exceptions), according to Spelman's analyses, can be described as "somatophobic," that is, they rest on the body/mind distinction, while at the same time disregarding the physical aspect of human existence as lower than the spiritual or intellectual one, and ascribe a privileged position to reason and mind. (It should be stressed that by dualism she does not mean only the view that there are separate substances but also the approach in which the physical and psychological aspects of one person are distinguished.[7]) If this philosophical presupposition is further combined with naturalization of women as closer to nature and more bound by their physiology than men, it will provide a philosophical justification for denigration not only of women, but also of children, animals, slaves, etc.

What Spelman suggests is especially dangerous and disturbing is the fact that many feminist philosophers, especially classical ones, adopt this "somatophobic" perspective in their own theories. As she puts it:

> various versions of women's liberation may themselves rest on the very assumptions that have informed the depreciation and degradation of women.... Those assumptions are that we must distinguish between soul and body, and that the physical part of our existence is to be devalued in comparison to mental.[8]

One of the examples she discusses is Simone de Beauvoir's philosophical views on the existential condition and emancipation of women. As Spelman observes: "De Beauvoir says that this attitude toward corporality has informed men's oppression of women, and yet her directions for women seem to be informed by just the same attitude."[9] Another example is Shulamith Firestone, who, on the one hand, criticizes the fact that men impose the beauty myth on women, and women torture their bodies (and, it should be added, their psyche) to fit into this imposed ideal, but on the other hand, describes pregnancy and childbearing as "deformation" of her body.[10] This leads Spelman to the conclusion that, if her initial statement (that from philosophical dualism combined with devaluation of the corporal aspect of human beings and identification of women with corporality follows the economic, social and political oppression of women) is correct, then it would mean that by adopting this view feminist theory is going down a blind alley, because it is tantamount to admitting that "men ... have been right all along,"[11] which paradoxically would be a justification of the very oppression feminists supposedly advocate against. This line of criticism towards the emancipatory projects of early stages of feminist theory, that is, based on adopting the same perspective that initially resulted in the oppression of women, may be put in a wider context of criticism of the Enlightenment concept of emancipation with its universalized reason, which, when applied to women, in short, welcomed them to participate in the public sphere and to engage in social or political life as long as they lived up to the universal ideal of a human being constructed in masculine terms. This is, for example, the line of criticism of postmodernist feminists against Mill's idea of the emancipation of women.

There exist feminist projects that try to demonstrate that it is not necessary to perceive the body/mind distinction as denigrating for women. They
recognize that it has been so historically and it was often politicized, but the
aim of feminism should be to change the interpretation of this distinction.
Adrienne Rich's project might serve as an example. But, as Spelman pointedly observes, the somatophobic attitude usually adopted by "classical" feminists leaves us with the impression "that indeed what women's liberation
ultimately means is liberation from our bodies."[12] This association of freedom
with being free from necessity in general, and the necessities of the body in
particular, is one of the limitations of classical feminism, which a somaesthetic approach may help to overcome.

In his essay Shusterman uses the classic feminist text—*The Second
Sex*—for a double purpose: (1) to find out what somaesthetics can learn from
Simone de Beauvoir: "Because body issues have always been central to feminism, I realized that feminist philosophy had a great deal to contribute to
somaesthetics and could do so from a perspective that my own male subject
position can hardly inhabit"[13]; and (2) to acknowledge what feminism, founded in large part on this classic book, can gain from somaesthetics .

He begins with explaining his project of somaesthetics and its fields. For
his analysis of de Beauvoir one distinction within somaesthetics is of special
importance: a distinction between representational somaesthetics, oriented
towards external appearance and concerned with the body's surface forms, on
the one hand, and experiential disciplines, oriented towards inner experience
aimed "to make the quality of our somatic experience more satisfying and also
to make it more acutely perceptive,"[14] on the other. A third category is also
distinguished: performative somaesthetics, focusing on building strength,
health, or skill.[15] "Feminists," states Shusterman, "...should be especially
sympathetic to experiential somaesthetics because it resists our culture's obsession with the representational domain of the objectifying gaze and can
offer an enriching alternative to specular body pleasures."[16]

As to his reading of de Beauvoir's classic text, Shusterman's starting point
is an observation which he describes as "strikingly ambiguous and paradoxical"
—the observation that although de Beauvoir's analysis and diagnosis of the
situation of women should encourage somaesthetic practices in the process of
emancipation, it seems that when it comes to the positive project, those practices
are explicitly excluded by her own words. To quote Shusterman:

> Beauvoir ultimately seems very critical of the basic approach of somaes-
> thetics as a tool for women's liberation, suggesting that an intensified
> focus on body cultivation is a distracting hindrance to women's progress
> toward greater liberation and well-being.[17]

In another part of the text we find the same observation:

Though her key arguments to explain the distinctive situation, sensuality, and oppressed status of women clearly imply the need for somaesthetics' potential for transformative liberation, Beauvoir persistently warns against dangers implicit in the sort of programmatic attention to the body that somaesthetics advocates, dangers that threaten to further enslave women in their oppressed condition of objecthood and immanence.[18]

In view of Spelman's account of how a somatophobic philosophical perspective initially diagnosed as responsible for the oppression of women is adopted by most classical feminist theories, this paradox seems more understandable.

According to Shusterman (and he is by no means alone in this interpretation), de Beauvoir's approach to woman's body is rooted in a dualistic metaphysics that she readily and unquestionably accepts, but this is not the only source of her theory. Shusterman notes that actually two different approaches to the body operate simultaneously in de Beauvoir's philosophical work. One is based on Merleau-Ponty's phenomenology: the body as a mode of being in the world and an instrument to experience the world. The other one—more persistent, but more harmful as well—is a Sartrean concept of the body as mere flesh, passive object. Therefore, Shusterman argues, metaphysical dualism is not enough to explain de Beauvoir's attitude to the body, especially woman's body, but has to be supplemented with the twofold approach to the body itself within de Beauvoir's work:

> In the case of Beauvoir, this asymmetry [of attention to mind and body] cannot be explained as merely a result of the dualistic mind-body hierarchy that so many philosophers inherit from Plato and Descartes. For Beauvoir clearly rejects such a simplistic dualism in order to affirm the ambiguity of the body as subjectivity and as object. Her worry about intensified attention to bodily feelings is better explained by the fact that the body symbolizes woman's inferior status (under patriarchy) as mere passivity or flesh, as a mere tool of natural reproduction and a mere object of man's desire.[19]

As a result, we receive a vision of emancipation described by another harsh critic of de Beauvoir, Sylviane Agacinski, in the following words: "freedom extolled by the philosopher is paid for by an absurd denial of nature, of maternity, and of feminine body in general."[20] How does de Beauvoir explain and motivate her position?

De Beauvoir wanted to uncover the cultural myths about women as mysterious and emotional beings. She wanted to reveal the way that women are trapped in social institutions and structures that are not theirs and that work against them. What is even worse, this cultural myth of a mysterious, irrational human "Other" is internalized by women and recognized as being rooted in and justified by precisely their biological or physiological construction. From

this perspective it seems that de Beauvoir's critical approach can be described
not as an essentialist or naturalistic, but rather as a biologistic one, if we understand these terms, after Elizabeth Grosz, in the following way:

> Essentialism is best understood as the postulation of a fixed essence, un-
> changed historically or culturally. ... Biologism is the postulation of a bi-
> ological universality, which is used to explain cultural and behavioral
> characteristics; and naturalism ... invokes some kind of nature—whether
> God-given, cultural or biological—to justify its universalist assertions.[21]

However, as de Beauvoir points out, biological facts do not have axiological value as such—their value is a social construct. Women are taught to
identify with their body and, in turn, perceive their body as a passive and
weak object. De Beauvoir describes women as physically weak, and shows
how lack of physical power reinforces further psychological and social weakness. Exactly at this moment of her argument Shusterman finds a starting
point for further argumentation of the kind that somaesthetics would provide;
but of course, in de Beauvoir's perspective that cannot be, because it would
mean going back to the body and finding the source of oppression in biology,
while it is not supposed to be in biology but its social interpretation. Still,
Shusterman advances his idea of the possibility for somaesthetics to take part
in emancipatory processes by applying somaesthetic techniques in order to
transcend the physical obstacles and therefore social and physical weakness
that worsen women's situation. So on this point I would say that de Beauvoir
is wrong and self-contradictory and Shusterman is right and consistent.

On the other hand, de Beauvoir believes that a woman who concentrates
on her body, which is always and necessarily imperfect from the point of view
of cultural requirements and ideals, will not develop her other skills and will
not engage meaningfully in the public sphere of social practice. It seems that
de Beauvoir might be right in her description of how women are forced by an
oppressive culture to devote so much time, effort and financial resources to
their bodies in order to fit into the sexual ideal, that there are no resources left
to engage into public life.[22] As she further observes: "In so far as a woman
wishes to be a woman, her independent status gives rise to an inferiority complex: on the other hand, her femininity makes her doubtful of her professional
career."[23] She will be passive and submissive, and will position herself as an
object of male gaze and male desire. But, if it is true that biological facts do not
have axiological value as such, but that this value is socially constructed, then
Shusterman is actually consistent with de Beauvoir's ideas when he writes:

> A creature whose life and bodily experience are shaped not merely by bi-
> ology, but by the changing historical situations in which she exists, woman
> is also an existent who can act to transcend and transform her initial situa-

tion. So the most important question about woman and her body is not what she historically or biologically is but what she can become.[24]

And this is the point at which somaesthetics should work. This sounds very optimistic and promising for women, but, again, there is not much that can be done about biological facts themselves.

In this context I think it might be instructive to refer to Sylviane Agacinski's analysis of de Beauvoir. She acutely demonstrates that there is in fact a double trap in de Beauvoir's thinking: one is based on historical and social conditions and relations of power of which womanhood is the product, and this one is expressed by her famous statement: One is not born, but rather becomes, a woman. However, the other trap observed by Agacinski is more dangerous:

> [A woman] is a *biologically trapped* being, above all a victim of her place in a species that destines her to fertility and procreation and thus dooms her to passivity.... the fabricated and alienated woman is the woman who remains in her *natural* alienation. In reflecting on this biological destiny she rejects, Simone de Beauvoir might just as well have said: *one does not become a woman, one remains woman.*[25]

If we continue this line of thinking about women and their bodies, it appears that it is not woman's physical weakness that is a problem, but its social valuation. When we direct our efforts to strengthening our body and to overcoming the weakness and passivity, we might be, paradoxically, strengthening the disadvantageous social interpretation of the woman's body, and so from the point of view of de Beauvoir this must be counterproductive, because the whole project of somaesthetics would be directed against a false enemy: the enemy is not the actual weakness and passivity of the woman's body, because even if strengthened and active it still remains the woman's body, trapped (as Agacinski wants it) in its biology. The real enemy would be the social structure and institutions that attribute negative value to it. At this point somaesthetics would not have much to say. Shusterman notices this problem and identifies a possible obstacle to somaesthetics in de Beauvoir's work in the idea that it is the collective situation that has to be changed, and not individual practices. But he thinks, and probably rightly, that it is precisely individual practices that might help to change the collective situation. As he puts it:

> There is no reason why individual efforts of consciousness-raising and empowerment through somaesthetics (especially when undertaken with an awareness of the wider social contexts that structure one's bodily life) cannot fruitfully contribute to the larger political struggles in which women are engaged and whose results will shape the somaesthetic experience of women in the future.[26]

Taking all this into account, Shusterman's application of somaesthetics to the feminist project of emancipation is definitely interesting and worth further elaboration, because it re-interprets the question of the complex and multifarious relations between feminism and women's bodies and this is something that requires constant rethinking within changing cultural and theoretical contexts. More than that, the general project of somaesthetics, with its postulate of re-evaluation of the human, individual body and its role in living a fulfilled life, is directed against the somatophobia characteristic of most influential philosophical traditions. As we have noted, the somatophobic approach, both in theory and in practice, works against women, so any effort to change that, even if not expressed explicitly (as in the case of somaesthetics), should be welcomed in the search for emancipatory perspectives.

The fact is, we do not know whether biological differences actually create other (psychological, social, intellectual etc.) differences between the sexes, or whether it is the other way around. But we can speculate about practical consequences of both hypotheses. It seems to me that in a way this is something that Shusterman is trying to do by his re-interpretation of *The Second Sex*. However, at the same time, we have to be aware that the "biological hypothesis," which somaesthetics seems to be favoring, has, at least from the historical perspective, worked against women, against equality of the sexes. Association of women with their body has been used against women at least since Aristotle. As Sylviane Agacinski, among others, observes, a woman is not "...absolutely *other* than man, no: rather always *less* 'man' than him, and thus less *human*. She has always been in the *lesser* position: *socially, naturally*, and even *ontologically*."[27]

So the real question, when we come down to the level of the "biology-culture" issue, is whether we should think in terms of sexual difference at all, or rather abandon this dualistic way of thinking about the sexes. In a 1979 interview, de Beauvoir stated:

> it comes to playing man's game to say that women are essentially different from the man. There exists a biological difference, but this difference is not the foundation for the sociological difference.[28]

Therefore, in the project of emancipation the body and biological difference should never be a focal point; this is in fact a very androcentric approach. As Agacinski observed,

> ... not only does the author of *The Second Sex* fail to criticize the classic description of sexual difference but she sustains it *as is*, as if woman had, logically in the end, suffered from a natural handicap linked to her body....[29]

It is true that de Beauvoir never questioned this "man's game"; she never questioned the passivity/activity opposition and its relation to freedom and the body. I think that, paradoxically, somaesthetics (if abused) might find itself in the same danger—the danger of forgetting the difference. And isn't that exactly "playing the man's game"? If we abandon thinking in terms of sexual difference, we go back to the abstract man, who is not sexless. We go back to the male norm and female "other."

So first we should find an answer to three questions: should we think of women's emancipation in terms of difference, or not? If so, what are the bases for this difference—biological or cultural? And then, are they changeable and contingent or permanent and constant? Only then can we discuss the possible benefit of somaesthetic practices and techniques for woman's emancipation. It seems to me that the paradox observed by Shusterman, that I mentioned earlier, has its source in different answers to these questions in de Beauvoir's and the somaesthetic approach.

One of de Beauvoir's famous statements is that "freedom will never be given; it will always have to be won."[30] And it has to be won also through the body, because this is how we exist in the world. As Shusterman claims:

> ...performative-representational somaesthetic activities oriented toward displaying power, skill, and an attractively dynamic self-presentation should promote de Beauvoir's goal of promoting women's confidence for engaging in greater action in the world.... somaesthetic's cultivation of the body should at least be endorsed for its contribution as a useful (though certainly not the only useful) means.[31]

Therefore, it seems to me that Shusterman's contribution may be said to overcome the theoretical obstacle connected with associating women with their bodies, because by re-evaluating the body he reconstructs the notion of freedom that I earlier pointed to as linked with being free from the necessities of the body in particular. As Andrea Dworkin claimed, standards of beauty and femininity are precisely the borders of woman's freedom: "In culture not one part of a woman's body is left untouched, unaltered. No feature of or extremity is spared the art, or pain, of improvement."[32] Therefore, freedom understood in these terms is much more difficult to achieve for women. In the case of Shusterman's proposal of somaesthetics the relation between body and freedom changes significantly: freedom to do what one wants because the empowered/powerful body allows it. I strongly believe that this reformulation of freedom is the most important contribution that somaesthetics might make to feminism. Gustavo Guerra commented on the somaesthetic project in the following way: "...not only does a heightened awareness create healthier individuals, who in turn produce an overall healthier society, but it also empowers the individuals to learn more about themselves and who they are."[33] In reference to women, it might be suggested that physical empowerment, and in-depth knowledge and awareness of the way a woman's body functions, may facilitate realizing the aim of making women's bodies the active subjects of politics, not its passive objects.

NOTES

1. Richard Shusterman, "Somaesthetics and *The Second Sex*: A Pragmatist Reading of a Feminist Classic," *Hypatia*, 18:4 (Fall 2003), pp. 106-136.
2. *Ibid.*, p. 126.
3. Susan Bordo, "The Feminist as the Other," in *Philosophy in a Feminist Voice: Critiques and Reconstructions*, ed. Janet A. Kourany (Princeton: Princeton University Press, 1997), p. 298.
4. Sherry B. Ortner, "Is Female to Male as Nature Is to Culture?" in *Woman, Culture and Society*, eds. Michelle Zimbalist Rosaldo and Louise Lamphere (Stanford, CA: Stanford University Press, 1974), p. 75.
5. Elizabeth Grosz, *Volatile Bodies: Toward a Corporeal Feminism* (Sidney: Allen and Unwin, 1994), p. 14.
6. Elizabeth V. Spelman, "Woman as Body: Ancient and Contemporary Views," *Feminist Studies*, 8:1 (Spring, 1982), p. 110.
7. *Ibid.*, 34, p. 131n34.
8. *Ibid.*, p. 125.
9. *Ibid.*, p. 121.
10. *Ibid.*, p. 123.
11. *Ibid.*
12. Spelman, "Woman as Body," p. 124.
13. Shusterman, "Somaesthetics and *The Second Sex*," p. 107.
14. *Ibid.*, p. 114.
15. *Ibid.*
16. *Ibid.*, p. 123.
17. *Ibid.*, p. 115.
18. *Ibid.*, p. 107.
19. *Ibid.*, p. 127.
20. Sylviane Agacinski, *Parity of the Sexes*, trans. Lisa Walsh (New York: Columbia University Press, 2001), p. 42.
21. Grosz, *Volatile Bodies*, p. 212.
22. See Simone de Beauvoir, *The Second Sex*, trans. Howard Madison Parshley (London: Vintage, 1997), pp. 698–710.
23. *Ibid.*, p. 708.
24. Shusterman, "Somaesthetics and *The Second Sex*," p. 117.
25. Agacinski, *Parity of the Sexes*, pp. 54–55.
26. Shusterman, "Somaesthetics and *The Second Sex*," p. 130.
27. Agacinski, *Parity of the Sexes*, p. 16.
28. Margaret A. Simons, Jessica Benjamin, "S. de Beauvoir: An Interview," *Feminist Studies*, 5:2 (Summer 1979), p. 343.
29. Agacinski, *Parity of the Sexes*, p. 43.
30. Simone de Beauvoir, *The Ethics of Ambiguity*, trans. Bernard Frechtman (New York: Philosophical Library, 1948), p. 119.
31. Shusterman, "Somaesthetics and *The Second Sex*," p. 122.
32. Andrea Dworkin, *Woman-Hating*, quoted in Bordo, "The Feminist as the Other," p. 299.
33. Gustavo Guerra, "Practicing Pragmatism: Richard Shusterman's Unbound Philosophy," *Journal of Aesthetic Education*, 36:4 (Winter, 2002), p. 81.

Ten

AESTHETICS AND CORPORAL VALUES

Krzysztof Piotr Skowroński

We can find many reasons why the human body should be considered in the realm of aesthetics, more than it has been in the humanistic tradition of the West. If we assume today's perspective and examine this juncture from a sociological point of view, we will realize the immense popularity of the cultivation and perfection of the body, by means of: bodily hygiene (for example, cosmetics, surgery aesthetics, and diet); bodily beautification (for example, hair styling, make up, adhesive nails, tattoos, and piercing); physical exercises (for example, jogging, fitness, and body building); body language (for example, smiling, friendly gestures, and others); and last but not least, fashion. From an axiological point of view, we can witness the present emancipation of the human body, along with a focus on hedonistic, intellectual, and spiritual potentialities. From a cultural point of view, we can see, especially since the Sexual Revolution of the late 1960s, a de-tabooization of sexuality and an eroticization of life by means of the hardly restricted presence of: nudity on beaches and at topless swimming-pools; the bikini-size costumes of sportswomen at sports contests; erotic clubs; pornography; and nudity in films and tabloids, on the Internet, and in advertisements, and commercial presentations.

Anthropologically, we can detect the techniques of the mass media in their grand-scale promotion of beautiful models of the female body. For example, we can see this promotion in Miss World Contests, by the Barbie doll, by movie stars and female television announcers. In all cases, women appear as slim, tall, long-legged, white-toothed, and smiling. From an epistemological point of view, we can examine the increase of bodily experiences generated by means of elevating corporal sensitivity in different ways, for instance in new types of experience (for example, in 3D cinemas and extreme sports) or in drug use. Finally, from a practical point of view, we can witness a boom in active models for everyday living. Here, the idea of self-creation consists, to a large degree, in working towards an attractive, strong, and healthy shape of our bodies.

At this point let me explain that, in my view, we can theoretically justify discussing corporal values by indicating that the human body can be seen as something in which, and by which, the realization of values is possible. We can discuss values and evaluations every time we deal with anything that can be, theoretically, made better or worse. More exactly, we deal with values whenever we perceive agents, living bodies, things (objects), states of things (facts and situations), and/or actions (deeds and activities) as: successful or unsuccessful, more or less appropriate, satisfactory or unsatisfactory to a greater or lesser number of people, or such that should or should not be like this or like that. We deal with values, in the context of the body, whenever we see the body as a place where latent potentialities can be actualized and developed, or when we see the body as a necessary tool (or set of tools) for the actualization of potentialities outside of the body itself (whether agents, other bodies, things, states of things, and/or actions). Ontologically, this understanding of the body does not necessarily imply an intrinsic or objective value of the body or its potentialities. Instead, it means that the body and its potentialities can be seen as the locus, or area, where greater or lesser values can be attained and cultivated. This depends upon the criterion or criteria that has or have previously been presupposed as the basis for the evaluation. The whole complexity of the problem of the basis for evaluation transcends aesthetics, and encroaches on moral, religious, economic, social, and political issues.

I wish to expand Aristotle's claim that ethics is a part of politics, into "aesthetics also is a part of politics,"[1] which also includes the human body. Namely, politics deserves a broader meaning, in a more profound context, since it takes place everywhere we deal with people, institutions, and centers of power exercising their might upon other people and other institutions. It influences their views, their behaviors, and their hierarchies of values. With this in mind, we can claim that the most intimate behaviors and the most personal impressions can be influenced, dominated, and regulated by external factors, such as: the system of education; the type of social hierarchy; the role of parents in the family; the scope of individual freedom; the threat of social expulsion for violating accepted behaviors; and so on.

These days, we take it for granted that the junction between aesthetics and the human body should be more and more explored in different aspects. All efforts in this direction, if profound and systematic, should be appreciated. For example, Richard Shusterman's idea of somaesthetics, as stated in "Somaesthetics and the Body/Media issue," introduces a discipline that deals with the betterment of corporal positive experience, in the context of sensorial and aesthetic perception, which makes life better.[2] I share his conviction about the significance of the practical dimension of body consciousness, and his reservations about the significance of purely theoretical speculations on the body-mind/soul problem. In the same way, I admire the importance that he places on the logic of gradation as a better way of approaching things than through categorical differentiations.

Also, I appreciate his idea of thinking about ethics and aesthetics in a more mutually related way, instead of treating them as separate and autonomous. I share his concern about the axiological dimension of the body, or the melioration and development of corporal potentialities. I also share his respect for the Epicureans, the Stoics, the Cynics, Michel de Montaigne, Henry David Thoreau, and Michel Foucault. We appreciate these individuals as philosophers, not professors of philosophy, and the attention they paid to non-discursive experience. I also agree with him regarding the significance of aesthetic phenomena commonly classified as low culture. As he writes about black music, such as rap and hip-hop, I wonder whether we could explore the specificity of, say, the Polish punk movement during the Communist regime as an expression of social tensions. Most of all, I appreciate Shusterman's efforts to show the theoretical and practical dimensions of the quality of life, and the ways to increase this quality here and now. Also, to some extent, I appreciate his construction of a postmodern type of auto-narration about life and its meaning.

However, I perceive some limits in Shusterman's published works. Shusterman and I agreed during a public discussion that took place during a conference devoted to his output, *Between Politics and Aesthetics; Richard Shusterman's Pragmatism* (Wrocław, Poland, March 8, 2008), that his published works do not present, for obvious reasons, the whole spectrum of his ideas. Accordingly, my interpretation refers only to his published works, instead of to what he may think about different issues. By "limits" in his published works, I mean three things: firstly, he writes more about troubled sexuality (homosexuality and sadomasochism), than about more "accessible" and practicable issues such as nudity, eroticism, and sexuality in general; secondly, he writes more about sophisticated techniques of breathing, than about physical exercises and non-professional sports in general; and thirdly, he writes more about particular drugs in Foucault, than about drugs, wine and spirits in general. The consequence of Shusterman's philosophical or somaesthetic message is, as I understand it, a promotion of: a "reasonable" or "controlled" or "limited" culture of nudity and sex; a culture of sports; and a culture of drinking. He does not explicitly promote these things, and I suspect that the moralistic restrictions of his cultural background (Jewish, American, and intellectual) might have influenced this restraint, although I am unable to judge this definitely. At any rate, my question is as follows: if somaesthetics is a discipline that deals with the body as sensorial and aesthetic perception (*aisthesis*), why not embrace all that could make for a richer, more profound, healthier, and happier life, including sex and wine?

I am also concerned by Shusterman's emphasis upon the specificity of philosophical life and its privileged role in the context of somaesthetics. I have a problem with delineating the confines of philosophical life and contrasting it with non-philosophical life (artistic, spiritual, scientific, political, etc.). Shusterman's message, especially in *Practicing Philosophy: Pragmatism and the Philosophical Life*, although interesting and worthy of analysis, appears "sectarian," if such a word can be used in this case. His message manifests something that I would call "philosophical partisanship," which I deem to be abortive or unsuccessful. I view it as abortive, because philosophers are no more predisposed than any other professional group to deal with corporal values in a special way. I believe that the perfunctory observation of this professional group can confirm that.

An approach towards corporal values, in their complexity and variety, can be worked out and cultivated by individuals irrespective of their professional affiliation, although, I must admit, the self-image of a given professional group, no matter how illusory, is a crucial attempt to elevate the meaning of the group, give it unity, and assume a special role in society. These attempts, in the context of the body, are made by priests (with their idea of the renunciation of corporal pleasures), mystics (claiming to be able to go through corporal obstacles), intellectuals (giving priority to reason over the flesh), sportsmen (with the idea of corporal perfectionism), soldiers (cultivating toughness), Yogis (cultivating corporal perseverance), karate masters (boasting of their staying power), and many others. It should be noted that philosophers have profoundly and systematically studied and articulated different theoretical models for a good life. Yet this does not mean that philosophers explore this issue better than non-philosophers, or that philosophers are happier and live better lives than non-philosophers.

Living in a typically gigantic Eastern European post-Communist housing estate, I often wonder how many unknown and unheard-of heroic actions and beautiful lives hide behind the windows of ten-story blocks of flats. I wonder how philosophers have created a self-image by referring constantly to the figure of Socrates, who lived twenty-five centuries ago, while failing to see the Socrateses in their own vicinity. For these and other reasons, I avoid any reference to the philosophical life. Instead, I treat the problem of somaesthetics in a more general context. Also, I would like to suggest some further developments, although I am unsure whether Shusterman would see them as acceptable. Three of these developments refer directly to a proposal put forward by Shusterman. Two other developments come from the Polish avant-garde writers Witkacy (Stanisław Ignacy Witkiewicz) and Witold Gombrowicz, who, in my view, are representatives of somaesthetics on Polish soil for two reasons: firstly, they stressed the significance of gestures, facial expressions, and corporal deformations in articulations of values; and secondly, they tried to unify life with philosophy and the arts.

The idea of somaesthetics is quite risky in one respect. Namely, talking about the body in an aesthetic context must, willy-nilly, lead us to confront controversial issues (such as nudism, eroticism, sexual promiscuity, and pornography) related to the beauty of the body and the intensification of corporal experience. In this respect, we should congratulate Shusterman for his intellectual courage, although I am unsure whether he has fully met these challenges. He does promote these (or some of these) controversial issues, but he does not write about them much. Yet, if we assume the principles of somaesthetics, we can see the body as a source for exploring impressions; as a seat of values to be actualized; as a vital site for experience; as a fertile field for the enrichment of aesthetic experience; and as an area for self-realization.

The body appears here as the center of somaesthetic experience. It is not merely an object to be used and, perhaps, abused as claimed by the moralists protesting against the objectification of body theory. For example, the idea of nudism, as I understand its promoters, attempts to eliminate conventional obstacles and to stimulate corporal sensitivity to better feel the omnipresent beauty of nature. As regards sexuality, we deal with the attractions of the body in aesthetic, emotional, cognitive, and intimate dimensions. These dimensions differ from mere copulation, and differ completely from rape and other forms of sexual abuse, including child pornography. In my opinion, the development of different sexual techniques, the perfection of love affair activities, the stimulation of emotions in lovers, and the cumulating experience can lead to the aims proposed by somaesthetics, with the conditions that the activities are carried out consciously, with consent, care, respect, and affection.

Drinking presents a similar situation. I would like to indicate, at the beginning, that by "drinking" I mean "the culture of drinking," or a moderated stimulation of the senses by means of tasting a beverage. In this respect, moderate amounts of high quality wine would be the best option, instead of the unfortunate intoxication of organisms that is practiced in various quarters. When consumed appropriately (in form, amount, and circumstances), alcohol excites the senses, animates the imagination, energizes the will, enlivens social relations, and sophisticates the sense of taste. I suspect that the danger of influencing volition and clarity of speculative powers, in a state of alcoholic excitement, is the main reason why thinkers have some reservations about wine and other beverages in the context of philosophy. This, however, does not explain why they tolerate other types of excitement, which no less influence volition and mind. For example, they tolerate love, happiness, unhappiness, and despair. There even exist philosophical movements, like existentialism, which emphasize the special role of extreme states, especially despair, both in life and in philosophy.

In the third example, non-professional sports in daily life, the perfective dimension of non-professional sports (stressed in the idea of the modern Olympic Games re-animated by Baron Pierre de Coubertin) strongly refers to the Greek idea of *kalokagathia*. This idea is the key issue for those, like me, who sympathize with the essential message of Olympicism or the current philosophy of the Olympiad. At the same time, we can wonder why Shusterman emphasizes two or three disciplines (or somatic techniques), which in his view are better than so many other ways of improving the quality of the corporal condition and the corporal consciousness. I confess that I might be slightly prejudiced since for over twenty-five years I have been a sportsman. Yet this long experience (both as a practitioner and instructor) has revealed that with few exceptions (ideological, sectarian, and mercantile) there exist no reasons to present an essential difference between particular disciplines (in sports that engage the exercises of the entire body, instead of its particular parts and functions, like chess, bridge, car-driving, golf, parachuting, etc.), as regards the overall condition of the body.

In my view, we cannot separate this or that discipline. We cannot elevate some techniques (for instance, breathing techniques, yoga, and the martial arts) over others (for instance, cross country running, gymnastics, swimming, athletics, dancing, and boxing). Also, I believe that it is wrong to claim that students of, say, yoga are more conscious about their body than students of, say, gymnastics. Instead, the real difference is whether we exercise actively and regularly (instead of sporadically), correctly (practicing under a good instructor instead of a bad one), consciously (instead of mechanically), systematically (with daily and weekly routine), comprehensively (for example, under dietetic regime, with no addictions), and suitably to our predispositions (mental, physical, and emotional). Instead of promoting certain disciplines and techniques, I would prefer an increase in the role of non-professional sports in everyday life, in general, along with its necessary ingredients. These ingredients include systematicity, discipline, dedication, and a modicum of technical, medical, and philosophical reflection in order to gain a deeper insight into what one practices.

Next, I propose that we briefly consider another dimension of somaesthetics, suggested by the most eminent representative of the avant-garde in Poland, Witkacy (Stanisław I. Witkiewicz). He examined what I call "private imagination," illustrated by the corporal deformation manifested in his arts. I wish to juxtapose Witkacy, by means of the term "private imagination," with Dewey's, and perhaps Shusterman's, ideas relating to the individual and the community. Namely, Witkacy has a catastrophic vision of the future due to his fear that mass culture will kill the individual spontaneity and spiritual singularity of each and every particular member of society by imposing more and more uniform norms, standards, and hierarchies of values. He articulated this fear in his art (especially in his painting) and also in his life (in which he provoked strange situations) by means of corporal deformities, pulling faces, changing countenance, suggestive facial expressions, manipulating visages, stressing the role of the look, assuming this or that posture, etc. If we agree that the term "form" means, among other things, rule, order, definition, shape, and regularity, then "de-formation" would mean a lack of rules, a rejection of an accepted definition, and a search for a new shape. In the context of corporal values, we will have a strong desire to construct or re-construct the self-image. Witkacy's aesthetics of deformation aimed to detect the potentialities of the body, including its dynamic plasticity and flexibility, in assuming different images in different social and political contexts.

Similar techniques, although used for different aims, appear in the philosophical literature of Witkacy's friend Gombrowicz, who wanted to show the crucial and conquering role of somatic aesthetics in inter-human relations. I suspect that we can see this in one of the issues that makes him so different from Shusterman, who in the last sentences of *Practicing Philosophy* claims that we do not have to deal with aesthetic auto-creation if we do not want to. In Gombrowicz, we must deal with it, and our only choice consists in striving to assume this or that form of self-image. For example, he preferred the term "mug" to "face," to express the power of the social image imposed upon each of us by others and by us upon others, at the cost of losing our face even in privacy when we deal with a mug or image of ourselves instead of the genuine expression As he explains in *Ferdydurke*, "[t]here is no escape from the mug, other than into another mug."[3] As an image creation strategy to produce one's mug, instead of waiting for one to be imposed, Gombrowicz practiced auto-narration in his diaries. They begin with a famous declaration of their main theme:

Monday
Me.
Tuesday
Me.
Wednesday
Me.
Thursday
Me.[4]

Let me conclude by stating that Shusterman follows the great masters of pragmatism, James and Dewey, in their anthropocentrism and focus on human bodies. The beauty of non-human bodies, both living (for instance, highly-developed Bonobo chimps) and non-living (for instance, the celestial sphere), awaits philosophical exploration.[5]

NOTES

1. Aristotle, *Metaphysics*, trans. William D. Ross. *The Internet Classics Archive.* URL= http://classics.mit.edu/Aristotle/metaphysics.html, 1094a–1095a.
2. Cf. Richard Shusterman, *O sztuce i życiu. Od poetyki hip-hopu do filozofii somatycznej* [On Art and Life. From the Poetics of Hip-Hop to Somatic Philosophy], trans. Wojciech Małecki (Wrocław: Atla 2, 2007), p. 75.
3. Witold Gombrowicz, *Ferdydurke*, trans. Danuta Burchardt (New Haven: Yale University Press, 2000), p. 281.
4. Witold Gombrowicz, *Dziennik* [Diary] *1953–1956* (Kraków: Wydawnictwo Literackie, 1989), p. 9.
5. A version of the present chapter was published in: Krzysztof Skowronski, *Values and Powers. Re-reading the Philosophical Tradition of American Pragmatism* (Amsterdam-New York: Rodopi, 2009).

Eleven

SAMPLING (NO)BODY

Robert Dobrowolski

The phenomenon of increasing aestheticization of contemporary culture has led to heated arguments between advocates of the autonomy of reason and those who perceive the chance for its salvation in submitting it to aesthetic treatment. With few mediators in this strongly polarized debate, one voice that deserves special attention is that of Richard Shusterman, who, standing on the ground of pragmatic philosophy, investigates the possible advantages of those opposing viewpoints for our individual and social life, showing at the same time the possibilities for their increased usefulness owing to experience-based revisions and transformations. The survivors from the clash of these competing claims with the demands of everyday practice would be those that stem from the reality of our actions.

The author of *Practicing Philosophy: Pragmatism and the Philosophical Life* opposes the predominant textualism, which deprecates the material, non-discursive elements of cognition. For Shusterman, the rejection of the extra-linguistic element is the result of ineffective identification of non-discursive references and an attempt to restore epistemological or metaphysical fundamentalism with a dogmatic temptation of the embodiment of some ultimate datum. The American-Israeli philosopher in his focus on somatic aspects of existence declares his aversion to universalist claims and attempts only to trace some regularities in this dynamic realm which would allow us to submit our somatic activity to careful reflection. This approach would result in pragmatic methodology, and finally, in the actual practice of rational corporeality. This turn towards somatic issues is apparently an obvious confirmation of rationalism as a standpoint capable of self-critical development.

To the advocates of "hard" rationalism, corporality is a kind of vicious matter which should constantly be disciplined and categorically repressed. It appears as a kind of natural evil which is beyond redemption. To postmodern aesthetes, however, it presents no difficulty; they do not perceive it at all (Rorty) or treat it as a base of attack for transgressive crusades against the tyranny of reason (Foucault). Among those diversely perceived bodies—damned, non-existing or vicious—there is no place for the ordinary body, modestly hiding, as it were, its commonplace existence. That absence is especially disturbing in times when the ordinary environment of our somatic experience is exposed to digital naturalization.

Modern technologies impoverish both inherent and culturally implanted rootedness, falsifying the human condition with delusions of immateriality. A typical modern Ulysses of digital interfaces, suffering from numerous psycho-somatic ailments, comes to mind here. The longer his cyber-odyssey, the further he drifts away from the completeness of his lost self. Blinded by the brightness of the screen, without the reassuring feel of solid ground under his feet, he be-comes an ever more submissive element of the objectifying mechanics of the system, rather than a super-subject liberated from the slavery of substance.

Notwithstanding this, we do not discard our already useless bodily co-coons at the door leading to the virtual world. The forgotten body follows, obstinately bereft of care, exposed to electronic shocks. It is not enough to wear an electronic glove to gain new handiness. What is needed is a reflection on the body and the new challenges it faces in a hitherto unfamiliar universum. Shusterman refers to a still very timely diagnosis by F. M. Alexander:

> Contemporary civilized conditions are unsuited to the inherited forms of somatic expression and moreover subject us unconsciously to new cus-toms and regimes of body control (like Foucauldian disciplines of bi-opower). The result 'is the larger number of physical disorders which in-flict themselves exclusively upon civilized man [for example, lower-back syndrome], and the large number of neuroses which express them-selves in intellectual and moral maladies.'[1]

Without an hysterical exorcising of our former "analogue" body, we should, nevertheless, redefine its functionality within the context of the deep-ening digitalization of our environment, and, while avoiding proselytes' fervor in support of the new at the cost of the old, we should strive for free transloca-tion between so-called "real" and virtual reality. "We must not let enthusiasms for new media convince us that the old ones can be abandoned as simply *aufgehoben*."[2] In this particular case, the multitude of horizons exerts a benef-icent influence on the considerate firmness of the body.

In his *Undoing Aesthetics*, Wolfgang Welsch describes California IT specialists who utilize this dual reality, preceding their online ecstasies with contemplation of the sun setting over the Pacific Ocean.[3] A person of sublime disposition could accuse them of an excessive inclination towards aesthetic platitudes. Obstinate dandies could use the following remark by Gilbert K. Chesterton as an appropriate riposte: "Oscar Wilde said that sunsets were not valued because we could not pay for sunsets. But Oscar Wilde was wrong; we can pay for sunsets. We can pay for them by not being Oscar Wilde."[4]

Indeed, the aesthetics of everyday life very seldom reaches the heights of genius. But on the other hand, genius itself often teeters on the verge of kitsch. This juxtaposition is actually one of the main ideas of Shusterman's somaesthet-ics. It is by no means praise of mediocrity but an incentive to knowledgeable tending and fertilizing of our down-to-earth elements. So his reflection on corporality is not developed in opposition to Foucault's exclusivity but rather as its complement or alternative. His somaesthetics appears not to show any deontological ambitions. Emphasizing the optional character of his concept, he points towards Foucault's aesthetics of transgression as an interesting counterpoint.

Stretching out on his bed of perversion not only his theoretical obsessions, but also his tangible body, the French philosopher tried to free himself, even if momentarily, from cultural *régimes*. Exposing himself to sadomasochistic experiments, he attempted to free his sexuality of any political context, drawing his own ephemeral maps of peripheral, extragenital sensual pleasures, far removed from their culturally prescribed centre. Although Foucault considers the body to be constantly immersed in some kind of social discourse of power which renders it political, he by no means slighted those momentary, even if delusive, ecstasies when the body, in transient suspension between the old and the new order, almost nonconforming, feels, as it were, its own innards.

Shusterman does not share Foucault's obsession with transgressions. In his view, the road to liberating self-transformation requires neither an excessive intensification of sensory perception, nor does it lead through the outskirts of perversion. Disdain for common, everyday pleasures does not contribute to the phenomenology of liberating somatic experiences. On the contrary, the "submissive body," despite Foucault's intentions, falls prey to yet another *régime* – that of Baudelaire's dandy, which few could stand up to.

What is more, the exclusivity of such perverted discipline weakens the ethical value of self-care, placing it within the confines of whimsical egotism. The concept of Shusterman's somaesthetics is apparently tailored to the needs of the contemporary everyman. Hard drugs and "laboratories of sexual experiments" would push him into greater discursive-sensory inertia rather than make him capable of self-creation, as pleasure is not meant as an object in itself.

> The aesthetic in somaesthetics is thus not confined to the narrow pursuit of immediate pleasure (however valuable that pleasure may be). Somaesthetics equally connotes both the cognitive sharpening of our aisthesis or sensory perception and the artful reshaping of our somatic form and functioning; not simply to make us stronger and more perceptive for our own sensual satisfaction, but to render us more sensitive to the needs of others and more capable of responding to them with effectively willed action.[5]

Like Foucault's, the ethical dimension of Shusterman's felicitology derives its depth from transcendence. This is not the transcendence available only in acts of transgression that annihilate rational self-control. On the contrary, transcendence as defined by Shusterman is a movement beyond habitual and ideological schemes, and it serves to enhance the power of self-control.

Finally, affect is the basis of empathy, which can ground communal living and progressive social action far more firmly and satisfyingly that

can mere rational self-interest. If experiential somaesthetics pragmatically provides techniques for the development, refinement, and regulation
of affect, it also has a social potential that should not be ignored. Bodily
rigidities and blockages are often both the product and a reinforcing support of social intolerance and political repression.[6]

According to Shusterman, it is possible to broaden our sensory self-
control without resorting to drastic methods of "avant-garde extremism" *à la*
Foucault. Everything depends on the values which we employ to construct our
corporality. For Shusterman, both the theory and practice of grounding our
corporality should serve as an opportunity for strengthening empathic abili-
ties, not as a tool for egoistic self-creation. If we are able to perceive our body
rationally, we can also discern our fellow man in another person. This is perti-
nent especially now, with the growing pressure of the media and the danger of
sensory deprivation which can transform us into an easily-manipulated zom-
bie society without cultivating our potential for empathy.

While an ancient philosopher strolled ostentatiously to disprove the Ele-
atic motionless being, Shusterman was led to the source of life by his own
body. It was on the dance floor of a music club, in the midst of Others, that he
experienced a sudden illumination, developing unforeseen intentional potentialities. It was then that unexpected bodily stirrings liberated him from cool
embrace of the rigorous purism of Critical Theory. It was not a bloodless
ghost of abstraction, but his own body, that led him in dancing motions to the
circle of enthusiastic advocates of pragmatism.

In dance clubs the "aesthetics of performance" cannot dominate the
"aesthetics of experience." A ballet master showing off his fanciful figures is
not welcome in a crowded discothèque where dancers whirl around to the
sound of unifying rhythms of common sense. The need for empathy, which
fills these places with crowds of strangers, seems to be expressed in a specifically egalitarian capturing of the aesthetic of experience by the common aesthetics of performance. Our being, rendering itself available, or as Hannah
Arendt claims, existing only on the surface of our body, loses its eccentricity
in an ever-tightening circle of dancers and becomes comprehensibly common.
Who would care to remember Fred Astaire or Ginger Rogers, when even
prosaic John Travolta, conforming to the spirit of the time, simplifies his film
dancing show to the level of a disabled consumer. After *Pulp Fiction,* even the
clumsiest dancer ventures to imitate his gestures.

The phenomenon of the desublimation of idols applies to the entire contemporary culture. Blurring the boundaries between high and low culture, and
aiming for their complete obliteration in protest against unjust stratification,
began many years before the emergence of hip-hop. "Roll over Beethoven"
called Chuck Berry in 1956, in his popular hit which was echoed at the beginning of the 60s by The Beatles. The turn of the 60s and 70s, likewise, was an
attempt to prove that progressive or symphonic rock (Pink Floyd, King Crim-

son, Emerson Lake & Palmer) was not inferior to the creative toil of the deaf old German. Finally, the inferiority complex shaken off, the 5th Symphony of "fate," transformed into electronic machinery, knocked at the doors of the biggest discos.

If there is a solution to this problem, it involves recognizing and developing a popular aesthetic that finds beauty and creative self-expression in more common, less spectacular forms. Though the sixteenth-century Montaigne could claim the greatest beauty for lives conforming to "the common human pattern ... without miracle and without eccentricity," this aesthetic has been undermined by modernity's quest for perpetual progress through singular genius and radical originality. For most contemporary philosophy, the notion of a popular aesthetic remains discredited yet unexplored. But its legitimation and amelioration (as advocated in *Pragmatist Aesthetics*) seem essential to the culture of democracy.[7]

For Shusterman, the practical and philosophical virtues of popular culture are not the issues of its anticipated development. They are already exerting their beneficent influence on culture as a whole, enhancing democratic tendencies in it. In his view, this is mainly due to the expansive hip-hop culture and its source, rap music, manifesting the triumphant body, which, liberating and invigorating the mind, serve as mediums for entirely rational and just self-creation. The techniques of cutting, sampling and scratching, common in rap music, not only undermine the historically sanctified integrity of the work of art, but also seem to ultimately discredit the romantic ideology of genius in a very attractive way, namely, by removing the indispensible originality and uniqueness. The ostentatious appropriation of musical themes blurs the boundaries between creation and reproduction. Artistic activity is no longer focused on achieving an inviolable, fetishist integrity; reconstructing and transfiguring techniques create a temporarily integral, incomplete work of art which invites further transmutations.

But, by rap's postmodern aesthetic, the ephemeral freshness of artistic creations does not render them aesthetically unworthy; no more than the ephemeral freshness of cream renders its sweet taste unreal.[8]

Owing to its dynamic intertextuality rap music can, in Shusterman's view, reanimate tradition in the form of a contemporary, living aesthetic experience. Politically committed hip-hop strongly undermines lofty aesthetic purism by integrating art with "the pursuit of knowledge in the aim of ethical growth and socio-political emancipation."[9]

The practical dimension of rap not only, as Shusterman claims, reflects the philosophical postulates of pragmatism but also makes useful amendments thereto. As opposed to some other theoretical pragmatists, hip-hop artists emphasize the links of aesthetics not only with cognition but also with practice. An aesthetic form of hip-hop derived from rap includes, apart from music, a form of dance (breakdancing), linguistic and extra-linguistic communication, graffiti, and other self-styling aspects. It presents a complete proposal—of life and certain philosophy—which can be submitted both to reflection and somatic experience. "It wants to be appreciated fully through energetic movement and impassioned dance, not immobile, dispassionate contemplation."[10]

Although the above-given outline of Shusterman,s characteristics of hip-hop may be valid to a large extent, it raises some doubts. First of all, it should be noted that all the features of hip-hop (excluding sampling and scratching techniques) mentioned by him are non-specific. Political engagement took place in music or popular culture much earlier. I do not intend to present the full genealogy of this phenomenon here. I will only limit myself to presenting some counterexamples relevant to these features as well as to others as indicated by Shusterman.

The very beginnings of 20th-century American pop-music, originating during the Swing era, are marked with highly political "political non-commitment." For a long time, white audiences craving syncopated rhythms listened to bands composed of white musicians made up in blackface.

> Along the same lines, consider the scene from Spike Lee's formidable *Bamboozled*, in which black artists themselves blacken their faces in the style of Al Jolson—perhaps wearing a black mask is the only strategy for them to appear white (that is, to generate the expectation that the "true" face beneath their black mask is white) In this properly Lacanian deception, wearing a black mask is destined to conceal the fact that we are black—no wonder, then, that the effect of discovering black under black, when they rinse off their masks, is shocking. Perhaps as a defense against this shock, we nonetheless spontaneously perceive their "true" face beneath the mask as more black than their mask—as if attesting to the fact that the blackening of their face is a strategy for their assimilation into white culture.[11]

With the passage of time, the genuinely black prototypes were admitted onto the stage, playing the parts of domesticated savages or comic butlers, sustaining the racial hierarchy. Every attempt to sublimate this artistic *emploi* ended in increased repressions. Tragic evidence is supplied in the biographies of such artists as Billie Holiday and Bessie Smith. Even the rock 'n' roll of the fifties, so vital for later moral changes, reacting to the Korean War, was quite restrained in this matter. The copulative movements of Elvis Presley (hence the jocularly ironic nickname Elvis the Pelvis) were no longer shocking but even the King himself was reluctant to reveal the origin of some of his early hits, such as "Hound Dog" which was originally performed by Big Mama Thornton. Finally the political element found its expression in James Brown's "Say it Loud, I'm Black, I'm Proud."

At the turn of the 60s and 70s the institutionally protected WASPs (White Anglo-Saxon Protestants) could hardly find a last shelter in the homely country farms and refuges of religious conservatism. Young Janis Joplin sneaked out of her house at night to listen to the singing of her remote black neighbors. When she matured, the signs of political rebellion could be traced even in her sentimental songs. The spectacular Woodstock festival, where a meeting for initiated beatniks and hipsters was transformed into the sweeping hippies' movement, is the best example of the scope and momentum that political commitment gained at that time.

This short reminiscence is by no means an attempt to lecture Shusterman, who admitted taking part in the electric guitar-amplified revolution. My intention was to restore the sense of proportion between hip-hop's political nature and that of the whole of contemporary popular music, on the basis of direct associations rather than on the assumption that everything is political.

Later on, at the end of the 70s, when in Silicon Valley the hippies metamorphosed into conforming and anti-social yuppies, the generational changing of the guard took place. Young rebels were swept by the counterculture of Punk—the last pop culture revolt before the emergence of hip-hop.

All the above-mentioned examples of political commitment should not be reduced to musical or artistic phenomena only. They should be analyzed within a much wider cultural context which confirmed a certain lifestyle and co-defined the entire hip-hop culture.

Another important feature indicated by Shusterman is the obliteration of the distinction between high and low elements in culture. As I mentioned before, the high aspirations of popular culture were evident in that culture since long before. Let me add that there have always been not only rock musicians who reached out for the high-culture repertoire (Emerson, Lake & Palmer and their album *Pictures at an Exhibition* with its version of Mussorgsky's composition) but also trying to refine their own productions by classical orchestration—an early example is Deep Purple and their recordings with symphony orchestra, while a relatively recent example is that of Metallica. On the other hand, classical musicians often manifest egalitarian attitudes by recording their own versions of rock compositions (an early example is Pierre Boulez adapting Frank Zappa; a more recent one, Nigel Kennedy and his violin transcriptions of Jimmy Hendrix).

According to Shusterman, hip-hop culture significantly supports the democratization of culture. He notes with satisfaction that the common philosophy of rap compositions, so close to everyday pragmatism, albeit simple, can be very inquisitive indeed. To illustrate this point he draws our attention to the French rap musician MC Solaar, who quotes Lacan himself in some of his works. The author of *Pragmatist Aesthetics* makes one reservation here, though: he is fascinated only by the brighter, nobler form of rap and makes a clear distinction between the dignified message of so-called "knowledge rap" and the commercialized, blunt aggression of "gangsta" rap. It seems that *vox populi* found an adequate means of expression in the simplistic, everyman-friendly technological aesthetic formula of rap, especially in not requiring any virtuoso sampling technique.

Rap is accessible to any performer, no matter how incompetent, thus opening wide the door to the musical stage. And since it is very common that lack of talent goes hand in hand with lack of inhibitions, very little space is left for unassuming, quiet artistry and exquisite taste. As Thomas Mann prophesied, democracy, apart from common happiness, brings the terror of the equalizing mass. T. S. Eliot and Ezra Pound were two other eminent modernist artists who warned against the dangers posed by that apparent simplicity of form. Although responsible for the propagation of free verse in English language poetry, they soon realized that the sad aftermath of their enthusiasm for *verse libre* was an alarming number of Sunday poets, among whom the voice of true talent was easily drowned. They resolved to discredit free verse temporarily and attempted to restore the old, rigorous forms of poetry.

The ever-progressing mediocrity of popular culture calls for similar, retroactive precautions. The injustice of established experts offends only against the backdrop of their generally ennobling activities. Contemporary degradation of the "experts' culture" has reversed the odds. Everything that conforms with the commercial and ideological matrix of the culture industry is raised to prominence while independent acts of a creative genius, that is, somebody who, setting new laws by the power of his or her creative act, breaks the transmission belt of automatic production, are doomed to media discrimination which attempts to abolish the prohibition on mechanical repetitiveness embodied in these works.

One specific symptom of this trend in popular culture was the divergence of the entertainment industry from the creation of so-called stars. Their apparent unattainability could be achieved not only by aggressive advertising campaigns but also by utilizing their specific charismatic qualities, skills or talent. Even if only a few stars came close to genius, their image always bore the stamp of originality. Outstanding actors of that time at least possessed an unusual appearance, which cannot be said about the ideally expressionless film celebrities of today.

At the beginning of the 1970s the film business realized that stars were the weakest link in the market chain of circulation. They became excessively fragile (drugs, alcohol abuse etc.) and on top of that very difficult to replace. Sex, drugs and rock'n'roll did not serve them too well. For instance, Jimmy Hendrix's virtuosity or the unusual voice of Janis Joplin originally contributed to their marketability, but became a kind of substantial burden, blocking free circulation of pop industry products after they died. Film studios faced the same problem—how to keep producing new stars when they are rare by definition, shining with unusual radiance. Hysterical idolatry created by marketing specialists backfired finally in the face of the film producers.

The first signs of the new marketing strategy became visible at the end of the 70s. Utilizing revolutionary elements of the Punk subculture, an army of talentless musicians was brought onstage and sold to the public. The best example that comes to mind here is Malcolm MacLaren and his product, the Sex Pistols.

Later on, uninspiring and blatantly commercial pop-music metamorphosed after the same fashion—the average consumer was fed with downright mediocrity and easily convinced that he was *cool*. Measured for his format in every field of entertainment, a new breed of celebrity appeared. Even a conscientious craftsman posed a threat to the industry, because he was not easily replaced.

The most radical way of dealing with this problem so far is the example of techno music. Just like rap, it does not require any specific, "analogue" artistry. Although comparatively free of immediate borrowings and translating all the outside themes into its electronic lingo, it is nevertheless extremely eclectic—a synopsis, rather than synthesis, of external motifs held together not by clear, individual expression but by the overpowering mechanical rhythm.

We can find anticipation of this phenomenon in the mercilessly exaggerated reflections of Theodor Adorno. The shamelessly coarse pop culture, along with the high culture that cajoles her rough charms, slide together into the ideal of the market. The result of these good relations is the stylistics of an assembly line which pervades both leisure time and entertainment forms. In the *metropolis* of today underground passengers hurrying to work listening to mechanical music on their portable players. The rhythmical continuum obliterates the distinction between work and holiday, free time and time sold. In Chaplin's masterpiece *Modern Times* a scientist-inventor demonstrates a device for feeding workers which allows the firm to save energy wasted during normal consumption. It seems that more effective ways of mobilizing production have been invented.

Somaesthetics, as well as the phenomenology of the body, is interested in its practical perfecting. To achieve harmonious growth of our embodied minds, it suggests developing techniques sensitive to cultural and civilizational changes as well as to the self-creating needs of particular individuals. Dangerous delusions of returning to the transcendentally "natural" forms of lost psychosomatic unity should be discarded here. Aesthetic upbringing modelled on Schiller's utopia could only too easily serve as the ideological basis for the terror of the one valid totality.

What can be said here about the so highly-praised hip-hop culture? Does it really serve the ambitious objectives of somaesthetics? Alas, whether standing by itself or as referring to the theory of the American pragmatist, it turns out to be, in its primitive monotony, the heavy, uninspired and aggressive fast food of the contemporary entertainment industry. Its alleged virtues are rather a corruption of virtues found elsewhere in popular culture. The aesthetic form of hip-hop is known equally for its allegedly nobler, kind, "full of clichés" and "knowledgeable" declarations, as well as for the shockingly degenerate gangsta rap. The brilliant, unbearably innocent original performance of "What a

Wonderful World" carries much more revolutionary potential. A naive, albeit generously gifted, artist can awaken our longing for paradise much more readily than can an aesthetic manipulability lacking moral backbone and confirming universal exchange.

Meliorative concerns about pop culture demand an increasingly pointed criticism of hip-hop; otherwise its uncultivated soil may turn into a wasteland. The "blond beast" of *Dialectic of Enlightenment* is replaced here by a "rap beast" equally ready for mindless aggression, and equally ready for mindless submission. Sampling defragmentation of the self seems to stem from a fear of excessive identification, that feature of late capitalism mentioned by Slavoj Žižek:

> The fear of 'excessive' identification is therefore the fundamental feature of late-capitalist ideology: the Enemy is the 'fanatic' who 'overidentifies,' instead of maintaining a proper distance from the dispersed plurality of subject-positions. In short: the elated 'deconstructivist' logomachy focused on 'essentialism' and 'fixed identities' ultimately fights a strawman. Far from containing any kind of subversive potential, the subject hailed by postmodern theories—the dispersed, plural, constructed subject, the subject who undermines every performative mandate by way of its parodic repetition, the subject prone to particular, inconsistent modes of enjoyment—simply designates the form of subjectivity that corresponds to late capitalism. Perhaps the time has come to resuscitate the Marxian insight concerning Capital as the ultimate power of 'deterritorialization' that undermines every fixed social identity, and to see 'late capitalism' as the epoch in which the traditional fixity of ideological positions (patriarchal authority, fixed sex roles, etc.) becomes an obstacle to the unbridled commodification of everyday life.[12]

Shusterman himself claims that since there is no unchangeable, constant reality, nothing can stop the body from changing. On the other hand, he regards the body as the surest center in the face of the changing media, convinced that by strengthening the body we strengthen our self.

When Shusterman refers to Alexander or Feldenkrais, suggesting bodily practice developed by himself, it is hard for someone who has never tried it to argue. The illusion of the innocence of such somapractical systematics, their purely pragmatic character, can be questioned. Such bodily regimes always bear the stamp of ideology. I do not wish to negate their potentially beneficent influence on the moral and intellectual sensitivity of a socially committed individual devoted to democratic values. My qualms are evoked by the fact that similar practices are very often utilized by those who despise such values. It may be relevant to mention here the training camps for members of some sects, or military use of some oriental physical exercises which can allegedly give peace and inner harmony to Western city-dwellers. (The bodily practice of Zen may be the same for a quiet psychoanalyst and for a worshipper of the divine wind, kamikaze).

From the pragmatic point of view I strongly oppose the bodily aspect of hip-hop; I object to the somaesthetic of a supposedly ownerless body writhing on a golden rapper chain of music producers. Let this rhetoric of aggressive, political canvassing give my reader a foretaste of the syllabized message of the hip-hop Master of Ceremonies.

If we accept the standpoint that the body transmits a direct reflection of the spiritual life of a given epoch, it is useful to consider whether the sampled body of hip-hop does not reinforce those current cultural trends that serve to dehumanize the contemporary individual and his social environment. I feel an aversion to the transgressions of Foucault, a strict follower of the inverse strategy of de Sade, according to which "one should inverse philosophy in order to reinvent it—so one should reinvent body by resorting to sodomy."[13] That reluctance about perversion does not always lead to "healthy" promiscuity. A rigid neck and resistance against health and happiness of the last people of whom "[o]ne has one's little pleasure for the day and one's little pleasure for the night: but one honours good health"[14] may be a better option here.

The hip-hop idea of body reflects the times—reversed Lacan mirror effect—in its flexibility which is devoid of substance; a psychophysical oneness of producer and recipient is being dismembered into replaceable modules, and all resistance is broken in the whirl of the break-dance.

Are we not more and more monads with no direct windows onto reality, interacting alone with the PC screen, encountering only the virtual simulacra, and yet immersed more than ever in the global network, synchronously communicating with the entire globe?[15]

The spreading cult of body is, paradoxically, accompanied by its loss. Only Malebranche's "madman," that is, a man who "directly feels this material body as his own"[16] is capable of laying claim for himself and for the Other. The same madman shrinks from desecrating dead bodies and from the gruesome delights of necrophilia. Marquise de Sade did not know the Other, but only our body as the machine of Nature.

It is through my body that I understand other people, just as it is through my body that I perceive 'things.'[17]

In the world of contemporary art, the *Korperwelten* plays of Hagens appear to be an immediate continuation of Enlightenment enthusiasm. The body was similarly unmasked at exhibitions organized in pre-war Germany where young people could admire scientific exhibits made of dead bodies. One can perceive here, as Adorno did, the looming shadows of the concentration camps and the production of human soap.

It is certainly undeniable that the technicization of the body results in a significant fortification of the human position, as well. We have to distinguish,

though, between the image of disabled persons taking part in "normal" sport com-
petitions thanks to sophisticated artificial limbs, and that of the body thoughtlessly
going limp in the embrace of invasive technology. Binary dematerialization and
virtual mediation of the body may lead to its specific cyber-larceny.

> Immersion into cyberspace can intensify our bodily experience (new sen-
> suality, new body with more organs, new sexes...), but it also opens up the
> possibility for the one who manipulates the machinery which runs the cy-
> berspace literally to steal our own (virtual) body, depriving us of the con-
> trol over it, so that one no longer relates to one's body as to 'one's own.'[18]

Daily surfing the ecstatic cyberspace weakens sensory identity and al-
ienates our body. It is submitted to neurotic avatarization when hardware
changes into software. "In the Internet era, when body becomes excluded as
the centre of our identity, it becomes a mere option."[19]
    The point is to make it an unusual option. The digitally infected sensuali-
ty of hip-hop, its aesthetics of unoriginal manipulation, and the dismantling of
the identity aiming at easy satisfaction becomes an ideal solution for the entertainment industry. The industry utilizes the fast food logic of production,
previously reducing its consumers to the primitive, digitalized level of its
products. If the body stands as a guarantee of the preservation of our self-
grounding,[20] hip-hop obliterates its uniqueness, offering us the opposite.
Whirling to the break-dance rhythms, with sampled mind, our body scatters
barely connected intentional threads which return to us in the form of a net of
affects not administered by ourselves.

> Thus, as opposed to the universal mobility and changeability of media-
> worlds, today we are learning to value anew the resistibility and un-
> changeability of the natural world and, in the same way, the persistence
> of the concrete as opposed to the free play of information, the massivity
> of matter as opposed to the levitation of imagery. In contrast to arbitrary
> repeatability, uniqueness gains value afresh. The electronic omnipres-
> ence awakens the yearning for another presence: for the unrepeatable
> presence of *hic et nunc* — for the singular event. And we are discovering
> anew the body's sovereignty and intransigence;—think, of, say, Nadol-
> ny's 'discovery of slowness,' or of Handke's praise of weariness.[21]

Sharing Shusterman's theoretical concern over the deteriorated bodies,
and consequently the minds, of contemporary bipeds, which confirms the
necessity of developing some kind of rational pragmatics in this field, and
trusting in the artistic and educational potential of popular culture, I also believe in his physiotherapeutic instructions. I will never stop wondering,
though, how it is possible that the author of the brilliant analysis of "Portrait
of a Lady" and recent rebel with causes which resounded in the Hendrix

Fender guitar can be so uncritical as to cherish hip-hop mediocrity and tediousness. But this *faux pas* does not rule out his dancing illuminations. What is missing in contemporary philosophy is the point of gravity, the right proportion between the "animal gravity" of abstraction and the insipid clowning of perversion, between body and mind, text and feeling. The American philosopher appears to be an interesting, neo-pragmatic continuator of Schiller's vision of the complete human being.

NOTES

1. Richard Shusterman, *Practicing Philosophy: Pragmatism and the Philosophical Life* (New York: Routledge, 1997), pp. 167–168.
2. Richard Shusterman, *Performing Live: Aesthetic Alternatives for the Ends of Art* (Ithaca, London: Cornell University Press, 2000), p. 150.
3. See Wolfgang Welsch, *Undoing Aesthetics*, trans. Andrew Inkpin (London: SAGE, 1997), p. 184.
4. Gilbert K. Chesterton, *Orthodoxy* (San Francisco: Ignatius Press, 1995), p. 63.
5. Richard Shusterman, "Somaesthetics and Care of the Self: The Case of Foucault," *The Monist*, 83:4 (2000), pp. 545–546.
6. Shusterman, *Performing Live*, p. 153.
7. Shusterman, *Practicing Philosophy*, p. 50.
8. Shusterman, *Performing Live*, p. 66.
9. Shusterman, *Practicing Philosophy*, p. 143.
10. *Ibid.*, p. 150.
11. Slavoj Žižek, *The Puppet and the Dwarf: The Perverse Core of Christianity* (Cambridge, Massachusetts, London: The MIT Press, 2003), p. 186.
12. Slavoj Žižek, *The Universal Exception: Selected Writings*, eds. Rex Butler and Scott Stephens (London, New York: Continuum International Publishing Group, 2006), p. 27.
13. Jean-Noël Vuarnet, *Filozof-artysta* (Gdańsk: Wydawnictwo słowo/obraz terytoria, 2000), p. 70 [original title: *Le philosophe-artiste* (Paris: Union Générale d'Editions, collection „10/18", 1977)].
14. Friedrich Nietzsche, *Thus Spoke Zarathustra: A Book for Everyone and Nobody*, trans. Graham Parkes (Oxford: Oxford University Press, 2005), p. 16.
15. Slavoj Žižek, *On Belief* (London, New York: Routledge, 2001), p. 52.
16. See Slavoj Žižek, *The Plague of Fantasies* (London: Verso, 1997), p. 142.
17. Maurice Merleau-Ponty, *Phenomenology of Perception*, trans. Colin Smith (London: Routledge & Kegan Paul, 1962), p. 186.
18. Slavoj Žižek, "Friedrich Wilhelm Joseph von Schelling," in *The Abyss of Freedom: Ages of the World*, trans. Judith Norman and Ann Arbor (University of Michigan Press, 1997), p. 65.
19. Hans Belting, *Antropologia obrazu. Szkice do nauki o obrazie* (Krakow: Universitas, 2007), p. 107 [original title: *Bild-Anthropologie. Entwürfe für eine Bildwissenschaft* (München, Paderborn: Verlag Ferdinand Schöningh GmbH, 2007)].
20. See Shusterman, *Performing Live*, p. 162.
21. Welsch, *Undoing Aesthetics*, p. 88.

Twelve

SOMAESTHETICS AND DEMOCRACY: DEWEY AND CONTEMPORARY BODY ART

Martin Jay

Perhaps no twentieth-century philosopher was as favorably inclined towards the role of aesthetic experience in building a democratic culture as was John Dewey, the preeminent public intellectual in America during the first half of the twentieth century. His vision of democracy necessitated a robust commitment not only to an open-ended process of unimpeded free inquiry, which emulated that of the scientific community, but also to the self-realization that came through active participation in the public sphere. The model of that self-realization he saw best expressed in the sensually mediated, organically consummated, formally molded activity that was aesthetic experience. "That which distinguishes an experience as esthetic [sic]," he wrote, "is conversion of resistance and tensions, of excitations that in themselves are temptations to diversions, into movement toward an inclusive and fulfilling close."[1] As such, it was the quintessential exemplar of what is meant when we say we "have *an* experience," rather than merely register an ephemeral sensation. In the words of Thomas Alexander, the foremost commentator on Dewey's aesthetics,

> ...in the idea of art we find the moment in which human alienation is overcome and the need for the experience of meaning and value is satisfied. Through art, in the aesthetic experience, the rift in the world that frustrates our primordial desire for encountering a sense of meaning and value is healed.[2]

Because aesthetic experience had as its *telos* consummation, closure, fulfillment, and inclusion, it could function as the model of a democratic politics that went beyond a thin proceduralism to a more substantive form of life. "Art is a mode of production," Dewey wrote, "not found in charts and statistics, and it insinuates possibilities of human relations not to be found in rule and precept, admonition and administration."[3] Thus, as one of his most eminent recent biographers, Robert Westbrook, has correctly noted with reference to Dewey's great work of 1934,

> *Art as Experience* was not incidental to the radical politics that absorbed Dewey in the 1930s. Indeed, it was one of the most powerful statements of that politics, for it clearly indicated that his was not a radicalism di-

rected solely to the material well-being of the American people but directed as well to the provision of consummatory experience that could be
found only outside the circulation of commodities.[4]

Or as another recent student of Dewey, David Fott, puts it,

> For Dewey aesthetic experience is the paradigmatic form of meaningful
> experience, occurring when the controlling concern in experience is the
> immediately felt relation of order or fulfillment. That relation may obtain
> in political matters as well as in any other sort; in fact, we can consider
> aesthetic experience the goal of our attempts to solve our political prob-
> lems, which arise when disorder is felt to occur.[5]

For Dewey, the full potential of aesthetic experience and of its political
counterpart would be realized only if three fundamental changes were effected. First, art had to leave the elite world of museums and private galleries
behind and become part of the everyday life of the masses. Life lived aesthetically would overcome the gap between means and ends and abet the inclusion
of the many in the pleasures heretofore enjoyed only by the few. What Peter
Bürger has seen as the historical mission of the avant-garde as opposed to that
of the modernists, the infusing of life with the redemptive power of art, was
thus also shared by Dewey.[6]

Second, aesthetic experience had to wean itself from the Kantian notion
that it was inherently contemplative and spectatorial. The claim in the *Critique of Judgment* that disinterestedness was the hallmark of the aesthetic had
to be abandoned, and the rights of need, desire, and yearning acknowledged as
just as inherent in aesthetic experience as in experience in general. In fact, to
the extent that the term "aesthetic" had contemplative connotations, Dewey
preferred to speak of artistic experience instead. For whereas the former suggested perception, pleasure, and judgment, and was thus relatively passive in
implication, the latter connoted production and action, making rather than
merely enjoying or judging what others had made. Both, Dewey argued,
should be acknowledged as complementary dimensions of politics as well as art.

Third, aesthetic, or rather artistic, experience involved the whole body
and not just the mind and imagination or even the senses as receptors of stim-
uli from without. Dewey thus resisted the time-honored hierarchy that still
subtended contemporary taste, which, so he charged,

> ...tends to reckon as higher the fine arts that reshape material, where the
> product is enduring rather than fugitive, and is capable of appealing to a
> wide circle, including the unborn, in contrast with the limitation of sing-
> ing, dancing, and oral story-telling to an immediate audience. But all
> rankings of higher and lower are, ultimately, out of place and stupid.
> Each medium has its own efficacy and value.[7]

For politics, it was therefore perhaps the performative arts that were even more important than those devoted to building permanent objects for posterity, an insight that anticipated Hannah Arendt's well-known distinction in The Human Condition between man as homo faber and as political performer.[8]

Although in eclipse for a generation after his death in 1952, pragmatism in general and Dewey in particular have had an extraordinary renaissance of interest in the past two decades. One of reasons for that renewed interest is precisely his theory of aesthetic experience and its larger implications.[9] Building on Dewey's argument, the contemporary pragmatist philosopher Richard Shusterman has proposed an ambitious project of what he calls "somaesthetics."[10] Hoping to efface the distinction between the fine arts and mere craftsmanship and undermine the exclusivity of art as an autonomous institution, Shusterman praises Dewey for his willingness to "…exchange high art's autocratic aura of transcendental authority for a more down-to-earth and democratic glow of enhanced living and enriched community of understanding."[11] Noting Dewey's fascination for the body therapeutics of F. Matthias Alexander, whose system of upper torso exercises were designed to enhance breathing, posture and motion, he argues that essential to aesthetic experience is prediscursive corporeal development.[12] Resisting the recasting of pragmatism in entirely linguistic terms urged by Richard Rorty, Shusterman insists on repairing the breach between mind and body:

> The most radical and interesting way for philosophy to engage somatics is to integrate such bodily disciplines into the very practice of philosophy. This means practicing philosophy not simply as a discursive genre, a form of writing, but as a discipline of embodied life.[13]

Looking around for a current example of realized somaesthetics, Shusterman hit on rap and hip-hop music as embodiments of a democratic and inclusive practice that repudiated the purist claims of aesthetic autonomy. "Hip-hop repudiates such purity," he writes. "It wants to be appreciated fully through energetic movement and impassioned dance, not immobile, dispassionate contemplation."[14] The politics of this music, an aggressive burst of outrage and protest against social and racial injustice, belies the stereotype of popular art as inherently conservative and conformist. What its performers calls "message" or "knowledge rap" is intended to integrate aesthetic with ethical and political concerns. Shusterman argues,

> Though few may know it, … rap philosophers are really 'down with' Dewey, not merely in metaphysics but in a non-compartmentalized aesthetics which highlights social function, process, and embodied experience.[15]

Whatever one may think of Shusterman's celebration of rap as a successful realization of the Deweyan ideal (he himself recognizes its distance from the irenic *telos* of consummation and order), it raises the question of the relation between contemporary artistic practices, broadly defined, and the realization of democracy. Rap and hip-hop are, to be sure, popular phenomena, which have introduced oppositional politics of a sort into the culture industry. At times, however, that politics has expressed itself in blatantly misogynist and homophobic terms, which Shusterman does not fully confront, although he acknowledges its dangerous rhetoric of violence. And to the extent that is has been commercially successful, it has perhaps lost some of its critical impetus.

It might therefore be useful to turn elsewhere for evidence of the plausibility of Dewey's ideas. We do not really have far to look. For a much more explicit attempt to combine somaesthetics with a critique of these impediments to democratic culture has, in fact, been made over the past forty years by artists who are not treated by Shusterman, perhaps because of their still esoteric appeal (if appeal is the right word).[16] I am speaking of a loose international community of performance artists who have experimented in often transgressive and provocative ways with their own bodies. With the recent publication of Tracy Warr and Amelia Jones's lavishly documented and graphically illustrated survey of what they call *The Artist's Body,* we can perhaps see for the first time the full extent and variety of this still vibrant movement.[17]

Although anticipations can be found in the performative impulse in Futurism, Dadaism, and Constructivism in the first decades of the last century and Antonin Artaud's Theater of Cruelty — perhaps they can even be spotted as early as the ancient Cynic philosopher Diogenes of Sinope — it was not really until the waning of High Modernism in the 1960s that it could fully develop. Inspired by the action painting identified with Jackson Pollock, which had drawn attention away from the canvas to the vigorous gesture of putting paint on its surface, and taking their cue from the foregrounding of the artist's complicated, often theatrically contrived, identity advanced by Marcel Duchamp, artists in a number of countries in Europe, Asia, and the Americas began to turn attention to their own bodies as sites of artistic expression. Rejecting the high modernist fetish of formal purity — which had still tacitly informed Dewey's aesthetics of consummation[18] — and impatient with the worship of art objects functioning as embodiments of value in both the economic marketplace and canonical history of art, they turned to ephemeral performances, which were site-specific, often outside of the gallery or museum, and designed to leave no permanent residue beyond the recording of their appearance on film, video, or photographs. Hostile to traditional notions of authorial sovereignty, they often worked collaboratively or anonymously, refusing the heroic, normally male-gendered version of artistic genius still so powerful in modernist movements like abstract expressionism. No less distrustful of conventional notions of beauty or sensual pleasure, they disdained, as had Duchamp, mere "retinal painting" in favor of an art based on ideas, theories, linguistic reflexivity, and social critique, while all the time using their bodies as the material on which these conceptual projects were realized.

Or more precisely, they paradoxically realized the de-materializing ambitions of conceptual art through the medium of bodies that were understood in terms of what Bataille would have called "base materialism," the body as a site of creaturely vulnerability, even abasement and decay, rather than ennobling beautification. In so doing, they intensified the anti-optical theatricalization of the aesthetic experience, that addressing of the body of the beholder in real time that formalist critics like Michael Fried were vigorously, if unsuccessfully, condemning in the Minimalist art of the 1960s.[19]

During the earliest phases of body art, there was often an ecstatic sense of release from normal constraints, sexual in particular, which expressed the celebration of polymorphous perversity characteristic of the sixties at their most utopian. Works like Carolee Schneeman's *Meat Joy* of 1964, described by Warr and Jones as "an orgiastic happening in which male and female performers grappled with one another in a variety of fleshy, messy materials in close proximity to the audience," sought to liberate the body from the constraints imposed by moral, aesthetic and social conventions.[20] That the artist was a woman willing to perform naked in public was itself a radical departure, although male artists like Yves Klein had already used nude female models writhing on a canvas covered in his trademark blue paint to produce what he called "anthropometric" paintings in 1960. The Italian artist Piero Manzoni, whose all-white canvases called *Achromes* registered the exhaustion of painting, had taken the process one step further by eliminating canvases entirely. In 1961, he exhibited what he called *Living Sculpture* in which nude models were signed by the artist and given a certificate of authenticity certifying that henceforth they were to be considered as genuine works of art.

Schneeman and other female performance artists who exhibited their unclothed bodies radicalized these gestures by wresting control of the aesthetic process from male artists. They explicitly sought the reversal of the sublimation of the naked, lust-inspiring body into the elevated nude, which had been a feature of Western art and the ideology of aesthetic disinterestedness for centuries. Following Duchamp, they urged the nude to descend the staircase from her pedestal and reveal herself, as she had done in Duchamp's final work, his infamous installation *Étant donnés (Given)*, as an explicit object of a voyeuristic gaze. Or rather, they sought to challenge the objectification of women through that gaze by pushing it to its limit and seizing control over the conditions of display and titillation.

Not only the objectification of women's bodies but the reification of their essence came under attack, as body artists anticipated the breakdown of gender boundaries later advocated by queer theorists like Judith Butler. In 1970, the New York artist Vito Acconci performed a piece called *Conversions* in which he pulled at each of his nipples to produce women's breasts, burned off his body hair and hid his penis between his legs in order to subvert his masculinity. The heady capacity to live beyond given gender categories, long a feature of drag queen self-fashioning, had been enacted by Duchamp in his celebrated self-image as Rose Selavy and then imitated by Andy Warhol's "Forged Image" a generation later. It inspired body artists like Paul McCarthy to masquerade both as a female sex object with a blond wig, mascara and black panties and a randy male sailor who has sex with hamburger meat and mayonnaise in a 1975 performance called "Sailor's Meat." A year before, Lynda Benglis photographed herself nude with an immense rubber penis protruding from her body in an advertisement for a gallery that she placed in the art journal *Artforum*, thus ridiculing the imperative to decide whether she was a male or female artist.

From virtually the beginning, however, body art evinced a darker, more troubled side, which went beyond merely calling into question conventional gender categories. It increasingly moved away from the wholesome vision of integrated, consummatory artistic experience defended by Dewey and still informing Shusterman's somaesthetics, a *telos* that perhaps with some license could still be seen underlying the androgynous experiments of artists like Acconi, Benglis, and McCarthy. Take, for example, the trajectory that led from Pollock's hyper-masculinist action paintings with their unavoidable evocation of ejaculatory frenzy to the Fluxus artist Shigeko Kubota's 1965 "Vagina Painting," in which she used a brush tacked on to her panties to smear red, menstrual-like paint on a canvas, to Rachel Lachowicz's "Red Not Blue" of 1992, in which men rather than Klein's women applied the color red, the color of menstrual blood, instead of his signature blue to a canvas via paint on their bodies and lipstick affixed to their penises, and finally to Keith Boadwee's 1995 "Untitled (Purple Squirt)," in which the artist somehow contrived to expel purple paint from his anus while lying on his back, in a gesture that mixed homo-erotic anal-eroticism with excremental aggression. Instead of the heroic expression of the male creative body, whose inspired actions left traces of their presence on canvases that were meant to be hung vertically on museum walls, the results were resolutely horizontal in implication, fully opposed to the elevating sublimation of the raw body, and explicitly hostile to conventional standards of heteronormativity. Those who watched these performances or their video records were thrust into the world of the *informe* — formlessness — and base materiality celebrated by Georges Bataille, rather than the realm of art as cultivation of the senses and elevation of the sensibility.

At the same time as the gender assumptions and formalist purism of high modernism was being challenged by artists like Schneeman, Kubota, Lachowicz and Boadwee, even more transgressive performances with highly charged political and religious implications were mounted by the group calling themselves Actionists in Austria, led by Hermann Nitsch, Günter Brus, Rudolf Schwarzkogler and Otto Mühl.[21] Here the dominant emotional effect was less lust than disgust, with meat not a source of joy, but of anguish. Nitsch's "Orgies-Mysteries Theater," which took place in the Schloss Prinzdorf,

> ...accommodated large numbers of performers and spectators for a three-day long Dionysiac orgy of blood and gore. Participants could

come and go at will: activities included ritual disembowelments of bulls and sheep, stuffing entrails back into hacked-open carcasses, the treading of huge vats of grapes mixed with entrails, blood and wine, blood-letting on to actors representing Christ and Oedipus, and nighttime processions around the castle with pigs, goats, sheep, horses, dogs and cattle and actors bearing flaming torches. Finally, buckets of blood, slime and entrails were dropped from helicopters on to military tanks, which then drove away.[22]

Contra Nietzsche, this was art as all Dionysus and no Apollo, a far cry from the glittering ornamentalism and precious elitism of the Viennese *fin de siècle* then being restored to its previous glory by the art establishment in the Austrian capital. Inevitably it provoked the strong reactions it so desperately sought, both from the state and from a confused and unsettled public, which worried about its dangerous identification with the regressive and nihilistic impulses it brought to the surface. Perhaps the most disturbing moment in the Actionist assault on bourgeois sensibilities, and as it turned out not on them alone, came in 1968 at the University of Vienna when Brus and his colleagues were asked to join a political meeting called "Art and Revolution," devoted to the role of art in late capitalist society. In what became known as "Action 33," Brus, standing naked on a chair, cut his body with a razor blade, urinated into a glass from which he then drank, defecated on the floor and smeared himself with his own excrement, masturbated while singing the Austrian national anthem and the university song "Gaudeamus Igitur," and capped it all off by inducing himself to vomit. Not only did this earn him an arrest by the state, whose still fascist essence he hoped to reveal, and exile to Germany, but also the wrath of the student militants, who thought he was mocking their pretensions to revolution.

However one interprets the highly ritualized spectacles of sacrifice and redemption staged by the Viennese Actionists with their echoes of German Expressionist pathos and violent reversal of everything held sacred in the traditional notion of *Kultur*, they foreshadowed powerful trends in the body art of the next two decades, in which masochistic self-mutilation, loss of boundaries between the interior and exterior of the artists' body, and a confusion of spectator and participant were all pursued with ferocious ingenuity. What was perhaps missing in the later work, however, was the attempt to create an ecstatic community, a communal festival rather than an alienated spectacle, a utopian goal that was a casualty of the post-sixties turn against redemptive politics and counter-cultural solidarity. What did remain, however, was the emphasis on the body in pain, to use Elaine Scarry's celebrated phrase, not the body in ecstatic pleasure.

Although it is dangerous to generalize about so heterogeneous a range of work, the body artists of the 1980s and 1990s seemed intent on foregrounding and even reveling in trauma, in both its physical and psychological senses, rather than trying to suppress or work it through. Self-abuse ran the gamut, metaphorical to literal, from Vito Acconci's *Seedbed* of 1971, in which he masturbated under a ramp in the Sonnabend gallery in New York, to the self-inflicted cuts to her hands, face and back by the French artist Gina Pane in 1972 or the Yugoslav Marina Abramovic's *Rhythm 0* of 1974, in which she provided instruments of torture to her audience and asked them to use them on her for six hours (after three, apparently, a fight broke out among the torturers, who had done a frighteningly thorough job of hurting and humiliating her, and the ordeal ended). In 1976 and a performance called "Event for Stretched Skin," the Australian artist Stelarc pierced his own back with meat hooks and suspended himself over various sites such as a street in New York or a gallery in Tokyo. In works like her live video operation-performance of 1993 entitled *Omnipresence*, the French artist Orlan showed plastic surgeons cutting into and rearranging her face to conform to traditional Western ideals of feminine pulchritude. Revealing how detachable and malleable the face can actually be in our increasingly posthuman world of prostheses and cyberization, she both mocked conventional standards of beauty and compelled the horrified viewer to share her self-inflicted pain. In many of these examples, in fact, the extraordinary discomfort of the audience, scarcely able to look at the horror before them in the face, was deliberately intended, thus evoking in a very different register Dewey's appeal to overcome the distinction between artistic and aesthetic experience.

Whether the intention was highlighting violence to women, the evils of political torture, the plight of the insane, or the ravages of AIDS, these works were meant to shock their audiences out of the anesthetic complacency into which they had fallen. Mobilizing aesthetics against anesthesia restored the original meaning of the term coined by Alexander Baumgarten in the eighteenth century, when it sought to draw philosophy's attention to the body and the senses. But now it was not the sublimated body, the beautiful body, the body of grace and proportion, but rather the abject body, the body of base materiality, the body invaded by technology, ravaged by disease, and unable to maintain its normal boundaries.

Whether or not the results were what can be called "great art" or even "art" by any normal definition of the word is not an issue I want to raise; there are obvious distinctions of quality, originality, and efficacy among the many exemplars of body art that have accumulated over the past forty years. And if we take an institutional approach to the issue of what is or is not art, that pioneered by philosophers like George Dickie and sociologists like Pierre Bourdieu, there can be little doubt that this work has passed the test and is now included in the canon broadly conceived. It is also clear that as in all projects of intended radical transgression, here too there are contradictions that vitiate the intentions of the artists. As I have tried to argue elsewhere in connection with the embrace of abjection as a term of approbation in the 1990s, the impulse to undermine the institution of art and privilege desublimation as an end in itself can court bad faith when it leads to the deliberate creation of abject objects for display in the very museums they are supposed to subvert.[23] Most body artists resisted leaving behind more than photographic records of their ephemeral events, but these too have found their way into the canonical embrace of the all-devouring art machine. It is also not always certain whether or not the willingness to challenge taboos is inherently liberating or simply a kind of acting out that demands ever more radical manifestations, thus duplicating the logic of incessant innovation and search for means to astonish the bored masses that is so much an engine of the capitalist production of desire. Herbert Marcuse may have been an inspiration to the body art of the 1960s, but it is important to recall his warning against what he called "repressive desublimation," in which apparent liberation produced its opposite.[24]

What is in any case abundantly clear is that we have moved a long way from Dewey's sunny vision of an art that presents attractive "possibilities of human relations" prefiguring a utopian form of realized life in the future. Even the hip-hop music extolled by Shusterman as an example of a liberating somaesthetics seems bland in comparison; rapping and sampling are, after all, pretty tame when set against the self-mutilation of an Orlan, Chris Burden, or Bob Flanagan. But it may be nonetheless arguable that the body art of the past generation, for all its remaining outside the mainstream, does have something useful to tell us about democratic culture, or at least the challenges to it. Without wanting to make inflated claims about its importance, let me suggest at least a few possible ways in which it can be understood in these terms.

Most obviously, body art does so by continuing and deepening that long-standing trend to expand the subject matter thought fit for aesthetic appropriation. By overturning any remaining hierarchical residues of aesthetic value and rejecting an organic notion of the integrated artwork, it also works against any residual belief in the body politic as an organic metaphor of naturally legitimated super- and sub-ordination. On questions of gender and sexual identity, body art has clearly been aggressively forcing us to confront on a visceral level issues that that the most advanced thinkers in these areas have only been able to raise in theoretical terms. Moreover, what Arthur Danto famously called the "transfiguration of the commonplace" has now been extended to those dimensions of human experience that were below all previous thresholds of respectability and suitability, except in the feverish imaginations of the dark writers of the Enlightenment like Sade or their twentieth-century descendents like Bataille.[25]

But rather than producing a problematic "aestheticization" of what should be confronted in moral or political terms, that danger against which Walter Benjamin famously warned in the case of fascist spectacle, this art refuses to beautify the hideous or sweeten the unpalatable in the service of formal pleasure (with certain exceptions aside like the coldly beautiful photographs of Robert Mapplethorpe, which make their way into the Warr and Jones anthology). Instead, it forces those with the stomachs to watch unflinchingly to realize that art need not transfigure or sublimate everything it touches, but rather can find ways to preserve its raw power and disturbing exigency. This is an art that resolutely resists the contemplative stance of disinterestedness associated with aestheticization at its furthest remove from moral and political problems, an aestheticization which paradoxically can have the anesthetic function of numbing us to the real pain outside. It makes us aware, as Dewey would have hoped it would, that the interests of life break through the frame of art, no matter how fierce the attempt to keep them at bay.

In a less obvious sense, the transgressive body art of the past three decades has also opened important questions about the limits and composition of the public sphere, which is taken to be the site of democratic will-formation. Against the assumption that there is a single public sphere in which citizens come together to argue about the great issues of the day, a modern version of the Athenian agora writ large, it shows us how fragmented and plural public spheres are in contemporary democracies. For there can be no doubt that this is art by and for a minority audience, an art that cannot even pretend to mass appeal. Unlike the rap and hip-hop musicians and wordsmiths celebrated by Shusterman, this is a body art without obvious roots in popular culture and very little ability to make its mark in the commercial market place. Although as shown by the dubious entanglements of the Brooklyn Museum of Art's infamous "Sensation" exhibition with its business sponsor, body art is not entirely safe from the lure of the marketplace, by and large, most of it has been able to avoid the temptations of commercial cooptation.[26]

When it does intersect with the more general public sphere, as it did when that show came under fire from the Giuliani administration for its alleged blasphemous implications, it was precisely its challenge to the reigning assumptions about decency, artistic value, and the role of state sponsorship of controversial art that had a democratizing effect. That is, by introducing ideas and artistic practices that could only have been nurtured in the permissive climate of an enclave public, a public that existed below the radar screen of the mass media, could it bring new issues to the more general public sphere, which could then make a start in sorting out their implications. Democracy, we might say, works best if such enclaves are allowed relative autonomy and allowed to serve as laboratories for unorthodox and even offensive ideas and practices, which can then invigorate, outrage, and provoke the general public, whose pieties need to be challenged from time to time. Although the more general public can easily dismiss what it finds objectionable as self-indulgent and exhibitionist acting out rather than anything worthy of the honorific title of art, and often has, in time, a kind of learning process can take place in which at least some of the provocations produce more general reflections on the cultural and political issues raised by the offenders.

There is also a powerful link between body art, indeed performance art of all kinds, and the fostering of a democratic culture. That is, the very gesture of resisting the reification of art objects and insistence on the transience and site-specificity of body art reminds us that democracy itself is a process, not a state of being, and a perpetually uncompleted project at that. To paraphrase Kant's famous description of the *Aufklärung*, we do not live in a democratic age, but in an age of democratization. Contrary to Dewey's stress on the consummatory quality of artworks, it is precisely the open-ended, unfinished quality of body art, its refusal to leave a fixed residue behind, that best serves democratic culture. If, as Habermas has famously argued, the goal of perfect consensus is an ideal *telos* of intersubjective communication, which is only asymptotically realized, the performativity of body-art, its insistence that even the body is a process, not a fixed object in the world, powerfully instantiates the way in which democracy is always in front of us, never fully achieved. The illocutionary promise of a consensus based on rational deliberation and the victory of the better argument is always just short of being cashed in, even as we may strive to attain it. One might even argue that the confrontational impact of this art pays homage to the agonistic moment in democratic practice which allows, indeed nurtures, creative dissensus rather than forcing a homogenizing consensus.

A similar conclusion follows from the complexity introduced by body art into the time-honored question of representation, which presents, of course, both a political and an aesthetic conundrum. By using the artist's body as a site of aesthetic experimentation, often taking real risks in so doing, the distinction between presence and representation is tacitly called into question. Although at times what seemed real was not — Nitsch and the Viennese Actionists dismembered only dead sheep, not live ones, and the legendary death by self-castration of Rudolf Schwarzkogler was just that, only a legend — at others the knife did really cut flesh and the blood was real. Some body artists did have themselves shot in the arm and did sleep with corpses and did nail their foreskins to boards. The result has been to undermine the privilege and self-sufficiency of the represented image over the actual activity, thus working against the extraordinary power that images have in the media-saturated mass democracy of the modern world.

Instead of providing a positive representation of the sovereign people, this art reflects the insight of recent political theorists like Claude Lefort and Jean-Luc Nancy that at the center of the political realm there is an absence, a void, a lack, which is filled only at our peril. In resisting sublimation, metaphorization and representation, body art thus helps us avoid trying to construct a mythical embodiment of "the people," an embodiment that can only be simulacral and deceptive because it covers over the inevitable distinctions, even conflicts, which always subtend it. It reminds us that the "demos" in democracy is only a fictional or counterfactual notion, never perfectly equal to an ontologically real object in the world.

Another way to make this point is to note the foregrounding of trauma in body art, which refuses to sugarcoat the violence that was so much a feature of the terrible twentieth century. It may not be accidental that both Nitsch and Schwarzkogler's fathers were killed fighting for the Nazis, while Mühl himself fought in the war and was a POW.[27] Their ritualistic orgies of mayhem and redemption were, it seems, designed in part to remind Austrians of a past they were not anxious to register. If, as Cathy Caruth has argued, trauma involves a kind of "unclaimed experience" in which the wound does not heal, but remains still festering beneath the scar, then the deeply troubled art we have been discussing expresses the belatedness of a traumatic event or events that have not yet been assimilated or reconciled.[28] As such, it brings to the surface those moments of founding violence that even the most democratic polity has difficult fully acknowledging. Much of the body art we have been discussing can thus be called, *pace* Dewey, art as unclaimed experience, in which the temporal fragmentation of belatedness and repetition go hand in hand with the disintegration of spatial integrity and the permeability of boundaries.

Yet another way in which body art might be seen potentially in tandem with democratic impulses is through its explicit resistance to the disciplining and normalization of the docile body — whether through the harsh regulations of factory labor or the soft inducements of mainstream conventions of beauty — of which Foucault has made us all so aware. This hope has recently been expressed in Michael Hardt and Antonio Negri's provocative book *Empire*, which explicitly cites body artists like Stelarc as models of a new "posthuman" refashioning of the body.[29] Although acknowledging its problematic colonization by mass culture in the service of the status quo, Hardt and Negri also manage to give it a positive potential. They write,

> Today's corporeal mutations constitute an *anthropological exodus* and represent an extraordinarily important, but still quite ambiguous, element of the configuration of republicanism "against" imperial civilization. The anthropological exodus is important precisely because here is where the positive, constructive face of the mutation begins to appear: an ontological mutation in action, the concrete invention of a first *new place in the non-place.*[30]

Whatever one thinks of Hardt and Negri's tentative mobilization of transgressive somaesthetics for positive purposes — Stellarc's performances may perhaps be best seen as instances of ascetic self-discipline rather than expressions of bodily vulnerability — it brings us almost full circle back to John Dewey's *Art as Experience*. But the detour has certainly complicated the assumptions that underlay it.[31] Dewey's aesthetics, it has been often been noted, lacked any sense of the sublime. It was inspired by a desire to make the world more and more available for sensual appropriation and aesthetic mastery, more and more a home for lives of beauty and meaning, and thus lacked an acknowledgment of the limits to representation presented by the sublime. Although there are, of course, obvious dangers in a politics that is based entirely on the experience of sublime horror and awe, it may be the case that a certain humility when it comes to our power to remake the world in the image of beauty is a valuable dimension of a democratic politics that knows it is perpetually falling short of the absolute realization of its goal. And while there may well be questions raised about the compatibility between the human rights discourse that is now so much a part of democratic culture, a discourse that has one of its foundations the inviolability of the human body, and an art that seems so intent on demonstrating its antithesis, there is sufficient warrant in much — albeit not all — of the work to read it as protesting rather than celebrating the pain it so powerfully evokes. And perhaps in so doing, it serves as a negative instantiation of the more substantive notion of democratic culture that Dewey has contrasted with its thin proceduralist twin. In short, for all its aggression against the mainstream *sensus communis*, for all its willingness to flirt with the violence and irrationality that would seem to be the antithesis of democratic politics, the body art so tenaciously performed in the enclaves of avant-garde culture over the past forty years may be a version of somaesthetics that has something to teach democracy after all.

NOTES

1. John Dewey, *Art as Experience* (New York: Capricorn, 1934), p. 56.
2. Thomas Alexander, "The Art of Life: Dewey's Aesthetics," in *Reading Dewey: Interpretations for a Postmodern Generation,* ed. Larry A. Hickman (Bloomington: Indiana University Press, 1998), p. 4.
3. Dewey cited in *Reading Dewey*, p. 349.
4. Robert B. Westbrook, *John Dewey and American Democracy* (Ithaca: Cornell University Press, 1991), pp. 401–402.
5. David Fott, *John Dewey: America's Philosopher of Democracy* (Lanham: Rowman and Littlefield, 1998), p. 109.
6. Peter Bürger, *Theory of the Avant-garde*, trans. Michael Snow (Minneapolis: University of Minnesota Press, 1984).
7. Dewey, *Art as Experience*, p. 227.
8. Hannah Arendt, *The Human Condition* (Garden City: Anchor, 1959).
9. See, for example, Philip W. Jackson, *John Dewey and the Lessons of Art* (New Haven: Yale University Press, 1998). Perhaps the best general study remains Thomas M. Alexander, *John Dewey's Theory of Art, Experience and Nature* (Albany: SUNY Press, 1987).
10. Richard Shusterman, *Practicing Philosophy: Pragmatism and the Philosophical Life* (New York: Routledge, 1997), p. 177. See also Richard Shusterman, *Pragmatist Aesthetics: Living Beauty, Rethinking Art* (Cambridge: Blackwell, 1992); and Richard Shusterman, *Performing Live: Aesthetic Alternatives for the Ends of Art* (Ithaca: Cornell University Press, 2001).
11. Shusterman, *Pragmatist Aesthetics*, p. 21.
12. Dewey wrote the introduction to three of Alexander's books, *Man's Supreme Inheritance* (1918), *Constructive Conscious Control of the Individual* (1923) and *The Use of the Self* (1932). He credited the "Alexander Technique" for having relieved his own problems of bad posture and stiffness, even his poor eyesight. Shusterman is himself a practitioner of Feldenkrais therapy, which continues this tradition.
13. Shusterman, *Practicing Philosophy,* p. 176. For Rorty's rebuttal, see "Response to Richard Shusterman," in *Richard Rorty: Critical Dialogues*, eds. Matthew Festeinstein and Simon Thompson (Cambridge: Polity Press, 2001).
14. Shusterman, *Practicing Philosophy,* p. 150.
15. Shusterman, *Pragmatist Aesthetics*, p. 212.

16. In an interview, "Self-Styling after the 'End of Art,'" conducted by Chantal Ponbrian and Olivier Asselin, *Parachute*, 105 (2002), p. 59, Shusterman does mention in passing several of the body artists discussed below. But he understands them as examples of "self-fashioning" and bodily discipline, rather than as challenges to normative notions of the self as active agent and the body as a fashioned aesthetic whole.

17. Tracy Warr and Amelia Jones, *The Artist's Body* (London: Phaidon, 2000). There have, to be sure, been earlier accounts, for example, RoseLee Goldberg, *Performance Art: From Futurism to the Present* (London: Abrams, 1988); Amelia Jones, *Body Art/Performing the Subject* (Minneapolis: University of Minnesota Press, 1998); and *Performing the Body/Performing the Text*, eds. Amelia Jones and Andrew Stephenson (London: Routledge, 1999).

18. Dewey's friendship with the collector Albert Barnes, who was a resolutely anticontextualist formalist, seems to have influenced his own judgments about the importance of form. For a discussion of Barnes and Dewey, which treats this issue at some length, see Alan Ryan, *John Dewey and the High Tide of American Liberalism* (New York: W.W. Norton, 1995), pp. 252–265.

19. Michael Fried, "Art and Objecthood," (1967) in *Art and Objecthood: Essays and Reviews* (Chicago: University of Chicago Press, 1998). In fact, this essay became an inevitable target in many accounts of the genesis of body art, for example see the following articles, all found in Jones, *Body Art/Performing the Subject*: Amelia Jones, "Art History/Art Criticism: Performing Meaning," pp. 42–46; Christine Poggi, "Following Acconci/Targeting Vision," p. 269; and Joanna Lowry, "Performing Vision in the Theatre of the Gaze: The Work of Douglas Gordon," p. 276.

20. *The Artist's Body*, p. 60.

21. For an analysis see Philip Ursprung, "'Catholic Tastes': Hurting and Healing the Body in Viennese Actionism in the 1960s," in *Performing the Body/Performing the Text*, pp. 138–152.

22. Warr and Jones, *The Artist's Body*, p. 93, here describe the eightieth of these in the 1984 series.

23. Martin Jay, "Abjection Overruled," in *Cultural Semantics: Keywords of Our Time* (Amherst: University of Massachusetts Press, 1998).

24. Herbert Marcuse, *One-Dimensional Man* (Boston: Beacon Press, 1964).

25. Arthur Danto, *The Transfiguration of the Commonplace: A Philosophy of Art* (Cambridge: Harvard University Press, 1981). For similar analyses, see Murray Krieger, *Arts on the Level: The Fall of the Elite Object* (Knoxville: University of Tennessee Press, 1981) and George J. Leonard, *Into the Light of Things: The Art of the Commonplace from Wordsworth to John Cage* (Chicago: University of Chicago Press, 1994).

26. Perhaps one exception is the recent self-marketing of Orlan, who has decided her art is not "body art" but rather "l'art charnel." See her website http://www.cicv.fr/creation_artistique/online/orlan/review4/revue4.html.

27. Ursprung, "'Catholic Tastes,'" p. 150.

28. Cathy Caruth, *Unclaimed Experience: Trauma, Narrative, and Experience* (Baltimore: Johns Hopkins University Press, 1996).

29. Michael Hardt and Antonio Negri, *Empire* (Cambridge: Harvard University Press, 2000), p. 448.

30. *Ibid.*, p. 215.

31. Fott, *John Dewey*, p. 118.

CONTINUING CONNECTIONS:
COMMENTS ON THE PRECEDING ESSAYS

Richard Shusterman

I

Responding to a collection of essays devoted to very different aspects of my work and treating a wide range of my books and articles presents a task that is both new and daunting. On several occasions I have had the role of replying to collected articles that critically focused on one of my books, but here the scope is much broader and the topics far more diverse. There is no way I could address all the issues and arguments here raised within the compass of a coherent and readably compact essay. The volume is not a *Festschrift* where my role would be to thankfully appreciate the essays that students and colleagues have written to honor me. None of the contributors has been my student or university colleague. Very grateful nonetheless for their efforts in writing about my work in pragmatism, I do not want to respond by adopting the familiar pugnacious stance of a philosophical gladiator whose main aim is to show that he is not only right in his views but also much smarter than his critics by polemically savaging their critical points and arguments with punctiliously detailed refutations or counterattacks. Though some enjoy such contentious hairsplitting (and I remember sometimes savoring it as a debutant first cutting my philosophical teeth), it usually strikes me as tedious, profitless distraction from real understanding and constructive dialogue.

Pragmatically, the most useful direction for my comments should be the one that best serves the primary purpose of this volume. If that purpose is to provide a deeper, richer understanding of my pragmatist theories, then let me focus my comments primarily on what these papers instruct me about those theories (their impact, uses, and limits, including those formulations of my views that invite misunderstandings and require clarification) and about the issues those theories address. These essays, taken collectively, are instructive in ways that go beyond the sum of points made by each individual contribution. Before providing any specific comments on the arguments of the individual essays, I should note two general points that their collectivity highlights in my mind.

The first is the theme of internationalism in philosophy, which I have often treated in my writings, including a guest-edited volume of the journal *Metaphilosophy* (in 1997) explicitly devoted to this theme. Philosophy, often pursued as an inquiry into the most basic, general features and meanings of experience, clearly seems to transcend national (and linguistic) borders and frequently claims to deal with universal truths. Yet philosophy just as clearly emerges from particular social contexts and national traditions. It may pretend to offer the God's-eye, absolute truth or "view from nowhere," but it always emerges from some location that somehow shapes its formulation and direction. Pragmatism, for example, is famous for its distinctive American origins, even if it can also be seen as a blend of philosophical ideas and insights already articulated in Europe. Context not only shapes the emergence of philosophical ideas, but can also significantly structure its reception. This collection of essay reflects some of the structures and constraints that shape the international circulation of philosophical ideas.

Because the volume originated with a conference held in Wocław (kindly organized by this book's coeditors), seven of the papers are from Polish authors. Poland has indeed been very receptive to my work, but certainly no more than France, China, or Germany (which have, like Poland, distinguished philosophical traditions of their own). It is not a performative contradiction to welcome wholeheartedly every one of the Polish contributions, while pointing out that there are interesting philosophical perspectives on my work from other cultural and linguistic traditions than those represented here. Another point that struck me when I considered the different essays together was that some were able to draw on my most recent publications while some of the Polish authors apparently did not have those texts at their disposal. Even with the internet, there unfortunately remains an economically based differential access to philosophical material, and such differences in access affect the production of philosophical work by determining the philosopher's range of bibliographical resources.

A second point that the collection brought home to me is the hybrid nature of my theorizing. By this I mean that my theories seem so intimately to combine different philosophical areas (ethics, aesthetics, political theory, etc.) that it is sometimes difficult to assign these theories a clear philosophical category. This is reflected in the fact that some of the essays appearing under one classificatory grouping in this book's table of contents might also fit in another. Does somaesthetics belong to aesthetics or to philosophy of mind? Does it not also have deep connections with epistemology, ethics, political philosophy, and nondualist metaphysics of human being as *soma*? Is my research on rap really aesthetics or instead a disguised form of politically motivated cultural criticism? Is my paper on faith and fallibilism (which forms the focus of Adam Chmielewski's contribution) an exercise in epistemology or philosophy of religion or indeed in ethics or philosophy of education? (Chmielewski even takes it in the direction of political theory.) When I argue for philosophy as an art of living, am I doing aesthetic theory, ethics, or metaphilosophy, or indeed even metaphysics (as Sami Pihlström here suggests)? It is hard for me to define my theories within a single philosophical category because I see the problems I treat as cutting across traditional philosophical areas.

When Arthur Danto told me several years ago that he considered me a systematic philosopher, I skeptically countered that I have never written separate monographs on ethics, epistemology, metaphysics, or political theory in the way that systematic philosophers traditionally do so that these different works combine to constitute a full system, architectonically built of separate rooms that together create a palace of knowledge. When I denied that I had such a systematic corpus, Danto explained that a separate book on each of philosophy's different areas was not needed because a systematically coherent position regarding these different areas was already evident in the way I treated specific issues within one area by also addressing and engaging their connections with other areas. I didn't need a multi-chambered palace; the necessary multiple facets were operative within a single room. For example, my work on rap is informed with philosophical theories and arguments that range from aesthetics and cultural theory to ethics, epistemology, politics, metaphysics, and the idea of philosophy as a way of life.

The world of experience that philosophy seeks to understand, interpret, and indeed even improve does not neatly divide itself into separate, autonomous philosophical compartments. If things are somehow connected in experience, even if far from smoothly unified, then my philosophical explorations tend to confirm such connections in working across philosophical disciplines (and traditions). If one graduate student (back in the days when my nights were filled with rap) described me (with a nod to my old school hero Grandmaster Flash) as a "philosophical mixmaster," then I hope that such philosophical mixing and hybridity do not entail mush and confusion. Let me now turn to the individual essays that demonstrate such imbrication of philosophical issues not only in *my* theorizing but in their own arguments.

II

If, since Aristotle, metaphysics is often considered first philosophy, while epistemology has also claimed primacy in modern times, then it seems fit to begin with the grouping of papers headed by these key topics. Sami Pihlström's paper provides an excellent start, not only because it is a model of clear analysis, insightful interpretation, and constructive dialogue but also because it highlights precisely the sort of philosophical imbrications that characterize my theories. It also usefully reminds readers that my efforts to revive philosophy as an embodied art of living with a robust dimension of real-world praxis do not imply that I disrespect or neglect philosophy's pursuit of theory (ethical, epistemological, metaphysical, etc.), which is often needed as a critical guide to practice.

Underlining such reciprocal supportive links of theory and practice among the ancient philosophers and some moderns in *Practicing Philosophy* and other works, I have also tried to exemplify this integration in my own philosophical efforts, not simply calling for practical change but exploring theories that provide reasons or tools to effect such change. I agree with Professor Pihlström that the idea of metaphysics as an inquiry delivering absolute knowledge "of ultimate reality, or Being qua Being ... urgently needs correction," and my frequent critiques of foundational metaphysics are aimed at such correction. But, as he notes, I also express and defend metaphysical views in my pragmatist theories.

When I was a student of analytic philosophy in Jerusalem, we used to distinguish between metaphysics (used pejoratively to indicate vague transcendental speculations) and ontology (used positively to indicate good metaphysical reasoning based on logico-linguistic arguments some of them being transcendental in character). Before my explicitly pragmatist turn, I did a great deal of work in analytic ontology, especially in the ontology of literature and art. I based my ontological conclusions on the entrenched (linguistic and more-than-linguistic) practices operative in our dealings in these domains. These practices can change through history and have ethical, political, and cognitive consequences that also provide reasons for maintaining or changing them.

After making my explicit pragmatist turn, I continued this line of ontological thinking in *Pragmatist Aesthetics*, presenting my views on the ontological status of artworks and how such ontology impacts our practices of interpreting art. But the book also proposes a general metaphysical position on reality as a whole, one that provides a pragmatist middle ground between analytic atomism and Hegelian, deconstructionist organic unity, while also suggesting another middle path between traditional foundationalist essentialism and a postmodern anti-essentialism of radical contingency that neglects the role of historical norms or historicized, mutable essences.

In *Surface and Depth*, I reformulate my view that, from the pragmatist perspective (a humanly situated point of view, not an impossible God's-eye view-from-nowhere), the ontological status of artworks ultimately relies on the diverse, intricately connected, and mutable ways in which our (changing) culture deals with art; and I expand this approach to cultural entities in general. If, to some extent, all the entities we discuss are identified, conceptualized, known, and in that sense shaped in experience through human languages and practices that are always already products of culture, then to that extent the ontological status and identity of those entities (even those we regard as natural objects) also depend on our human practices. This, as Sami Pihlström recognizes, does not preclude advocating a level of realism. In such realism, the world we really experience is an indissoluble mix of what is independent of the human (beyond the control or shaping of human practices) and what is shaped by those practices or conventions. As W. V. O. Quine, one of the pragmatic analytic heroes of my student years metaphorically put the point (that William James earlier made), our reality "is a pale gray lore, black with fact and white with convention," but without "any quite black threads in it, or any white ones."[1] Because I believe that the metaphysics of our cultural objects are so thoroughly dependent on our cultural practices (as I explain in the chapter on "Pragmatism and Culture" in *Surface and Depth*), I am far less interested in providing abstract definitions and formal classifications of their ontological status than I am in analyzing more precisely those cultural practices and even in trying to change them for the better.

Pihlström's paper connects pragmatist metaphysics with religious thought, noting that Dewey's naturalism does not preclude his being a religious thinker. If this view seems right to me, it is because I appreciate Dewey's important distinction between being "religious" and practicing or affirming a particular institutional religion. Dewey argues that religion needs a process of purification through which its "ethical and ideal content" is separated from its unhealthy connection with belief in a "Supernatural Being" and with the often unsavory and outmoded, ideologies, social practices, and ritual forms of worship that are simply the "irrelevant" accretion of "the conditions of social culture" in which the various traditional religions emerged. He therefore recommends that we distinguish and preserve what he calls "the religious" in contrast to religion in the concrete traditional sense. Defining the religious as an experience or attitude "having the force of bringing a better, deeper and enduring adjustment in life" that is "more outgoing, more ready and glad" than stoicism and "more active" than mere submission, Dewey affirms that "any activity pursued in behalf of an ideal end against obstacles and in spite of threats of personal loss because of conviction of its general and enduring value is religious in quality," while noting that artists and other kinds of dedicated inquirers display such activity.[2]

In this sense, I would not object to being described as a religious thinker, for I unabashedly admit to a spiritual dimension, interest, or motive in my philosophical work. Indeed, despite my critiques of institutional religion, I acknowledge a spiritual yearning that has occasionally led me to experiment in some varieties of religious practice, including some outside the Jewish faith into which I was born. In any case, I am less optimistic than Dewey that we can purify the religious from its outmoded institutional accretions, and less confident than G. E. Moore, Richard Rorty, Arthur Danto, and others that art can somehow replace religion in a new post-religious culture. I argue for these points in an essay "Art and Religion," which treads a delicate middle path between institutional religious orthodoxy and vehemently anti-religious secularism, while also contrasting Catholic notions of transfiguration and transcendence with those of a number of East-Asian religions.[3]

Adam Chmielewski's interesting paper highlights just how far my views of faith are from the official Vatican line, but he bases his critique of my philosophy of religion entirely on a short article "Faith and Fallibilism" that I was asked to write for a special issue of the journal *Common Knowledge* in response to Cardinal Ratzinger's last homily before he was elected to the papacy and became Pope Benedict XVI. Deftly situating the homily and the reactions it generated within the broad history of the Catholic Church and contemporary issues of religion and multiculturalism in contemporary Western culture and politics, Chmielewski explains the historico-political reasons why Ratzinger, as a Catholic churchman, should insist on infallibility as the only way to ground the Catholic faith. Absolutism and infallibilism may be the reigning orthodoxy and best *Realpolitik* for the Church of Rome, but my essay's argument was aimed more at issues of epistemology and the ethics of belief, that faith and fallibilism are, in principle, very compatible and that religious belief might be rendered more mature, more tolerant, and even more resilient through a fallibilist perspective. Fallibilism strengthens epistemological resilience by consoling us, when we learn we were wrong about some belief, that we were at least right to know that we could, in principle, be corrected.

If this seems more an *Idealpolitik* than a pragmatic *Realpolitik,* then I happily confess that making logical space for ideals even when we know that present institutions will not currently allow them actual space is part of my sense of the pragmatist agenda of using philosophical argument to sustain or indeed inspire social hope. Moreover, if clerics and their lay supporters try to argue more specifically that faith and fallibilism are simply incompatible with Catholic doctrine, I could respond that they both are found in its holy canon.[4] When Chmielewski argues that religion's job of creating collective identity works better through an infallible exclusivity of faith than through the inclusivity of Asian religions like Buddhism (and grounds this on our essential human nature: "the constitution of humans"), I wonder how he would explain why Asian communities are socially more tight-knit and collectively minded than our Western societies seem to be. But I prefer not to discuss such matters at this high level of generalization, with homogenizing notions of human essence or of East and West, because each of these cultural categories contains incredible diversity, though I realize that there is sometimes a useful economy in such gross dualistic distinctions.

Don Morse appeals to my interest in Confucianism to explain what he calls my erotic pragmatism in a paper that shows how somaesthetics cuts across issues in epistemology, metaphysics, and environmentalism. I am happy to be identified as an erotic pragmatist (a description that nicely complements my being labeled a pragmatist of "con-sensualism" by a Parisian female philosopher[5]). But my meanings and advocacy of eroticism are very different from what Professor Morse portrays, and they have no immediate connection with the Confucian idea and ideal of the fundamental unity of heaven, earth, and man. My vision of eroticism may be less edgy than Foucault's, but it is far steamier than the asexual notion of "Human Eros" that Morse invokes: the mere desire "to experience the world as a fulfillment of meaning and value." There seems to be a simple (but also productive) misunderstanding in Morse's reading of the closing sections of *Body Consciousness* that I should clear up here.

Its criticisms of F. M. Alexander (whose work I otherwise much admire) focus on his one-sided, individualistic rationalism, whose repudiation of free emotional expression made him wary not only of sex but also of music and dance. I speculate that perhaps Dewey did not distance himself enough from Alexander's critique of emotional excitement because Dewey at that time was himself struggling in his personal life against the free expression of passion, at least in its erotic form. More generally, Dewey gives very little attention to sexual expression; while William James indeed speaks of "the *anti-sexual instinct.*" One aim of my recent research in somaesthetics is to provide a contemporary pragmatism that takes sexual eroticism as seriously and positively as French philosophers of the body often do, while also treating it in the melioristic pragmatist spirit as a tool for improving the quality of our experience. Confucianism (which is one of the most prudish of East-Asian philosophical traditions) would not be the best way to do this. Thus, in critically contrasting Alexander's insistence on radical self-autonomy to the Confucian ideal of connecting the human person (through his body) with heaven and earth, I am not suggesting a sexual threesome of coital union but rather simply expressing the Confucian (and Deweyan) recognition that the individual body derives its powers (and is made whole) from its connection with the wider world of forces and things beyond it. I then construe this dependence ecologically by arguing that enlightened care for the self must include care for the environment that surrounds us.

Professor Morse interprets this as a sort of cosmic, ecological eroticism, which seems a metaphorically creative and metaphysical reading of what I more simply described as more conscious openness to the transactional self's relation to the wider world and the need for the self to harmonize with the environment. However, this openness to greater harmony of connection does not mean erotic contact or fusion with the environment, and certainly not all the universe in its unbounded vastness. (Dewey, I think, is erotic enough in this transactional sense, though not adequately concerned with the erotic in the more basic interpersonal, sexual sense). I agree with Morse that, practically speaking, our experience and treatment of our situation are always bounded in some way (even though the penumbra of connections and interrelations extends indefinitely in principle), and I repeatedly affirm the body's role as helping to constitute the center and boundedness of our experience[6] I likewise insist that somaesthetics' heightened awareness achieves its greater awareness through a focus that involves bounded attention that includes some proximate environment but never too much of it. If we are trying to feel the vertebrae of our thoracic spine by the contact it makes with the floor, our focus is indeed engaged with the floor but not with the ceiling or the walls that emerge from the floor or the furniture in the adjoining room.

Finally, when *Body Consciousness* suggests that somaesthetic skills of enhanced awareness can improve our lives in many ways by augmenting, through greater consciousness, our resources for meaning and pleasure, "including an uplifting sense of cosmic unity" by making us more productively aware of our contact with the environment, I am not affirming a monistic metaphysics of a perfectly unified, harmonious, seamless universe. Nor am I advocating a mysticism of fusion. My own sense of cosmic unity might be described as a vaguely felt, undefined unity involving a dazzling, confusing variety, a unity that is far from fully unified and harmonious. As William

James described it, "a world imperfectly unified still … in which we find things partly joined and partly disjoined," a world in continuous transformation, as we humans indeed are.[7]

Jerold J. Abrams' work on posthumanism takes this notion of transformation seriously and treats it with great skill. Though he does not really contest my views or challenge my arguments, I consider him one of my sharpest and most useful critics. This is because in deploying my theories in relevant issues where I have not yet deployed them—issues relating to nanotechnology, genetic engineering, robotics, performance-enhancing implants or drugs, and other radical forms of somatic intervention, Abrams powerfully shows the limits of somaesthetic theorizing while also helping it overcome those limits through his unique and important contributions to this field. He is right to recognize that Peirce has important insights for somaesthetics, and though I could not include them in *Body Consciousness*, I have subsequently discussed them in detail.[8]

Somatic transformations toward the superhuman or posthuman raise issues of what aspects of the soma will be privileged for enhancement and what will be relegated as obsolete and discarded. Abrams affirms very generally that the superhumans must retain "the basic look and experience of the face and the body" since this look is "essential" in terms of historical continuity to "recognize each other and themselves in this form." Even though I am happy to grant this assumption, so many hard problems remain. Does this basic look include sexual difference; is it only a matter of looks regardless of other sensory aspects of somatic style and behavior?[9] Even if we looked roughly the same, would we still be considered humans if we behaved or functioned completely differently? What if, for example, we never laughed or cried, did not need to eat or sleep or dispose of bodily wastes, were devoid of bodily feelings of hunger, thirst, pain, fatigue, and have neither sexual desire nor the need for such desire or behavior for procreation. Indeed, for all the joys of sex, there are also many people who deeply suffer because of its powerful place in our lives. Certain visions of the future would like to marginalize or discard it, so one task for an advocate of erotic pragmatism is to highlight and improve the value of erotic experience, a project I am now pursuing within the framework of somaesthetics. But the more important general lesson here is that how we design ourselves in the future depends on our evaluations of what we should design for; here the links between aesthetics, ethics, and metaphysics are once again salient.

III

Turning to the essays grouped under literature and aesthetics, we find the same feature of transdisciplinary imbrications. Anna Budziak begins her contribution by locating it "at the frontiers of philosophy, psychology, and literature." Her erudite and insightful essay is a real gift to me because it connects the philosophy I long ago developed when writing on T.S. Eliot with my much newer research in somaesthetics. Because I saw my Eliot book as essentially part of my analytic, pre-pragmatist period, before I developed my interest in popular art and somatic philosophy, I never thought of connecting Eliot and somaesthetics. Professor Budziak reminds us that Eliot (despite his personal anxieties about embodiment) recognized that even the rarified realms of poetry and criticism are grounded in human physiology and could profit from being connected with the scientific precision of that field. As she likewise points out, not only does Eliot recognize (with James) the bodily grounding of emotion but he also insists that emotions, despite their somatic nature, can nonetheless be educated.

Somaesthetic perception and reflection (higher forms of explicit and critical somatic awareness that I explain in *Body Consciousness*) are, I argue, useful tools for educating our emotions because they enable us to discern more clearly what those emotions are by improving our awareness of their somatic dimensions, which in turn can also shed light on their other aspects. Reeducating the emotions begins with knowing what emotions we have and how we feel them. Budziak, in discussing somaesthetic spirituality and the special body-mind harmony of mysticism, alludes to Eliot's essay on "The Metaphysical Poets." I should recall here that in that essay Eliot formulates his famous theory of the dissociation of sensibility that affirms, in its own distinctive way, the value of somaesthetic intelligence and perception. The metaphysical poets were exemplary in uniting feeling with thought, in sensing things with critical intelligence. They did not divide their thinking and feeling into different times or compartments of mind. Somaesthetic perception and reflection aim at such discriminating, thoughtful feeling or sensation. We need to learn not to feel and think separately but, as it were, to combine them in a single perceptual act that might be expressed by the rather silly-sounding term "flinking"—to convey the idea of thoroughly blending feeling and thinking, of sensing with thoughtful attention or thinking with and through our feelings and sensations.

Kacper Bartczak's contribution also examines my work through the focus of a poet, though one I have only very briefly discussed in my corpus. Professor Bartczak's essay is especially valuable in the way it places my views on self-development in critical dialogue with those of Richard Rorty, who in introducing me to Deweyan pragmatism also helped introduce me to these questions of self-creation or self-stylization. I regard Rorty, along with Pierre Bourdieu and Arthur Danto, as the major thinkers whose exemplarity and interest in my work made my career possible. Rorty not only opened my eyes to the resources of pragmatism but also showed how its insights could be combined with those of analytic and continental philosophy and literary theory. Nonetheless, my version of Deweyan pragmatism is very different from his in many ways that I articulate elsewhere and cannot pause to rehearse here.[10]

Rorty and I frequently discussed our differences, and he long ago admitted in conversation a problematic tension between his Bloomian strong poet and his liberal ironist that his last writings try better to reconcile, as Professor

Bartczak deftly demonstrates. I find Rorty's final position still deficient not only because its narrow focus on self-creation through literature neglects life's somatic dimension as a site for self-fashioning but also because his scope of literature seems too limited. He essentially focuses on philosophy and the novel with only a rapid nod at poetry, and he explicitly rejects the literatures of the social sciences (which he condemns as "dreary" and "grim").

My stance is more nuanced and pluralist. Reading novels does not necessarily make us better, kinder, or wiser (as certain novels point out themselves). Novels can also be dreary and morally dubious or even noxious in their values (abusively pornographic fiction, for instance); so reading novels even for pleasure demands a second stage of reflective critique so that we don't simply absorb its world view unconsciously in our pleasurable identification with its fictional world. Conversely, the literature of social science need not be dreary and dismally abstract; some works of social, anthropological, or psychological analysis describe with beautiful prose and psychological insight the colorful details of particular cultures, social worlds, and diverse (often unconventional) individuals whose depicted experience enlarges our own.

If I differ with Rorty in how to develop Dewey's legacy, I also differ on some matters from Dewey himself, even in aesthetics. Dorota Koczanowicz perceptively notes some of those differences, while emphasizing the common ground I share with Dewey. She especially focuses on our advocacy that art and aesthetic experience should be more deeply integrated into life rather than simply cherished as a separate, sacred domain where people retreat from life to be healed. She rightly points out that Dewey and I recognize the therapeutic value of art and aesthetic experience but argue that such therapy does not require a quarantined recuperation clinic set apart from the "contamination" of real-life practices and energies. The pragmatist goal, I would add, is more positive than therapy (which implies ailment or disease); it is rather the direction of growth, enrichment, and flourishing. At the end of Dr. Koczanowicz's paper, we find an apparent paradox for pragmatist aesthetics: that in bringing the special quality of aesthetic experience to everyday life, such life is in an important way no longer ordinary, everyday experience but instead special. There is, however, no contradiction here because everyday does not imply ordinary in the sense of blandness, dullness, or routine. With the proper mindfully perceptive attention or artistry, many everyday events and objects can be transfigured into special aesthetic experiences without losing their ontological status of belonging to the everyday world and becoming through such aesthetic transfiguration (of perception or performance) an object of some putatively transcendent and compartmentalized artworld.[11]

Wojciech Małecki concludes this section with an essay that brings the focus back to literature's role in the philosophical quest for self-knowledge and self-development that Bartczak's essay raises from the angle of poetic self-creation. Professor Małecki (author of the first English monograph on my pragmatist writings) focuses on the role of autobiography in my philosophical work in an article that displays his characteristic erudition and polemical critique. Canvassing the breadth of my corpus, he not only helpfully formulates the reasons I give for using biographical and autobiographical material in interpreting a philosopher's thought and self-fashioning within the project of philosophy as an art of living, but he also provides a perceptive account of the different ways I use elements of my own autobiography in my philosophical writings. If one of these uses belongs to "the tradition of philosophical self-purification and confessions of guilt," then let me make the further confession that there remain many experiences and misadventures whose purification through philosophical writing still await their turn for cleansing.

I do not feel guilty (though sometimes embarrassed) about registering in print how my affection and admiration for certain people have shaped my philosophical thought, but such explicit avowals help make the point that my devotion to aesthetics is not limited to the appreciation of beauty and meaning in artworks. I admire personal beauty, especially the radiance of character that can shine in the intelligent grace of a dancer as well as in the eyes of a philosopher. If I have a twinge of guilt in subjecting unsuspecting readers of philosophy to some personal confessions, I willingly bear the guilt in the hope that those confessions redeem themselves by making my views more comprehensible and attractive. When I offer justifications for using autobiographical insights in writing about issues of self-examination and self-development that I faced in recommending and practicing philosophy as an art of living (where writing also forms part of that practice), this is not by way of compensating for feeling guilty that my work "never provides any precise definition of autobiography," which Dr. Małecki admits is "the slipperiest of literary genres."

I feel no such guilt because I do not think such vague, slippery genres admit of precise definitions, and I was anyway not interested in literary genre definitions. This includes the definition of literature itself as a genre associated with the fine arts versus the broader definition of literature as writing in general. My case for philosophy's ultimately needing literature is essentially based on the broader sense of literature that includes not only fine art but all thoughtfully composed verbal discourse (written or oral). I was also not "primarily" interested in convincing some unspecified, hypothetical group of "theorists" identified as "the opponents of philosophical autobiography" that autobiography is always needed or always useful for treating all problems relating to the self. The scope of my plea for the pertinence of autobiographical reflections was within the project of examining and practicing one's own philosophical life, where the concrete shape of one's past experiences seems useful for understanding who one is so that one can steer a better path forward toward improving oneself. My own autobiographical marks were also introduced in that context.

It would not trouble me if there were a group of theorists who maintained their rigid refusal to use autobiographical material (implicitly or explicitly) in doing philosophy and who instead insisted on studying issues of the self (even issues that relate to their own personal selves) in impersonal, logically universal

terms. I have not encountered such a group, but I am a metaphilosophical pluralist who recognizes that philosophy is a contested concept with rival methods
that may be differently successful with different problems. As a pragmatist, I
think we should judge our theories and methods principally by their results; and
thus my pluralist stance as well as my affirmation and use of autobiographical
material for certain philosophical projects should also be judged by their results—not only in making my views more comprehensible (and perhaps more
convincing and attractive to readers), but also, of course, in providing me with
better self-knowledge for leading my philosophical life and relating more fruitfully to those people in whose ambit I live it. I am happy that my autobiographical remarks illuminated some points for a critic as penetrating as Professor
Małecki and that he finds my "textual persona" to be of the "dynamic, suspenseful" type. (On whether my fully-embodied, real-life persona is similarly exciting
or instead dismally boring, he diplomatically withholds judgment.)

    As to the philosophical benefits of an interesting biography, my limited
experience suggests mixed results. An interesting life narrative certainly at-
tracts more readers, but they are often then distracted from one's books and
arguments which are not as easy or exciting to read as one's life story. When
the French version of *Body Consciousness* came out, I was given an entire
page of *Le Monde*, with two articles and two pictures of me.[12] The article on
the book was roughly four times shorter than the article on my life; and that
life profile compressed into a breathless narrative as many "hot points" as it
could find (Israeli military intelligence officer, political resistance activist, rap
advocate, Zen practitioner, etc.) without trying to see how (or if) they hung
meaningfully together and how they illuminate my philosophical ideas.

IV

My comments on the essays grouped under the category of somaesthetics will
be more limited because my recent research has increasingly concentrated on
this field while the essays of this final section hardly treat that new research or
even the extensive treatment of somaesthetics in *Body Consciousness*. Nonetheless the essays make some instructive points by highlighting how somaesthetics intersects with ethics, feminist politics, contemporary fine art, democracy, sport, and popular culture. Insightfully analyzing my critical study of de
Beauvoir's *The Second Sex* to advocate somaesthetics' potential for promoting
feminist liberation, Monika Bokiniec provides a nice balance to Martin Jay's
concern in the final essay that my appreciation of rap's aesthetic of movement
and métissage suggests a complicity with its expressions of misogyny. She is
right to underline that somaesthetics and feminism share a meliorative orientation that closely links theory and practice, and I am happy that she is essentially sympathetic to my approach, though prudently skeptical about the extent to
which it can indeed provide liberation. As Professor Bokiniec realizes, I fully
and explicitly recognize somaesthetics practical limits here and thus advocate

that its work of sociocultural critique and self-cultivation needs to be combined with other more distinctively political, economic, and social reforms.

Somaesthetics should not be identified simply with what she calls the "biological hypothesis," because it sees the soma as more than biological and thus includes socio-cultural critique (enlisting historical and social science research) as central to its project. If our positions diverge, I think it is because my pragmatist perspective sees much greater interdependent continuity between nature and culture while she seems more inclined to follow de Beauvoir in accepting the conventional dualism between the socio-cultural and the biological-natural with respect to human bodies. Without invoking Abrams' futuristic somatic transformations of our physical form and somatic functioning, we already know how culture (with its technology) reshapes nature, including human nature. Not only do drugs reshape our biology, but our physical size and somatic development are affected by the material culture of what we eat and the social forms of living in which we grow and age. The use of growth hormones in foods have changed the parameters and rhythms of human growth, such that girls in the United States are beginning to menstruate much earlier than before (and also earlier than their counterparts in regions where such hormones are not used.)

I really like the spirit of Krzysztof Skowroński's essay, and I welcome his interest in exploring somaesthetics and taking it into directions I have not yet considered. As I have often said, the somaesthetic project is so vast that it needs a host of researchers, and I happily welcome Professor Skowroński among them. I share his appreciation of the somatic intelligence of athletes and dancers, and agree with him that the somaesthetic goal of attentive awareness can be pursued and achieved through sports like long-distance running or bodybuilding, not just through yoga or meditation. I also share the concern he notes (with Witkacy) of the somatic conformism of ideal body stereotypes propagated by the advertising industry of mass culture. Combating this trend not only by critique but also by searching for other models and modes of somatic beauty (experiential as well as representational) is one of aims of the somaesthetic project as articulated in *Performing Live* and *Body Consciousness*, books to which Professor Skowroński does not refer. He maintains that my published works do not discuss eroticism and sexuality (except for the "troubled" sexuality of "homosexuality and sadomasochism"), although I informed him (at the 2008 Wroclaw conference) of a detailed study I devoted to the aesthetics of heterosexual eroticism that was published shortly before.[13] Perhaps he could not obtain the article or instead found it irrelevant to his critique, but other readers may think otherwise.

Professor Skowroński radically misreads me when he says my approach to the philosophical life is "sectarian" and meant only for "professional" philosophers. My book *Practicing Philosophy* urges the contrary view that artists, scientists, saints, poets, and ordinary people with other employment (or even unemployed) can live the philosophical life, if they pursue in practice "the ideal of critically reflective self-care as self-improvement through the disciplined pursuit of the relevant knowledge. ... Democratizing the philosophical life means that anyone could make this ideal her guiding principle in life."[14] Of course, as I also point out, philosophical readings can help us here, but they are not sufficient. Moreover, for me, such readings include a wide-range of "wisdom" literature from religious and literary traditions that are part of the common cultural heritage available to non-specialists. Finally, though I share Professor Skowronski's aesthetic appreciation of certain forms of "the culture of drinking" and their stimulation of imagination and social feelings, it seems useful to point out that alcohol physiologically works as a depressant, and its perceived effect of temporary excitation is in fact the result of its depressing inhibitory neural mechanisms.

The two final essays, like Bokiniec's, explore somaesthetics' political dimension, but usefully link that dimension to the realms of art and popular culture. Both essays, unfortunately, take rap music as my preferred paradigm of somaesthetics, while most readers have instead identified disciplines such as Zen meditation, t'ai chi chuan, Alexander Technique, Feldenkrais Method as being more paradigmatic. Let me set the record straight. My vision of somaesthetics is pluralistic and cannot be confined to any particular somatic discipline. I never intended rap as my somaesthetic ideal in life or in art, though I did indeed commend its celebration of vigorous bodily movement for a fuller aesthetic experience as one of rap's refreshing features. When Martin Jay first showed me his paper (originally written and published in a different context) back in 2002, I could understand his identifying somaesthetics with rap, since my research on other somaesthetic disciplines had only recently appeared, and had not yet been properly assimilated. By now, Professor Jay—my favorite intellectual historian (and a good friend)—has a broader view of somaesthetics, which in his magisterial *Songs of Experience* (2005) is no longer linked to rap but instead related to the somatic therapy that Dewey learned from Alexander.

Before considering Professor Jay's instructive look at Deweyan democracy through somaesthetics and contemporary body art, I should respond to Robert Dobrowolski's essay which seems to be written under the powerful influence of Adornian philosophy, rhetoric, and plaintive passion. He is sympathetic to somaesthetics' emphasis on embodiment, diversity of values (including those of improved ethical understanding) that can be furthered through greater somatic awareness, and the plurality of methods (not only those of radical limit experiences) for realizing embodied values. But he is vehemently critical of the culture of rap. Always ready to recognize certain dangers and contradictions in hip hop culture (and noting them in print even in my initial affirmations of that culture), I have lamented how its early energies have been excessively commercialized, homogenized, and gangsterized and thus rendered less interesting aesthetically, cognitively, and politically. Moreover, I never argued that rap was the only form of politically-engaged popular

music that used its lyrics, ideas, and intertextual allusions to challenge dominant ideologies (including aesthetic ones) and promote democracy.

Rap, however, did combine, in the freshest, most salient, and most controversial way, many of the ideas I was exploring (ideas about aesthetics,
popular art, embodied experience, the cultural politics of artistic legitimacy,
postmodernism, and ethics as an art of living) at the time when I was writing
Pragmatist Aesthetics and rap was struggling to establish itself in a culture
where even the official entertainment industry was willing to exclude it. For
all its current faults, I still would defend rap against the charge that it displays
no artistry or talent and that its sampling techniques and interest in passionate
movement imply a dismantling of personal identity, an abandonment of the
project of self-development. In high culture's artistic, religious, and romantic
domains, momentary self-abandon is frequently seen as a necessary step to
embracing a wider, fuller, richer self; reading philosophy can work the same
way. Self-growth implies a double movement of opening up or letting go but
then reasserting one's critical powers to assess and reconstruct oneself.

Though I applaud Martin Jay's attempt to link Deweyan democracy and
somaesthetics to contemporary body art, I find it hard to imagine Dewey appreciating this genre, not only because of its more "esoteric" character but
also because of its frequent emphasis on sex, transgression, abjection, and
violence. All these features go against what I elsewhere criticize as Dewey's
one-sided fixation on the wholesome, unified, and harmoniously consummated form of aesthetic experience. For similar reasons I also doubt if Dewey
would have grooved on rap. But I feel sure he would have admired the skill
and energy of breakdancing, would have affirmed rap's democratic identity as
a popular art and its close links with the real life of ordinary people, and
would have appreciated the sense of community that hip hop, at its best, pro-
moted as an alternative to gang warfare—until it succumbed to its own increasingly destructive tradition of violence. Audible violence was always an
important part of rap's aesthetic, even in its "stop the violence" tracks.[14] But
let me immediately add that art is full of violence and that violence is not
always bad or destructive.[15]

For all their differences, contemporary body art and rap share an underlying logic of violence. One likely reason (that has both artistic and democratic import) is the need to shock audiences out of their complacency, to make
them pay attention to their message by transgressing customary boundaries of
perception and of taste. The analogies with Foucault's somaesthetics of transgression (but also with mainstream sensationalist films and advertising in their
competition for viewer attention) are obvious. Among the central themes of
Body Consciousness is that such violence will be increasingly pervasive in a
culture that seems to be losing its capacities for attending to subtle messages
and losing its perceptual skills for appreciating fine differences.

I believe that somaesthetics, as a discipline of theory and practice, not
only explores fruitful methods and strategies for cultivating improved powers

of awareness and perception, but also provides helpful perspectives for criticizing the troubling social, political, psychological, and cultural results of our attention deficits and perceptual insensitivities. There is so much work to do in this area, and so little time; too little to take more of it in response to these essays, besides this final word of grateful thanks.

NOTES

1. W. V. O. Quine, "Carnap and Logical Truth," *in Ways of Paradox and Other Essays* (Cambridge: Harvard University Press, 1976), p. 132.
2. John Dewey, *A Common Faith* (Carbondale: Southern Illinois University Press, 1986), pp. 3, 6–8, 11–13, 19.
3. Richard Shusterman, "Art and Religion," *Journal of Aesthetic Education* 42:3 (2008), pp. 1–18.
4. In discussing my "Fallibilism and Faith" paper, Olli-Pekka Vainio affirms this point, citing on the one hand, "now we see through a glass, darkly; but then face to face: now I know in part" (1 Cor 13:12) and on the other hand, "you must continue in the things which you have learned and been assured of" (2 Tim 3:14). See Olli-Pekka Vainio, "On Believing and Acting Fallibly," *Studia Theologica*, 64 (2010), pp. 97–109.
5. Antonia Soulez, "Practice, Theory, Pleasure, and the Problems of Form and Resistance: Shusterman's Pragmatist Aesthetics," *Journal of Speculative Philosophy*, 16: 1 (2002), pp. 1–9.
6. Besides *Body Consciousness* and with special respect to Dewey, see my "Dewey's Art as Experience: The Psychological Background," *Journal of Aesthetic Education*, 44:1 (2010), pp. 26–43.
7. William James, *Pragmatism and Other Essays* (New York: Simon and Schuster, 1963), p. 76.
8. Richard Shusterman, "Somaesthetics and C. S. Peirce," *Journal of Speculative Philosophy*, 23:1 (2010), pp. 8–27.
9. For a detailed analysis of the sensory modalities of somatic style, see Richard Shusterman, "Somatic Style," *Journal of Aesthetics and Art Criticism*, 69:2 (2011), pp. 147–159.
10. See, most recently, Richard Shusterman, "Pragmatism and Cultural Politics: From Rortian Textualism to Somaesthetics," *New Literary History*, 41:1 (2010), pp. 69–94. For my principal critiques of Danto and Bourdieu, see, respectively chapters 10, 12 of *Surface and Depth* (Ithaca: Cornell University Press, 2002), and a more recent paper on Danto, "Arte come religione: la transfigurazione del Dao di Danto," *Rivista d'estetica*, 35 (2007), pp. 315–334, forthcoming in English in the second edition of *Danto and His Critics* (Oxford: Blackwell).
11. See Shusterman, "Art and Religion."
12. See *Le Monde* (November 30, 2010), reproduced in PDF at http://www.fau.edu/humanitieschair/Lemondedeslivresentiernovfrontback.pdf.
13. Richard Shusterman, "Asian Ars Erotica and the Question of Sexual Aesthetics," *Journal of Aesthetics and Art Criticism*, 65:1 (2007), pp. 55–68.
14. Richard Shusterman, *Practicing Philosophy* (London: Routledge, 1997), p. 61.

15. See Richard Shusterman, "Pragmatism, Art, and Violence: The Case of Rap," in *Philosophical Designs for a Socio-Cultural Transformation*, ed. Tetsuji Yamamoto (Tokyo and Boulder: E. H. E. S. C. and Rowman & Littlefield, 1998), pp. 667–674; and "Rap Aesthetics: Violence and the Art of Keeping it Real," in *Hip Hop and Philosophy*, eds. Derrick Darby and Tommie Shelby (Chicago: Open Court, 2005), pp. 54–64.

ABOUT THE CONTRIBUTORS

JEROLD J. ABRAMS is Associate Professor of Philosophy at Creighton University in Omaha, Nebraska (USA). His research focuses on pragmatism, aesthetics, film, and popular culture. His essays appear in the journals *Philosophy Today*, *Human Studies*, *The Modern Schoolman*, *Film and Philosophy*, *The Transactions of the Charles S. Peirce Society*, and several volumes on philosophy of film such as *The Philosophy of Stanley Kubrick*, *The Philosophy of Science Fiction Film*, *The Philosophy of Film Noir*, *The Philosophy of Neo-Noir Film*, *The Philosophy of Martin Scorsese*, *The Philosophy of the Coen Brothers* (University Press of Kentucky); *Woody Allen and Philosophy*, *James Bond and Philosophy*, and *Star Wars and Philosophy* (Open Court); *House and Philosophy* and *Battlestar Galactica and Philosophy* (Blackwell); and *Hitchcock as Moralist* (SUNY, forthcoming).

KACPER BARTCZAK is the author of *In Search of Communication and Community: the Poetry of John Ashbery* (Peter Lang, 2006) and *Świat nie scalony* (Biuro Literackie, 2009). A Visiting Fulbright Scholar at Stanford University (2000-01) and at *Princeton University* (2010-11), a Kościuszko Foundation Scholar at Florida Atlantic University (2008), he did research under Richard Rorty, Richard Shusterman, and Alexander Nehamas. He is assistant professor at the University of Łódź, Poland, where he teaches American literature. He is also a poet in the Polish language.

MONIKA BOKINIEC, Ph.D., Institute of Philosophy, Sociology and Journalism, University of Gdańsk (Poland), has published a number of articles on the aesthetics of popular art, media art and feminist aesthetic theory. Currently her research concentrates on two topics: the cinematic representation of the figure of an artist and the ethical criticism of art. She is a member of the Polish Society of Aesthetics.

ANNA BUDZIAK teaches English literature and literary theory at the University of Wroclaw, Poland. She has authored two book-length studies: on T.S. Eliot and, recently, on Walter Pater and Oscar Wilde. The latter, *Text, Body and Indeterminacy: Doppelgänger Selves in Pater and Wilde*, was on the final shortlist for the biennial ESSE (European Society for the Study of English) Book Award in 2010.

ADAM CHMIELEWSKI is Professor Ordinarius in the Institute of Philosophy, University of Wrocław, Poland. He is also a social activist and political columnist. He studied philosophy ans social sciences at universities in Wrocław, Oxford, and New York. He authored several books, among them *Popper's Philosophy: A Critical Analysis* (1995) *Incommensurability, Un-*

translatability, Conflict (1997), *Open Society or Community?* (2001), *Two Conceptions of Unity* (2006) and *Psychopatologies of Political Life* (2009). He translated from English into Polish a number of books, among them works by Bertrand Russell, Karl Popper, Alasdair MacIntyre, Richard Shusterman, Slavoj Žižek, as well as some works of fiction. He is the Editor-in-Chief of the *Studia Philosophica Wratislaviensia*, and a member of editorial boards of several Polish and international journals.

ROBERT DOBROWOLSKI (Ph.D. in Philosophy), is the author of a number of articles on aesthetics and contemporary culture and art. Recently he published an article entitled "Inna śmierć [Another Death] (Blanchot, Levinas, Bezuchov)" in the prestigious Polish periodical *Teksty Drugie*. He is currently doing research on the presence of the body in the modern and post-modern culture and working on his book *Contemporary Experience of Body: The Study in Aesthetics*. He works at University School of Physical Education In Wrocław.

MARTIN JAY is Sidney Hellman Ehrman Professor of History at the University of California, Berkeley, where he teaches Modern European Intellectual History. Among his works are *The Dialectical Imagination* (1973 and 1996), *Marxism and Totality* (1984); *Adorno* (1984); *Permanent Exiles* (1985), *Fin-de-siècle Socialism* (1989); *Force Fields* (1993); *Downcast Eyes* (1993); *Cultural Semantics* (1998); *Refractions of Violence* (2004); *Songs of Experience* (2005); *The Virtues of Mendacity* (2010), and *Essays from the Edge* (2011).

DOROTA KOCZANOWICZ, Ph.D., is the author of *Doświadczenie sztuki, sztuka życia: Wymiary estetyki pragmatycznej* [The Experience of Art and the Art of Living: Dimensions of Pragmatist Aesthetics] (2009). She also co-edited *Między estetyzacją a emancypacją. Praktyki artystyczne w przestrzeni publicznej* [Between Aesthetisation and Emancipation. Artistic Practices in Public Sphere], (2010). She did research in John F. Kennedy Institute in Berlin and in Norway at The Wittgenstein Archives at the University of Bergen (WAB). Currently she is working on a food and art project.

WOJCIECH MAŁECKI is Assistant Professor at the Institute of Polish Philology, the University of Wrocław, Poland. His research interests include pragmatism (both classical and contemporary), continental philosophy, literary theory, aesthetics, philosophy of the body, and popular culture. He is the author of *Embodying Pragmatism: Richard Shusterman's Philosophy and Literary Theory* (Peter Lang, 2010), the editor or co-editor of three collections of essays, and an associate editor of the journal *Pragmatism Today*. He has published numerous book chapters and articles in journals such as *The Oxford Literary Review, Angelaki, Deutsche Zeitschrift für Philosophie, Journal of Comparative Literature and Aesthetics, Foucault Studies, Teksty Drugie*, etc. He has been a visiting fellow at the Institute for Advanced Studies in the Humanities (the University of Edinburgh), the John F. Kennedy Institute for North American Studies (the Free University of Berlin), and the Center for Body, Mind, and Culture (Florida Atlantic University).

DON MORSE teaches at Webster University in St. Louis, MO, USA, where is Associate Professor and Chair in the Department of Philosophy. His work explores connections between American and European thought. He is the author of *Faith in Life: John Dewey's Early Philosophy* (Fordham University Press, 2011).

SAMI PIHLSTRÖM received his PhD from the University of Helsinki, Finland, in 1996. He is, since 2006, Professor of Practical Philosophy at the University of Jyväskylä, Finland, and since 2009 Director of the Helsinki Collegium for Advanced Studies at the University of Helsinki. He has published widely on pragmatism and related topics, including metaphysics, ethics, philosophy of science, and philosophy of religion. His recent books include *Pragmatist Metaphysics* (Continuum, 2009) and *Transcendental Guilt* (Lexington/Rowman & Littlefield, forthcoming 2011). He is the Book Review Editor of *Transactions of the Charles S. Peirce Society*, as well as one of the Executive Editors of *Sats: North European Journal of Philosophy*. He is actively involved in international networks of pragmatism scholars, including the Nordic Pragmatism Network and the Central European Pragmatist Forum.

RICHARD SHUSTERMAN is the Dorothy F. Schmidt Eminent Scholar in the Humanities at Florida Atlantic University (Boca Raton) and director of its Center for Body, Mind, and Culture. Author of *Body Consciousness* (Cambridge, 2008), he has also written *Surface and Depth* (2002); *Performing Live* (2000); *Practicing Philosophy* (1997); and *Pragmatist Aesthetics* (1992, 2000, and translated into fourteen languages) as well as other books. A graduate of Hebrew University of Jerusalem (B.A. and M.A.) and Oxford University (D. Phil), he has held academic appointments in France, Germany, Israel, Japan, and China, and has been awarded research grants from the National Endowment for the Humanities, the Fulbright Commission, the American Council for Learned Societies, the Humboldt Foundation, and UNESCO. The French government has bestowed on him the title of Chevalier in the Ordre des Palmes Academiques. His research in somaesthetics is nourished by his work as a certified somatic educator in the Feldenkrais Method.

KRZYSZTOF (CHRIS) PIOTR SKOWROŃSKI, Ph.D., currently teaches Contemporary Philosophy, Aesthetics, Cultural Anthropology, Polish Philosophy, and American Philosophy at the Institute of Philosophy, Opole University, Poland. He authored books: *Values and Powers: Re-reading the Philosophy of American Pragmatism* (Amsterdam-New York: Rodopi, 2009) and

Santayana and America. Values, Liberties, Responsibility (Newcastle: Cambridge Scholars Publishing, 2007). He also co-edited books: *Under Any Sky. Contemporary Readings of George Santayana* (with Matthew Flamm; Cambridge Scholars, 2007), *American and European Values: Contemporary Philosophical Perspectives,* (with Matthew Flamm and John Lachs; Cambridge Scholars 2008) and *The Continuing Relevance of John Dewey: Reflection on Aesthetics, Morality, Science, and Society* (with Larry Hickman, Matthew Flamm, and Jennifer Rea; Rodopi, 2011).

Index

VIBS

The **Value Inquiry Book Series** is co-sponsored by:

Adler School of Professional Psychology
American Indian Philosophy Association
American Maritain Association
American Society for Value Inquiry
Association for Process Philosophy of Education
Canadian Society for Philosophical Practice
Center for Bioethics, University of Turku
Center for Professional and Applied Ethics, University of North Carolina at Charlotte
Central European Pragmatist Forum
Centre for Applied Ethics, Hong Kong Baptist University
Centre for Cultural Research, Aarhus University
Centre for Professional Ethics, University of Central Lancashire
Centre for the Study of Philosophy and Religion, University College of Cape Breton
Centro de Estudos em Filosofia Americana, Brazil
College of Education and Allied Professions, Bowling Green State University
College of Liberal Arts, Rochester Institute of Technology
Concerned Philosophers for Peace
Conference of Philosophical Societies
Department of Moral and Social Philosophy, University of Helsinki
Gannon University
Gilson Society
Haitian Studies Association
Ikeda University
Institute of Philosophy of the High Council of Scientific Research, Spain
International Academy of Philosophy of the Principality of Liechtenstein
International Association of Bioethics
International Center for the Arts, Humanities, and Value Inquiry
International Society for Universal Dialogue
Natural Law Society
Philosophical Society of Finland
Philosophy Born of Struggle Association
Philosophy Seminar, University of Mainz
Pragmatism Archive at The Oklahoma State University
R.S. Hartman Institute for Formal and Applied Axiology
Research Institute, Lakeridge Health Corporation
Russian Philosophical Society
Society for Existential Analysis
Society for Iberian and Latin-American Thought
Society for the Philosophic Study of Genocide and the Holocaust
Unit for Research in Cognitive Neuroscience, Autonomous University of Barcelona
Whitehead Research Project
Yves R. Simon Institute

Titles Published

221. John G. McGraw, *Intimacy and Isolation (Intimacy and Aloneness: A Multi-Volume Study in Philosophical Psychology, Volume One)*, A volume in **Philosophy and Psychology**

222. Janice L. Schultz-Aldrich, Introduction and Edition, *"Truth" is a Divine Name, Hitherto Unpublished Papers of Edward A. Synan, 1918-1997*. A volume in **Gilson Studies**

223. Larry A. Hickman, Matthew Caleb Flamm, Krzysztof Piotr Skowroński and Jennifer A. Rea, Editors, *The Continuing Relevance of John Dewey: Reflections on Aesthetics, Morality, Science, and Society*. A volume in **Central European Value Studies**

224. Hugh P. McDonald, *Creative Actualization: A Meliorist Theory of Values*. A volume in **Studies in Pragmatism and Values**

225. Rob Gildert and Dennis Rothermel, Editors, *Remembrance and Reconciliation*. A volume in **Philosophy of Peace**

226. Leonidas Donskis, Editor, *Niccolò Machiavelli: History, Power, and Virtue*. A volume in **Philosophy, Literature, and Politics**

227. Sanya Osha, *Postethnophilosophy*. A volume in **Social Philosophy**

228. Rosa M. Calcaterra, Editor, *New Perspectives on Pragmatism and Analytic Philosophy*. A volume in **Studies in Pragmatism and Values**

229. Danielle Poe, Editor, *Communities of Peace: Confronting Injustice and Creating Justice*. A volume in **Philosophy of Peace**

230. Thorsten Botz-Bornstein, Editor, *The Philosophy of Viagra: Bioethical Responses to the Viagrification of the Modern World*. A volume in **Philosophy of Sex and Love**

231. Carolyn Swanson, *Reburial of Nonexistents: Reconsidering the Meinong-Russell Debate*. A volume in **Central European Value Studies**

232. Adrianne Leigh McEvoy, Editor, *Sex, Love, and Friendship: Studies of the Society for the Philosophy of Sex and Love: 1993–2003*. A volume in **Histories and Addresses of Philosophical Societies**

CPSIA information can be obtained at www.ICGtesting.com
Printed in the USA
BVOW061159150312

285212BV00001B/74/P